SHADOW OF A CONTINENT

SHADOW OF A CONTINENT

The Prize That
Lay to the West — 1776

LARRY L. MEYER

AMERICAN WEST PUBLISHING COMPANY
PALO ALTO — CALIFORNIA

Library of Congress Cataloging in Publication Data

Meyer, Larry L   1933–
  Shadow of a continent.

  Bibliography: p.
  Includes index.
  1. The West—Discovery and exploration. 2. The
West—History—To 1848. 3. United States—Territorial
expansion. I. Title.
F592.M49   978'.01   75–6324
ISBN 0–910118–62–0
ISBN 0–910118–63–9 deluxe

FIRST EDITION

Contents

To Nancy

Acknowledgments

Debts in other than specie can never be repaid, only acknowledged. Mine begin with those to my wife, Nancy, who worked so closely with me on this book as fellow researcher, uncompromising editor, and constant encourager. For her, indispensable seems an inadequate word.

As an amateur historian, I owe much to the countless professionals, living and dead, who have invested their lives in sifting the past for fact and meaning. But I'm particularly grateful to those who gave me expert guidance and counsel in the preparation of this book: Ray A. Billington, Senior Research Associate of the Huntington Library; John C. Ewers, Senior Ethnologist of the Smithsonian Institution; George P. Hammond, Director Emeritus of the Bancroft Library; Abraham P. Nasatir, Research Professor of History at San Diego State University; and Doyce B. Nunis, Jr., Professor of History at the University of Southern California.

Thanks also go to the staffs of all the libraries I consulted, with special gratitude to those at the Huntington, the Bancroft, the Denver Public, and, foremost, my alma mater, UCLA, where my old and good friend Everett T. Moore, Research Librarian, opened so many doors.

Finally, I would like to thank my friend Tom Watkins for his phone call on a Denver winter's night in 1972. It made all the difference.

Introduction

WHEN THE BELLS RANG OUT in Philadelphia that July 4, 1776, heralding the birth of a new nation and portending a new age, the New World was no longer very new. European colonizers had been busy for more than two hundred fifty years in Columbus's accidental find, first exploring for a way around the obstacle to India, then exploiting it, reducing what parts of it they could into subservient extensions of the nations they had come from. Cordilleras had been crossed and rivers run and forests and savannahs north and south cleared to make way for the plow. Just as the land was altered, so too were its native peoples, many of whom were humbled or sent packing or eliminated. Tenochtitlán had been razed and looted, and the Inca top lopped off by Spanish steel; French *voyageurs* had pushed far north, west, and south from their Saint Lawrence River stronghold in search of beaver; stolid Englishmen, long tied to Atlantic tidewater to produce the basic stuffs of a tired economic system, were at last wandering westward in significant numbers. Already old were the ruthless *encomiendas* that were the foundation of Spanish settlement; so, too, was the cruel trade of Englishmen and Frenchmen and Dutchmen in black men who labored and died on plantations to provide what Continental fashion and palate desired.

Only the western half of North America—the trans-Mississippi West and its Canadian counterpart—remained *terra incognita*, or, more accurately, a little-known land. Only west of the long-grass prairie and north of New Spain's fragile frontier was there left a land to match the white man's seemingly limitless capacity to dream dreams and make myths. Spain had probed hesitantly

9

and sporadically at it from the south, only to back off time and again for lack of men and resources. Dauntless Frenchmen, goaded by a profitable Indian trade, had crisscrossed the Great Plains for half a century before the first meeting of the Continental Congress. Through the daring of the sea rovers Drake and Cavendish, even the cautious English were aware that the land had an end — a far western front with the Pacific. Yet, of all the men, remembered and forgotten, who had entered and seen the American West, none had taken the measure of this vast land still largely in shadow.

Historians generally agree that the early story of America — and the trans-Mississippi West — is mostly a European one. Europeans were its dominant characters from the first, and their influence was to survive the breakaway of their colonies. This Old World dominance can be traced back to the sixteenth century when Europe burst its borders. The epidemic of the Renaissance had spread north from Italy to inspire men's minds, freeing them from traditional views of the globe and their small place on it. This new knowledge was not merely theoretical, but applied also to the practical science of making new tools and machines. Printing presses spread the word. Technologies gathered steam before there was steam. New advances in navigation and shipbuilding, such as more masts, larger keels, and double oak planking that could suffer the recoil of heavy cannon, virtually turned over the waterways of the world to Europe. Change-resistant Islam, static China, and lesser civilizations were to prove no match for the strangers who had come so far to trade and, eventually, to conquer. The travelers brought back to their homelands gold and silver, silk and spices, and yet more new knowledge. In return they exported ambitious men, religious beliefs deeply held, habits of violence, and diseases lethal to isolated peoples with no immunity to them.

Close on the heels of the Renaissance came the Reformation, a final fracturing of Christian unity, which had shown widening cracks for more than two hundred years. Nor did the break stop with a single split. The Reformation produced Lutherans in rebellion against Rome, then Calvinists in disagreement with both, Anabaptists against the world, and countless other schismatics convinced that they alone possessed the Word. Many would have to cross the Atlantic to escape persecution and to be free to practice what they preached. The Counter-Reformation had its own divisive effects within the Church of Rome which carried even to the North American wilderness, where Jesuits were in sharp competition with Franciscans, Sulpicians, and Capuchins in missionary work.

With the Renaissance and the Reformation came the maturation of mercantilism, a form of primitive state capitalism that was to shape the New World and the West from their colonial beginnings. Gold and silver mined in Mexico and Peru and channeled through the ports of Spain had altered the economies of all Europe, making mercantilism a credo for the Continent, though with as many variations as there were nations subscribing to the system. Among its tenets was the equating of wealth with the possession of precious metals, which were to be hoarded or plowed back into home industries. To that end, each nation tried mightily to export much and import little, thus assuring a favorable balance of trade. This meant high import duties, economic diversification, and the coddling of local manufacturers — all to be rigidly enforced by an increasingly powerful centralized authority.

Working at its best, the system required a concentrated urban labor force, greatly improved communications and transportation (chiefly, more and better sailing vessels), and the granting of lucrative privileges and subsidies to private companies, which were expected to increase the national honor while lining their pockets. Possessing colonies — preferably blessed with what Europe lacked — was, of course, crucial. Not only would these distant holdings supply the raw materials to be finished in the homeland, but they made convenient dumping grounds for surplus production — keeping the wealth in the family, as it were. So that the arrangement remained closed and tidy, colonists were forbidden to trade with rival nations. Economic practices had become means to purely political ends.

It all made good sense in London, Paris, and Madrid. It made somewhat less sense in New England, New France, and New Spain. In fact, the system never worked according to the theory. New World colonists increasingly traded with one another when they thought they could get away with it, until the eighteenth century became known as the golden age of smuggling. It was but one indicator that mercantilism had run its course as a viable economic system.

In the watershed year of 1776, Adam Smith published his *Wealth of Nations,* describing a mature capitalism that would—again in theory—be no respecter of national boundaries. But England had not had the benefit of a pre-publication reading; outdated policies survived and assured the secession of its thirteen North American colonies and the formation of a new nation that would, from its first imperial breath, covet the western no-man's-land.

Mercantilism had found ready ground in the sixteenth century, a time when Englishmen increasingly thought of themselves as Englishmen, Frenchmen as French, and Spaniards as Defenders of the Faith and subjects of the most powerful monarch on earth. Destinies had assumed a national *gestalt;* warfare, a new dimension. The importation and cultivation of New World foods—particularly maize and the potato—now sustained greater populations than Europe had ever known. All conspired to further the concentration of power in a few cities and in the hands of a few men. Expensive bureaucracies developed under monarchies worth their salt, standing armies became necessary to a nation's survival, and supportive taxation fell heavy on the drab, stable, and circumscribed agriculture of the homeland. The glamor was in the new lands that usually dwarfed in size and resources those of their transoceanic owners. If further new lands could be acquired, preferably at the expense of the enemy of the moment, so much the better. More was the goal of strategy; less was a national disgrace.

It had not started that way. The discovery and exploration of America, and the first commerce with her, had been a pan-European effort. The new knowledge came from no one people. Copernicus, Galileo, Bacon, and Descartes spoke the common language of genius. Curiosity did not stop at arbitrary borders, and the courage and enterprise of individual men had nothing to do with where they were born.

Italians had made the maps and captained many of the great

The world's oceans belonged to Europe by the early sixteenth century, its sea-lanes opened mainly by the vessels of Iberia.

voyages of discovery. German mathematicians and cartographers had contributed their scholarship, though the tragic religious wars that raged for more than a century in central Europe would remove the fractured states of Germany from participating in the New World experience, save for the religious refugees who left them to cross the ocean.

Portugal's Prince Henry the Navigator assembled an international company of savants and seamen at Cape Saint Vincent, that questioning thumb of land thrust into the Atlantic. But Pope Alexander IV did Portugal no favors in 1493 when he cut the new lands lengthwise into two grossly unequal parts for the Iberian powers. Spain got all but the bulge of Brazil, and the Portuguese looked elsewhere to extend their empire—in the East Indies, Africa, and Asia. The United Netherlands, the remarkable little quasi-republic that had freed itself from Spain by 1609 and drew phenomenal vigor from its militant brand of Protestantism, established itself in Guiana and Brazil, as well as in New Amsterdam. Yet its strength was always more commercial than political, and in time the Dutch found their place as the bankrollers of Europe, who for a price would underwrite the wars and imperial hopes of larger states or carry their cargoes across the oceans.

Throughout the sixteenth and seventeenth centuries a weeding-out process took place in the New World. The age of discovery was past; the age of earnest colonization under way. Power in Europe took a westward bias that would not cease for centuries. Spain, France, and England, each populous and each with a sense of national purpose and easy access to the critical ocean, became the contenders for the New World prize. The other nations, disqualified for reasons of geography, internal ills, or whatever, found themselves out of the contest, lesser forces in an ever shifting game of power equalization in Europe. And on the other side of the Atlantic Ocean, the imperial struggle was down to three.

It was Spain, triumphant after some six hundred years of almost continuous fighting to clear the Iberian peninsula of Moors, which first colonized the New World a century before her future competitors. The timing is telling. Spain was still very much a feudal kingdom then, and despite its military preeminence and the veneer of modernity, it remained largely untouched by the profound changes taking place in the rest of Europe. Yet there is no gainsaying the enormous energy of those fading knights, the gilded men, the *conquistadores* whose early penetration of the trans-Mississippi darkness remains a monument to man's audacity, will, and greed.

In May of 1539, Hernando de Soto, heroic veteran captain under Pizarro in Peru, blond as the sun, as courageous as he was cruel and as arrogant as he was obstinate, led a well-provisioned force of six hundred men north from Cuba in the wake of Ponce de León and Pánfilo de Narváez for yet another exploration of Florida. He was after riches he would not find, and the quest took him and his second-in-command, Moscoso, westward from their southeastern landing into the future Louisiana, Arkansas, and Texas before the folly of it all finally became plain. When it did, the burnt-out leader of the expedition, the pride of Peru and Estremadura, was already dead and his body surreptitiously committed to the waters of the Mississippi. The sadder and wiser

The personification of the gilded man, Hernando de Soto was bold and brutal—and buried in the Mississippi he discovered.

Moscoso took about half of the once elegant six hundred to Mexico by sea.

A year after de Soto's departure from Havana, the properly credentialed Francisco Vasquez Coronado, in charge of more than two hundred mounted men, sixty-odd infantry, and several hundred Indian allies, marched north from interior Mexico in pursuit of gold and glory, but instead found buffalo and Kansas before turning back again. While Coronado was embarked on a magnificent failure, Hernando de Alarcón, following in the wake of Francisco de Ulloa, who had sailed the same way the year before, took three vessels up the Sea of Cortez and two smaller boats up the Colorado River to its junction with the Gila, only to be disappointed in not making contact with Coronado by land.

The final probe north in this brief but extraordinary flurry of Spanish activity was a two-vessel expedition out of Navidad on Mexico's west coast under the command of Juan Rodríguez Cabrillo. In July of 1542, the voyagers were scraping the shin of Baja California; in September they discovered San Diego Bay. Cabrillo continued northwest in the teeth of the trying winds, and somewhere north of San Francisco Bay (which he missed), he turned about. Later, during a Santa Barbara Channel landing, the captain broke a leg that did not mend. When Cabrillo died, the survivors tried north again, sailing beyond Cape Mendocino before returning to Navidad on April 14, 1543. They brought back news of a populated and fertile coast, but not the mineral riches that Spain was looking for.

The expeditions into what New Spain called the Northern Mystery had given her additional geography, which she already had in unhealthy abundance, without the instant wealth that would have made its occupation worthwhile. So interest in the north, the American West, faded . . . for a while.

Sir Francis Drake put England in the contest with his 1579 voyage to the California coast.

INTRODUCTION

In 1579 the privateer Francis Drake, later to be knighted by Queen Elizabeth for his exploits, went on a spree of pillaging Spain's Pacific ports from Chile to Mexico, then hied far upcoast to find a safe anchorage until winds were right for a trans-Pacific trip home. The sea dog reported that he put in some miles north of present San Francisco, trafficked with the natives, and claimed the land he called New Albion for England. Since he had been charged with finding the western portal of the Strait of Anian, that had-to-be shortcut to India, and since his route home by way of the Cape of Good Hope had been kept secret, it was feared by the Spanish that he had used the mythical waterway.

King Philip II was alarmed. At the least he had been out-flanked, and that proved to be the first stimulus of many to follow that would goad Spain into defensive action. Already there had been a rewakened interest in the north among the Catholic clergy in Mexico, who were pressing for conversions among the Pueblo Indians; silver strikes at Zacatecas and Durango, up the spine of Mexico, had shortened the long, arid in-between. When the digging got as far north as Chihuahua in 1567, Coronado's land was not that unreachable anymore.

Several petitioned the Crown to assume the expenses of a conquering expedition north. The command eventually went to Don Juan de Oñate, a man with years of experience on the northern frontiers of Nueva Galicia and Nueva Vizcaya, a man with a wife whose lineage named Cortés and Montezuma—the best of both bloods. The year was 1598; their strength ran to four hundred, including eight missionaries and excluding seven thousand domesticated beasts—perhaps the best evidence of all that where they were going they meant to stay. Where they were going was to be called, in a flight of optimism, New Mexico.

Oñate quickly reduced the placid tribes along the Rio Grande del Norte and established a temporary headquarters at San Juan on the river. The priests were immediately dispersed among the maize-growing Pueblo peoples, while Oñate occupied himself with exploration. First he went west to the Hopi mesas of Arizona, then back to the river valley and northeast for a place called Gran Quivira, where he discovered neither more nor less than Coronado had found six decades before. Upon his return to the

"ONATE ENTERS NEW MEXICO" BY CARL OSCAR BORG. WESTWAYS

Spain was first to settle in the West. Conquistador Juan de Oñate brought Cross and Sword to New Mexico in the year 1598.

Rio Grande, Oñate found the colonists desperate for food and in an ugly mood. In a move to recoup his reputation, he went west again in 1604 to see the California (which he concluded to be an island) that Sebastián Vizcaíno had only recently visited by sea. He found no gold there, no silver, none of the rumored pearls.

New Mexico became a royal province after Oñate's removal in 1608, but that did not improve its status as a poor, sleepy outpost a thousand miles from anywhere important, kept half-alive by a subsistence agriculture and the zeal of priests.

The seventeenth had been an unkind century for Spain in northern latitudes. She was joined in colonizing North America by her competition: Protestant England and Catholic-but-rival France. The English established Jamestown in 1607; a year later the French under Samuel de Champlain settled themselves in chill Quebec. It would be the more distant French who posed the first threat to New Spain in the American West.

At first France was too enfeebled by internal religious conflicts and her off-again, on-again wars with England to do more than cling by a thread to Canada, with its fisheries and timber and furs and six-month-frozen access up the Great River of the East, the Saint Lawrence. Eastern Canada never did become truly a paying proposition. It was too frigid and soil-poor for that. But it had just enough of what France could use, fostered a much-needed maritime boom in the ports of Bordeaux and La Rochelle, buoyed hopes of a Gaulish El Dorado, and denied England what she would otherwise have.

Under French colonial policy, faith and flag had to coexist with men who meant to make money, by whatever means. As with Spain, the modus operandi was essentially feudal—grants of seigneuries to aristocratic scions who crossed the Atlantic to do well for themselves. The lesser folk who went along, the *habitants,* would provide the labor to firm up estates and thereby increase the royal power of France. The influential Jesuits, with sponsors deeply entrenched in court, were also to be given their head: let them bring the red man into the True Church if that made them happy. It could only harm England, not France.

Of the parties to the French imperial mission—the noble military caste, the pious clergy willing to undergo martyrdom

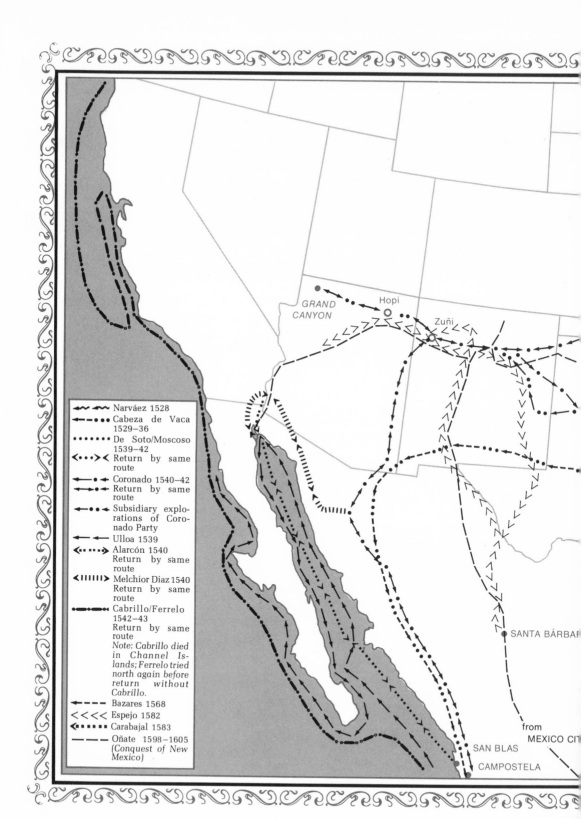

Narváez 1528
Cabeza de Vaca 1529–36
De Soto/Moscoso 1539–42
Return by same route
Coronado 1540–42
Return by same route
Subsidiary explorations of Coronado Party
Ulloa 1539
Alarcón 1540 Return by same route
Melchior Diaz 1540 Return by same route
Cabrillo/Ferrelo 1542–43 Return by same route
Note: Cabrillo died in Channel Islands; Ferrelo tried north again before return without Cabrillo.
Bazares 1568
Espejo 1582
Carabajal 1583
Oñate 1598–1605 (Conquest of New Mexico)

GRAND CANYON

Hopi

Zuñi

SANTA BÁRBAR

from MEXICO CIT

SAN BLAS

CAMPOSTELA

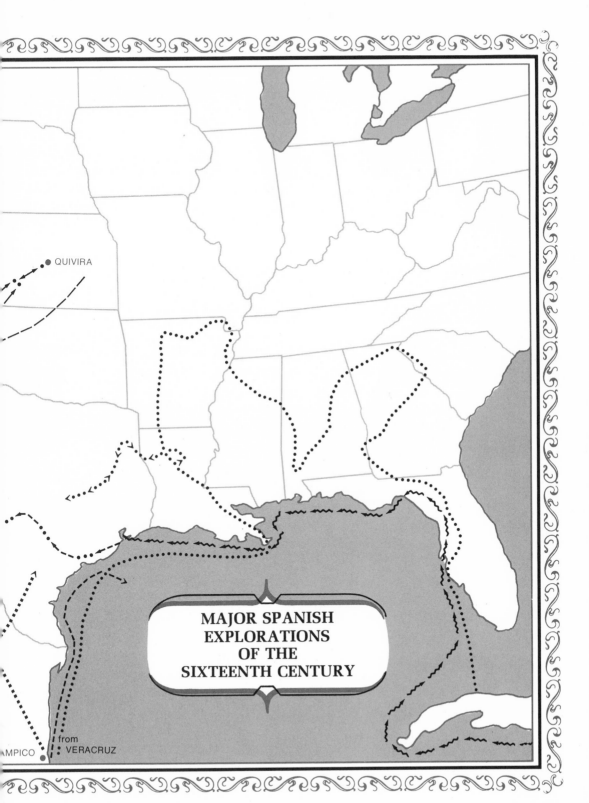

QUIVIRA

MAJOR SPANISH
EXPLORATIONS
OF THE
SIXTEENTH CENTURY

from
VERACRUZ

MPICO

among the *sauvages* (and so often accommodated), and the dependable *habitant* who was to drudge it — the last mentioned was at once the weakest and strongest link. Those who volunteered to come to New France, and those who decided to stay, became free men breathing free air. Their religion was old and so comfortable as to be stifling. The social strictures of Quebec and Montreal were precisely what they had crossed an ocean to escape. So the west drew them — a Turnerian suction operative long before the Scotch-Irish made their entrance. They were *coureurs de bois:* woodsmen, fur men, squaw men, natural men.

Throughout the seventeenth century it looked as if France would be the first to divine the mystery of the West. She moved in that direction with astonishing speed, her vehicle being fur trade with the Indians. It began with barter for pelts with the Hurons and Ottawas, then quickly followed the setting sun to the Sauks, Foxes, Potawatomis, and Miamis of the western Great Lakes region. As early as 1659 the French were entrenched in the far western finger of Lake Superior — thanks to a gifted pair of explorer-traders, Médard Chouart Groseilliers and Pierre Esprit Radisson. But it was not until 1665, with Louis XIV's appointment of Jean Talon as intendant, the king's personal representative in legal matters, that New France got going. Each year Talon sent twenty-five licensed traders westward; also pressing west were Jesuits without the least interest in beaver. A not-surprising coolness developed between priest and *voyageur*. The use of alcohol in the fur trade, with its devastating effects on the Indian, widened the rift, and churchmen seeking its ban met little success with a Crown scratching for *livres* to finance costly wars on the Continent. In 1673, in a peace-keeping gesture, Talon sent Father Jacques Marquette along with layman Louis Jolliet in search of the mighty river *Messipi,* of which the Indians had spoken. On June 17 they found it, and prospects looked bright for the new would-be claimant to the western lands.

But the health of New France was never robust. A chronic ventral affliction kept flaring up in the person of the five-tribe Iroquois nation. Though the French treated the native peoples more humanely than other colonizers, they had made the innocent mistake of befriending the Hurons and the Ottawas — sworn enemies of the Iroquois grouped strategically on the south and east shores of Lake Ontario. By association, then, New France was in receipt of an enmity she could ill afford. If the Iroquois had been just another band of *Peaux-rouges* it would not have been a grievous matter. But the Iroquois were a warrior confederacy who "came like foxes, attacked like lions, and fled like birds," scattering their Algonkin-speaking foes like frightened geese. Incited first by the Dutch and subsequently by the English, who correctly feared French encirclement, the Iroquois launched periodic, ferocious war on the *fleur-de-lys,* broken only by brief years of uneasy peace. With each new attack, the westward reach of the French constricted in painful spasm; what was in their grasp was lost and had to be seized again.

Louis de Baude, Comte de Frontenac, dealt the Iroquois confederacy a severe beating after he became governor in 1672. He knew what was at stake—knew almost as well as his favorite courtier, Robert Cavelier, Sieur de la Salle. La Salle remains largely an enigma, one of history's noblest failures. Intelligent, courageous, relentlessly determined, he was perhaps the first white man to understand what possibilities lay in the great interior river valley. As he saw it, the colonies of North America would form along north-to-south axes rather than east-to-west as the nations do now; there was an empire to be won and he would be its emperor.

After years of strengthening his position along the lower Great Lakes, following up on his fur trade monopoly granted in Paris but seldom honored in Quebec, he set out in 1683 with his resourceful and loyal second-in-command, Henri de Tonty, to take the Mississippi for good—and for France. He went all the way down it, to the Father of Waters' silty debouchment into the Gulf of Mexico. The key to the continent was, indeed, in the mouth of the great river. With its possession, the French would contain traditional enemy England on three sides and would have a forward base from which to stage assaults on New Spain with its rich mines.

Still dogged by bad luck and harassed by jealous countrymen, particularly the fat merchants of Montreal, La Salle carried his dream to Paris and rallied support. In 1684 he returned with four

The visionary La Salle took formal possession of the Mississippi Valley for Louis XIV on April 9, 1682. France would hold Louisiana for nearly a century.

hundred men to plant France firmly on the southern entrance to the West. But he missed the river. He overshot it (there is good reason to believe he did so deliberately, thinking to steal a march on Spain) and landed with his unruly colonists on the inhospitable Texas shores of Matagorda Bay. The party was dispirited, faction-ridden, and frightened; and a petty rogue put a bullet in the head of its leader to hide another crime. La Salle—the visionary, the lonely man more than a century ahead of his time—was

gone. French designs on the West had received a serious setback.

England had not exactly been sleeping. But neither had she moved west from her seaboard colonies at more than a snail's pace. The settlers, whether in colonies royal, proprietary, or underwritten by a joint-stock company, were a stolid lot, whose mission was to grow crops for England, to purchase the Scepter'd Isle's manufactured goods, and to stay close to the ports. But England envied France her fur trade. Some enterprising Englishmen became engaged in the lucrative barter, chiefly in New York through their allies the Iroquois. Still, they remained a distant second to the westward-pressing French, even after the defection of Radisson and Groseilliers, who went to London in 1668 and showed receptive England the way to the great beaver grounds of Hudson Bay. "The Governor and Company of Adventurers of England Trading into Hudson's Bay," with its vague claims to lands west, gave England not only a healthy piece of the action but a strategic northern position and a straddle of New France. But if the Mississippi—the all-important river that divided the continent—became French, those advantages would be small consolation indeed. Only England's navy could be relied upon to prevent total encirclement.

England was not alone in its worry. Spain again had reason to stir from its torpor. In 1680 the Pueblo peoples of New Mexico united under Domingo Naranjo (a black slave brought from Mexico and freed) and an Indian medicine man called Popé in revolt against their overlords, slaughtering some four hundred of them and driving the rest south to El Paso. For the next twelve years the Indians worked to purify their culture of everything that was Spanish and Christian. The laundering ended only when Don Diego de Vargas led an army north in 1692 on a reconquest that would take six years. Even before the revolt the viceroys in Mexico City were nervously aware of French expansion in the north—wherever that was. But in 1685, reports of La Salle's presence in Texas, where New Spain had been sending trading, slaving, and missionary parties since the 1630s, were something else. Spanish paranoia was piqued anew.

At the close of the seventeenth century, the imperial attention of three nations was directed to the mouth of the Mississippi. Clearly, mastery of the river led to mastery of the continent. In October 1698 a Spanish force left Veracruz; Dr. Daniel Coxe sent two shiploads of Huguenot colonists from England; and Pierre LeMoyne d'Iberville sailed from France with two hundred soldiers and settlers. The Spanish secured Pensacola Bay instead of the Mississippi's mouth, Coxe's party got sidetracked in the Carolinas, and Iberville prevailed. He established himself first at Biloxi before exploring and then fortifying the Mississippi proper. Louisiana, so named by La Salle in honor of Louis XIV, now had a small permanent population, and it spoke the Sun King's language.

By 1700 the white man's knowledge of the trans-Mississippi West was still pitifully small. A relative handful had wandered into its fringes, the lucky ones to wander right back out again. No European power had had but the remotest brush with a rival within its vast expanse. Yet they were all closing in on the great empty space on their maps.

In the eighteenth century there would be many more intruders in the West and even direct contact and conflict among people who had at least a nominal allegiance to different crowns. Again the Mississippi Valley would be focal. But the centuries-long contest of the imperial powers, which included among its prizes the American West, did not take place in the West. Rather, most of the blood would be spilled elsewhere, at remote stations girdling more than half the globe. Spain and France and England knew the stakes in the context of their times. The American West was no more than a pawn of unknown value on a multi-continental chessboard. The three nation-players involved in the game might view it as expendable to win an advantage elsewhere, but they would not surrender it for nothing.

In 1776 they would be joined in the contest by a fourth nation, the first nation of the New World, conceived as much in cupidity as in liberty, which would assume in its infancy an aggressive posture regarding all lands to its west.

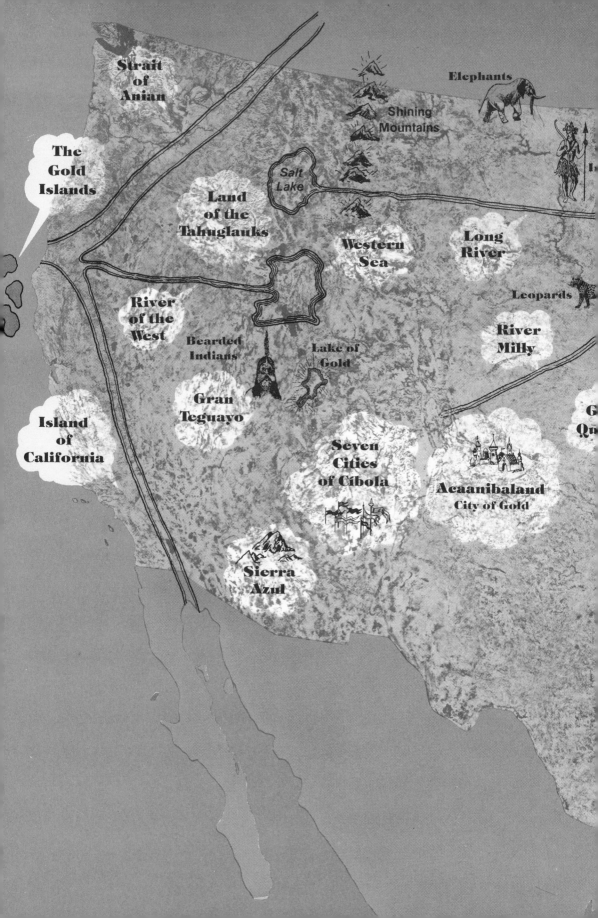

PART I: FANTASYLAND

Tigers

iffins

New World Myths

PART I
FANTASYLAND

November 22, 1803. Thomas Jefferson had a problem. He had only recently concluded a secret treaty with Napoleon that would give his young republic a million square miles of additional real estate for a mere fifteen million dollars. Louisiana was a bargain any way one looked at it; the trouble was, Jefferson had consulted the United States Senate neither about the merits of the acquisition, nor about the Senate's willingness to fund it. Moreover, Jefferson, a firm upholder of the Constitution, was not sure his action was legal. Something had to be done. So on this day the third president of the United States sent a message to an incensed Congress extolling the vast lands which he had admittedly never seen, the boundaries of which were at best uncertain, and the title to which lay under a Spanish cloud. The soil bordering the Mississippi River was the most fertile in all the world, Jefferson assured Congress. And beyond, the earth of those western prairies was so rich that it would not support the growth of trees. Moreover, lead was available in such quantities as to satisfy the needs of all Europe, and was easily recovered because it lay only two or three feet below the surface of the ground. In the north there were caves of saltpeter and, so he had heard, many silver and copper mines. Also out there was a tribe of giant Indians and — wonder of wonders — a mountain of solid salt! This was no piddling pimple on the face of the land, but an enormous mountain 180 miles long and 45 miles wide, and located only one thousand miles up the Missouri River. "The existence of such a mountain might well be questioned," Jefferson conceded, "were it not for the testimony of several respectable and enterprising traders, who have visited it and exhibited several bushels of the salt to the curiosity of the people of Saint Louis. . . ."

Not everyone — in or out of Congress — was impressed, though some were openly amused. The *New York Evening Post* of November 28 wondered whether there might not be salt birds sitting on salt trees atop that salt mountain and feared that the glare from the mountain on a sunshiny day must be dreadful. The *Evening Post* further speculated that "it would have been no more than fair in the traveller who informed

Mr. Jefferson of this territory of solid salt, to have added, that some leagues to the westward of it there was an immense lake of molasses, and that between this lake and the mountain of salt, there was an extensive vale of hasty pudding, stretching as far as the eye could reach, and kept in a state of comfortable eatibility by the warmth of the sun's rays, into which the natives, being all Patagonians, waded knee deep, whenever they were hungry, and helped themselves with salt on the one hand to season their pudding, and molasses with the other, to give it relish."

It seems incredible now, looking back, that Thomas Jefferson, son of the Enlightenment and product of the Age of Reason, practical farmer and amateur scientist, could have swallowed such nonsense. Perhaps he did not. Perhaps it was all a ploy to gain support for absorbing the western lands he had long wanted. At least he had the advantage of knowing as much about that distant territory as any of the senators, perhaps more, and it did not much matter that collectively they knew very little. When you buy a pig in a poke with someone else's money, why not have them believe the hog's hooves are of solid silver and its bristles of wire gold?

Whatever Mr. Jefferson's private state of mind, he was publicly following an old and honorable tradition — that of investing the American West with the marvelous, the miraculous, and the monstrous. As Europeans established themselves in the New World and gradually extended their frontiers, digesting the wonders of novel flora and fauna, discovering exotic peoples and a topography that bore little resemblance to their home continent, expectations rose of what was yet to be found. Not surprisingly, the best was saved for last, and what was last was the trans-Mississippi West.

Any yarn that Jefferson could spin about that faraway land had already been surpassed in fancy by Spaniards, Frenchmen, and Englishmen before him. The Spanish in the Southwest had heard early of a stream in which swam fish as large as horses; of a tribe of Indians with ears so large that they used them to shade themselves from the heat of the sun; of another tribe who lived out their lives under water, and still another who never ate food but were sustained by merely sniffing it. The French had first been drawn into the New World contest partly on the testimony of a Canadian Indian brought back to the court of Francis I by explorer Jacques Cartier. The wily chief Donnaconna filled impressionable ears with tales of pygmies, people who could fly like birds, those who dressed in gold and copper, and unipeds who traveled in great bounds over a tropical landscape on a centrally situated foot. Englishmen avidly read fictitious accounts of voyages through the fabled Strait of Anian that led to Cathay. It was even said that griffins and leopards and unicorns had been seen "out there," as were Chinese and a race of baldheaded folks who may or may not have been one and the same.

Something there was about the West that set a man to lying. It might have been the sheer immensity of sky, the heightened visibility of a sub-humid atmosphere (mirages were as common then as now), or the enormity of landforms on an often treeless expanse that either scrambled his sense of proportion or so humbled him that he had to exaggerate what he saw to regain his self-esteem. By having been among wonders, he himself had become more wonderful, and friends back home should know it. The world was also shrinking, and man perhaps needed at least one unknown corner of it to house his wildest hopes and fears. The real wonder is not that the myths were concocted in the first place, but that belief in them persisted among so many for so long.

Chapter 1

The Metal Lovers

IT WAS THE EXPECTATION of mineral riches that first lured Spaniards north out of the civilized Valley of Mexico. They were looking for an *otro México,* and the quest would take them far and deep into the shadowlands of the American West.

It all began with a true adventure tale to beggar the imagination of a Daniel Defoe. Alvar Nuñez Cabeza de Vaca, of Spanish yeoman stock, sailed in 1528 from Cuba as treasurer to Pánfilo de Narváez, a red-haired, one-eyed blusterer who had failed to distinguish himself under Cortés in the conquest of Mexico. Their voyage had as its end the exploration of the ill-defined land called Florida, and the expedition was a disaster. Hostile red men and fetid swampland saw to that. The beleaguered Narváez built boats from the hides and sinews of his slaughtered horses to effect a retreat, but nature was unsympathetic and all the craft were lost to storms off the Gulf Coast. The men who manned them were to undergo an ordeal in survival that ultimately reduced their numbers from two hundred shipwrecked to a mere four, wandering inland from the shores of Texas. Cabeza de Vaca was among them, a natural leader from all that we read. For eight years he wandered westward among the Indians as a sometime slave and revered medicine man, traversing what is now Texas, New Mexico, and a corner of Arizona before turning south to Mexico, recording with a clear mind what he saw and what he heard.

It is ironic that de Vaca, by most accounts an intelligent, modest, and humane man, should have passed on to his gullible Mexico City questioners some hearsay information of cities that had turquoise, copper, and emeralds in abundance. Gold could

Shipwrecked Cabeza de Vaca wandered with Indians before reaching Mexico with tales to tell (depicted by Frederic Remington).

only be inferred by a people who already had Peru and Mexico as precedents. The *hidalgo* mind was predisposed to think in terms of trinities.

What de Vaca had to say seemed to confirm what an Indian slave had already said about seven cities called Cíbola. Golden they were. Not unlike those seven cities on the island of Antilla that Portuguese navigators had vainly searched for in the Atlantic in the fourteenth century. So they had been on the new continent all along, then, in the obscure northwest country, the houses with their turquoise doors and golden walls gleaming in the sun, waiting to be stripped.

Mexico was infected with a fresh case of the gold itch. From the meanest street idler to Viceroy Antonio de Mendoza himself, few were immune. When de Vaca and Andrés Dorantes, a fellow

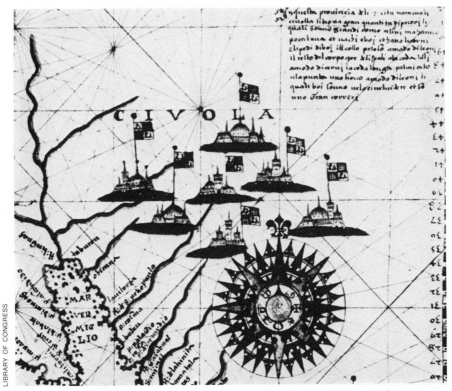

Gold and turquoise were to be found in the Seven Cities of Cíbola, placed in New Mexico by Juan Martines on his map of 1578.

survivor of the Narváez expedition, declined to lead the way north, the guide's role to a reconnaissance party fell to one Estévanico—Dorantes' garrulous Negro slave who had survived, even thrived, in the years of suffering with his master. He would show the way to Fray Marcos de Niza, who was wise in the matters of conquest by virtue of having been in Peru with Pizarro. It made more sense to Mendoza than it should have when he sent them out from Culiacán in 1539 with a few Indian bearers.

For all his qualities of strength, resourcefulness, and influence among the Indians, Estévanico had a fatal fondness for native turquoise and native women. It was not long before he leaped ahead of the main body with his harem and hangers-on, sending back to the trepid de Niza encouraging messages of his progress— eventually crossing the Rio Grande and reporting his approach to the seven cities called Cíbola. When Estévanico reached the Zuñi village of Hawíkuh in the outlandish garb of a self-proclaimed prince and announced that he, a black man, was an emissary from powerful white men to the south who meant to come north, it was a failure in diplomacy. The Zuñis immediately imprisoned him. Three days later they killed him.

Word of his death reached Fray Marcos through Estévanico's retainers. De Niza probably never got closer than one hundred fifty miles to Hawíkuh, the mesa-top village in what is now western New Mexico. But that did not stop him from gilding the cholla. His report to Mendoza became one of history's great lies believed. Included in the embroidery was the friar's claim that he had looked down on Cíbola from an eminence: "Judging by what I could see from the height where I placed myself to observe it, the settlement is larger than the city of Mexico. . . . It appears to me that this land is the best and largest of all those that have been discovered."

Francisco Vasquez Coronado led the army north in 1540. In July he avenged Estévanico by taking Hawíkuh. But what he took was chiefly mud piled high; Marcos de Niza, along for the ride, discreetly excused himself for a quick return to Mexico.

A less credulous Coronado now sent exploration parties out from his base camp at the discredited Cíbola. One went northwest to discover the Grand Canyon and to be befuddled by earthforms

The fabled gold of Gran Quivira became the common dust of Kansas for Don Francisco Vasquez de Coronado in 1541.

that abided by no known standards of perspective. Another expedition probed eastward from Zuñi to the mesa fortress of Ácoma and were well received and replenished. The journey continued on to the Rio Grande north of present-day Albuquerque, where the men in armor wintered among the Pueblo peoples, who soon found the Spaniards' weapons more believable than their word. There, on the banks of the Great River of the North, was hatched one of the first deceptions of many that would become commonplace in the American West. Out of self-preservation, no doubt, when white men came asking the way to gold and silver and such, the aborigine invariably pointed "that way," which more often than not happened to be in the direction of his enemies or some inhospitable wasteland that might do the interlopers in.

A man called the Turk, an Indian captive of the Spaniards, filled Coronado's head with a dream to replace the shattered Cíbola. Off to the northeast was a place known as Quivira, so rich its inhabitants drank from jugs and bowls of gold. Need more be said? Spring saw Coronado leading his sanguine band onto the short-grass plains and into thick herds of buffalo — "shaggy brown cows," as the Spaniards described them. Their leader soon sent most of the army back to the Rio Grande, while he led the rest to what is thought to have been southern Kansas, where he found a chief wearing a copper necklace. But there was no gold. The Turk got his, by garroting. In 1542 an ailing and disillusioned Coronado returned with his legions south to Mexico and a personal disgrace.

Coronado's failure did not put a stop to wishful thinking among the metal lovers. Mexico's conquered Aztecs had among their legends one that described their origins in a land far to the north, where there were seven caves (that magic number again) and a lake around which lived a people with plenty of gold (that magic word again). This place was called Copala. The Spanish did not immediately set off in large numbers to find it; in the mid-sixteenth century the location was still too obscure, the distance known to be great, and Coronado's disappointment still fresh in many minds. Yet, the legend persisted like a low-grade fever. It flared up again as Spaniards moved north up Mexico's central plateau to rich silver strikes at Zacatecas.

Francisco de Ibarra, who was to become the first governor of the northern mining province of Nueva Vizcaya, went hunting for Copala in the 1560s and may have reached the Gila Valley of Arizona before giving up. In 1582, while leading a band of soldiers and priests to the pueblos of the Rio Grande, Antonio de Espejo heard from the Indians of a lake of gold north of Zuñi. A prospector at heart, he took a small group to find it. The *Laguna de Oro* eluded him, but following other leads he went west beyond the Hopi mesas, deep into Arizona, where he claimed to have discovered ores "said by those who know to be very rich and contain much silver." (Upon viewing the same rocks, a companion on the journey dismissed them as "worthless.") Espejo returned to the Rio Grande and dallied a while longer to explore and prospect far afield, claiming more finds before returning home to Nueva Vizcaya with the inflammatory news.

Curiously enough, it was neither the haughty *conquistador* nor the common hustler who gave the Copalas of the West an aura of authenticity, but priests, men of God and the cloth, who wished to interest the Crown in far-off riches to further their own Christianizing efforts among savages in need of salvation. Over and over, the same ecclesiastics, on what for them was an inviting and fertile frontier, gave each illusory dream of worldly riches the help of their pens and the support of their learning. None put his motives more concisely and candidly than Father Antonio de la Ascensión, a Carmelite chaplain who accompanied the 1602 expedition of Sebastián Vizcaíno up the California coast. What he saw of the Pacific shores was pleasing; it complemented perfectly what he had heard of New Mexico: "Each will stimulate the other to discover new lands and riches, and all may enjoy very good pearl fisheries and mineral wealth, those of New Mexico enjoying the wealth from the Lake of Gold, and those of the Californias that from such rich mountains which are on that border or near it and have an abundance of rich silver ore. Both of these God created for the service of man, as lures, I think, so that in the interest of these temporal things the king, our lord, might send his vassals to discover and enjoy thém, and in their company, friars and ministers of the Gospel to undertake the conversion of those natives."

One believer, Fray Gerónimo Zárate-Salmerón, wrote that the conqueror of New Mexico, Don Juan de Oñate, on his 1604 journey to the Colorado River, was told by Indians of other Indians "who spoke the Mexican language" and wore gold bracelets on their arms and wrists. Copala again, which Zárate located "more than 400 leagues in a straight line" from Mexico City. Beyond Moqui (Hopi), he collected more secondhand evidence of an Aztec past in the ruins of cities, irrigation canals, and ore tailings similar to those found in Sinaloa and Culiacán.

Before the end of the seventeenth century, Copala became entangled with yet another myth—that of Gran Teguayo, a kingdom as imaginary as Gran Quivira and with as much alleged gold as all the rest. It did not matter that no Spaniard had seen

Copala-Teguayo with his own eyes. It had to be there and it would be found in time. Credit for coining the name Teguayo seems rightly to go to Don Diego de Peñalosa, a cocky Peruvian-born liar-adventurer who became governor of New Mexico in 1661. Peñalosa's administration was brief. In 1664 he had a final falling out with the Franciscans, and the following year he was recalled to Mexico City to answer charges brought against him by the Inquisition. There, in 1668, he was adjudged guilty, fined, and banished forever from New Spain. Don Diego was humiliated but not defeated; he had a dream to peddle, and if Spain would not underwrite his conquest of Teguayo, then maybe there were other buyers. Garbed in the dress of a knight of Alcantara, the "Count of Santa Fe" wandered first to London, then on to Paris, where he informed Louis XIV that he had been to both Quivira and Teguayo, and was willing to lead a fleet to liberate their gold and silver. Louis put him off, saying the present war with Holland made it impossible for France to consider that proposition just now. He would have to wait.

Don Diego waited, feeding Louis schemes from time to time — in 1682 one for establishing a French base at the mouth of the Rio Grande, and two years later another proposing the conquest of Tampico on the Gulf of Mexico as a staging area for taking the lucrative mines of Santa Barbara (in the present state of Chihuahua), which had been objects of French and English envy since about 1580. Louis listened, passing the information on to La Salle, who was preparing to grab for France the mouth of the Mississippi and all the strategic advantages that would provide for controlling the continent. In short, Peñalosa was pumped and then dumped. So it was the Frenchman, not the Spaniard, who sailed off to the coast of Texas in 1685.

Spain meanwhile had got wind of Peñalosa's treachery, and it brought on a case of the jitters. There were foreign designs on her territory — territory from which she had just been ejected by the Pueblo Revolt of 1680. What, the Council of the Indies wanted to hear, did anyone in New Spain know of this northern kingdom of Teguayo? The answer came from Alonso de Posadas, *custodio* of the New Mexico missions during Peñalosa's tenure. Fray Posadas' report placed "the land which the Indians of the north call Teguayo and which the Mexican Indians traditionally call Copala" west of the Rocky Mountains, in the vicinity of what would later be called the Great Salt Lake. In the Mexican language, Posadas explained, Copala meant a gathering place of many nations. It was all in keeping with Aztecan pre-anthropology, which went even further: "By the same ancient traditions it is said that from Teguayo comes not only the Mexican Indians, which were the last, but all the other nations which in different times were inhabiting these lands and kingdoms of New Spain. They say that Guatemala and all the other kingdoms and provinces of Peru and those close by have their beginnings here." Teguayo was populated by many different peoples and with the wild cows called *cíbolas*, Posadas wrote, and was not far from Quivira. "This is not only presumable but certain, and all the nations of the north affirm it, especially an Indian named Don Juanillo from the town of Jémez. When I was minister of that frontier he told me several times of having been prisoner in the said provinces of Teguayo for two years, and that there are many people in that region, speaking diverse languages, some of which were spoken in New Mexico; and also there is a large lake there. . . ."

Spain did not dispatch an army to find Teguayo, but it did send an expeditionary force under Alonzo de León to Texas to intercept La Salle's party. By the time they arrived, the French leader had been murdered, and his turbulent colony scattered to the insalubrious winds of the Gulf Coast. The immediate threat had passed. Nevertheless, Spain was moved to reconquer New Mexico. This was accomplished by Don Diego de Vargas Zapata Ponce de León in the 1690s. Teguayo then lapsed for a time into a limbo of *cantina* gossip. There were simply not enough Spaniards in New Mexico to do more than hold their own against the depredations of the Comanches, Apaches, and Utes, let alone to go tramping off into the hostile hinterlands.

It was pressure from the Utes who came raiding out of the northwest—the direction of Teguayo—that finally brought some Navajos to ask their sometime enemies, the Spaniards, for protection. The Spaniards obliged. In the 1740s they sent Franciscan missionaries west from the Rio Grande to minister to those nomads willing to leave their canyon hideouts and settle in the new pueblos of Encinal and Cebolleta. One of these was Fray Carlos Delgado, a prelate advanced in years but burning still with evangelical zeal who wished to proceed northwest two hundred leagues to a wonderful place he had heard of. "Some of the natives tell how this Teguayo, so renowned, is made up of various nations, for in it are found people from all of them, both civilized from among those whom we are governing as well as others who are heathen. One division, or city, is so large that, after their manner of expressing themselves, they say that one cannot walk around it within eight days. In it lives a king of much dignity and ostentation, who, as they say, neither looks nor speaks to anyone, except very briefly, such is his severity. He rules all the nations in those regions, and I am sure they desire to be acquainted with our holy habit, for they say that in former times a religious went there and contracted a fatal illness. After his death they kept him in a box, which they give one to understand is of silver. The said religious merited this honor because of his having catechized the king. All his successors regard as relics a shrine of gold, and the articles used in saying mass."

It was an attractive proposition Delgado sent to Commissary General Fray Pedro Navarrete, with something for everybody—the man of God, the man of gold, and the just plain inquisitive. To occupy Teguayo would also put the Franciscans one up on the Jesuits in their competition to please God with conversions. The priests in black were themselves on the move. In 1744, Jesuit Jacobo Sedelmayr had invoked the mystery of Teguayo, with its caves whence the Aztecs came, to promote settlement in the Gila-Colorado river area. Sedelmayr longed to find the cradle of Aztecan civilization and possibly learn the roots of their remarkable organization and governmental methods. But he tempered his intellectual curiosity by wondering aloud whether the French might not already have discovered Teguayo. The French! A tried and true bugaboo to raise. Yet nothing came of these clerical schemes, Jesuit or Franciscan, except more elaboration on the legend—until 1776. Then, as momentous events were taking place on the other side of the continent that would be crucial to the fate of the American West, Father Silvestre Vélez de Escalante struck out from New Mexico for *terra incognita*, into the Great Basin, where for more than two centuries Copala-Teguayo had been said to exist. Escalante's party went as far as Utah Lake and found Indians living around its shore, but none of the splendors of the fabled Teguayo. "It is nothing," wrote Escalante, "but the land by which the Tihuas, Tehuas and the other Indians transmigrated to this kingdom; which is clearly shown by the ruins of the pueblos which I have seen in it, whose form was the same that they afterwards gave to theirs in New Mexico."

Also in the Spanish bag of myths was that of an interior tribe of bearded Indians who wore armor just as the Spaniards did — descendants, perhaps, of their own shipwrecked people. Escalante told of seeing Indians wearing rabbit-skin cloaks (probably Paiutes) who had "thicker beards" than the Lagunas of the Lake region. Capt. Don Bernardo Miera y Pacheco, the secular commander of the expedition, could not resist adorning his fine maps with drawings of them. As for Teguayo, he moved that *más allá* — beyond Utah Lake to the nearby Great Salt Lake, which the explorers had not reached. There, related Miera, were large tribes who dwelt in organized communities and "tipped their arrows, lances and *Macanas* [war clubs] with a yellow metal, as it was done anciently." Thus did the legend limp on, into the nineteenth century and the coming of the Americans.

THE MEN OF METAL had other legends to lead them into the northern wilderness. Prominent among these was Sierra Azul, the blue mountain of silver that bemused some Spaniards almost as long as Copala-Teguayo and was in many ways its mythological parallel — almost a mirror image in silver of the gold. Elements of it can be traced back to the first Spanish *entradas* into the American Southwest, when Sierra Azul was believed to lie near Zuñi; later it was placed farther west, on the sunset side of Oraibi; finally it retreated into the heart of what would one day be the state of Arizona.

One of the first to give the legend substance was Capt. Marcos Farfán, who, serving under Oñate during the New Mexican conquest of 1598–1605, was sent west of Hopi to check on Espejo's old reports of mineralization there. On what is now thought to be the east side of either the Aquarius or Hualpai ranges, Indians showed Farfán many veins of black, brown, blue, and green ores, samples of which were returned to New Mexico for assaying. One showed silver in eleven ounces per hundredweight. Farfán raved "The said mountains are without doubt the richest in all New Spain," and "the veins are so long and wide that half the people of New Spain can have mines there."

But half the people in New Spain never made it to Sierra Azul. In fact, virtually everyone in New Spain proceeded to forget the very accurate geographical information that Oñate and his officers had provided on the northern territories. What was not forgotten was the part about that mountain of silver, though its whereabouts had become lost and its particulars sometimes confused with Teguayo. In 1626, Gerónimo Zárate-Salmerón, the padre who had "located" the Lake of Copala, muddied other waters somewhat by reporting that "in the province of Zuñi are deposits of silver of so fine a blue that they use it for paint and carry it to the settlements of New Mexico." Fray Zárate said that he had brought some "stones" to Mexico City and was told by painters there that "it was the best blue in the world" and that "each pound of it was worth twelve pesos." From this and from what had been said before evolved the legend of Sierra Azul, given that name by Domínguez de Mendoza, who claimed to have accompanied Peñalosa on his apocryphal journey to Gran Quivira in 1662. The blue mountain never suffered from quite the same remoteness as Teguayo, but it too became a carrot of the clergy to whet the royal appetite for extending New Spain's boundaries.

Fray Alonso de Posadas, who had such encouraging things to say about Teguayo in his 1686–87 report to the king, also put in a good word for Sierra Azul, "so famed for its wealth because its ores have been assayed many times, but never possessed because of our negligence and timidity." Posadas placed the silver mountain 100 leagues southwest of Santa Fe

With but a toehold in the West,
Carlos II feared France.

Louis XIV, his powerful rival,
encouraged French expansion.

and 50 leagues north of Sonora. A few years later a charlatan named Toribio de Huerta made an attractive offer to Spain's King Carlos II. He was prepared to undertake the reconquest of New Mexico at his own expense. All he asked in return was a marquisate stretching from El Paso in the south to Taos in the north. That he was the man for the job his record would attest: he had served his king for forty years as a conqueror in New Spain; he had "discovered" Gran Quivira; and he knew of a "place called Sierra Azul more than 200 leagues long and full of silver." Huerta mentioned something else that must have struck a responsive chord: at Sierra Azul there was also quicksilver—literally ponds of it. It just happened that Spain was then facing a critical shortage of mercury for the refining of silver from its mines in Mexico. Though Huerta proved to be without funds, the Crown was sufficiently impressed to authorize the man to draw six hundred pesos and head the expedition. Somehow, for reasons unknown, the project never got off the ground. Huerta was denied a place of honor in the pantheon of *conquistadores*, and was relegated instead to a paltry and puzzling historical footnote.

Coronado conquers Ácoma, Flemish style. New Mexico's landscape might pass for Tuscany's in this painting by Jan Mostaert.

The larger role was to go to Don Diego de Vargas Zapata Lujan Ponce de León, an ambitious young man of the blood with conquest on his mind. For him Sierra Azul held no personal attraction, but that did not keep him from playing on the hopes others had for it in order to achieve his own objective—that of being the man to reconquer New Mexico. Testimony taken from twelve former residents of the territory agreed that west of Oraibi was an extremely heavy red (one said blue) substance, slightly liquescent and of a greasy consistency, which the Indians

used as paint. It sounded like cinnabar, the most important ore of mercury. "I repeat, your Excellency," de Vargas wrote to the viceroy, "that I shall take the risk at any cost to find the said mine, and dispose of the apprehension about these stories, all of which appear so wonderful." De Vargas was at the time unhappily anchored in El Paso, having been ordered not to proceed north but to stand by and assist in putting down Indian uprisings in Sonora and Sinaloa.

Finally, in 1692, the restless de Vargas got his long-awaited orders. The invasion was *go*. Santa Fe was to be retaken first; then a small party was to visit the mines and send back to Mexico City twelve loads of ore — six of red and six of blue — for analysis. De Vargas carried out the plan until he moved west toward the putative mine. An Indian he met told him that the red earth pit was very hard to get to, being ten days' travel from Awatobi in the Hopi country, in a waterless wasteland frequented by the fierce Cosninas Apaches (Havasupai), high on a mountain that would take at least a day to climb. De Vargas decided not to go but instead obtained some samples of the red earth from the natives at Shongopovi on the Second Mesa, which were duly forwarded to the capital. An assay showed no quicksilver. Royal interest in the blue mountain with the red earth dimmed.

But the legend never died on New Spain's northern frontier. When it was not ballyhooed in Santa Fe, it was discussed in Pimería Alta, the mining-ranching-mission region, extended from northern Sonora, which reached close to the present Arizona border by the early eighteenth century. The intrepid Father Eusebio Kino heard of Sierra Azul and named a stream the Río Azul because he had been told that it flowed through a multicolored mountain that was partly blue. Kino, a man schooled in Germany and well educated in the sciences, never took seriously stories of a lake of quicksilver, and other geological monstrosities. But men of Kino's background were rare in the wilds. A colleague, Lt. Juan Matheo Manje, was less skeptical and described again the heavy, red, greasy earth being used by the Indians, who said its source was more than a five-day journey northwest of Casa Grande. He could provide no more intelligence than that "years having passed, there only remains the story of Sierra Azul, rich in silver, without anyone at the present time having any knowledge of its whereabouts."

Toward the middle of the eighteenth century, Sierra Azul made a comeback through a combination of circumstances. First, there was the *bolas de plata* silver strike at Arizonac in 1736, which drew attention to modern-day Arizona, where Sierra Azul stood in blessed isolation, somewhere in the heart of a triangle formed by the Hopi pueblos on the north, the Colorado River on the west, and the Gila River on the south. Then, in 1740, a small contingent of French-Canadian traders arrived in New Mexico from the northeast by way of the Great Plains. What and where, they wanted to know, was this Sierra Azul? Word had certainly gotten around.

Father Juan Miguel Manchero, on a formal visit to the missions and presumably present when the Frenchmen arrived, saved his answer for four years, and then it was not for French ears: "It is called Sierra Azul because the earth, rocks and the whole region is blue, with green, red, yellow and scarlet veins . . . and at the top there is a rock two varas long and a vara and a half wide which shines and looks exactly like gold. . . . Sierra Azul is four days' journey from Moqui, and the road is rough and dry. . . . The nation which inhabits the Sierra Azul is called that of the Cosninas Apaches." Something old, something new, much that was borrowed, and, as always, blue.

At the same time, Sierra Azul got good notices from another, not unexpected, quarter. They came from Franciscan fathers stationed among the Navajos, including Fray Carlos Delgado again. As with the touting of Teguayo, the father's motive was transparent. The Jesuits were making alarming progress north from Sonora, and the Franciscans wanted to keep the spiritual harvest to themselves. Significantly, after the Hopi mission field was withdrawn from the Jesuits in 1745, the Franciscans made no serious efforts to preach on their western mesas for another thirty years.

None of the metal lovers ever found Sierra Azul, though the myth was still kicking in the nineteenth century when the Anglo-Americans arrived and went off chasing the blue mountain of hearsay. Ironically, it was they who took wealth—gold, silver, and quicksilver—from the earth in central Arizona, around Prescott, where Sierra Azul might have been.

Chapter 2

Jumping Geography

NO LAND EVER SUFFERED MORE abuse at the hands of geographers than the American West. Contrary to what one might expect, knowledge of the dark side of the North American continent did not progress with the passing of years. Throughout the seventeenth century there was actually an almost steady regression into error, and the misconceptions about the land's shape and size and what was on it were not entirely cleared up until deep into the nineteenth century.

The reasons were many. Before the Anglo-American invasion only a relative handful of men had reached the shadowlands at any one time, and the ones that had were often uneducated, untrustworthy, or both. Moreover, since their sponsors back home were willing to believe the preposterous, those who had been west, or pretended to know something about it, often catered to that weakness for the enrichment of their pockets or reputations. Nations with accurate information tended to keep it away from others with whom they were in imperial competition. This was especially true of the one that knew most — Spain, already in decline in Europe by the opening of the seventeenth century but still seemingly secure in the New World as the eighteenth century came to a close. A lid of official secrecy was clamped on New Mexico and lands adjacent.

European geographers, drawing up charts in the comfort of their studies, thousands of miles from the land they were depicting, suffered under empirical handicaps and an intellectual legacy that was perhaps even more crippling. They had not outgrown medieval concepts of geographical symmetry: if there was a southern ocean, they reckoned, there had to be a northern ocean. If there was a great river of the East, then there had to be one — and only one — in the West. The methodology was deductive, analogues were eagerly sought, and unverified scraps of information were accepted so long as they fit preconceptions. The old habits did not die easily, and remnants survived into the Enlightenment, when logic dictated a bisymmetry for earth forms as it did most natural phenomena.

It might have been different, too, if mariners upon whom the mapmakers relied had had better navigational aids. It had long been possible to make fair approximations of latitude by measuring the sun's angle above the horizon at noon and then referring to tables showing the sun's declination at known latitudes on a given day, but longitude remained a headache. A reasonably accurate marine chronometer was not in use until 1760. Consequently, the breadth of the uncrossed North American continent fluctuated according to the whim of the mapmaker.

Europe's cartographers were guilty of another bad habit: they could not abide a vacuum. So when they weren't doodling or dropping a fanciful drawing or a cartouche into the empty places on their maps, they borrowed place-names to plug the holes. The 1539 journey of the prevaricator Marcos de Niza and the bona fide report of Coronado gave them a selection of names from which to draw. From de Niza there were Cíbola, Tabursa, and Tontonteanch; from Coronado, Axa, Tiguex, Cicuic, and Quivira. These and other place-names in variant spellings wandered back and forth across a West of fluctuating width, to be dropped suddenly, then resurrected to fill a void.

Gran Quivira set the style and precedent for future loose play with the facts. Coronado found his disappointment in south-central Kansas in 1541, but it did not stay there long. The Spanish chronicler Francisco López de Gómara was partly to blame for the mix-up that followed. Though he had not been with Coronado in Quivira, he nevertheless had a lot to say about it in his *Historia General de las Indias,* published in 1544: "Quivira is in 40 degrees, a temperate country, well-watered, with many herbs, plums, mulberries, nuts, melons and grapes which mature well. . . . They [Coronado's party] saw on the coast ships with merchandise which

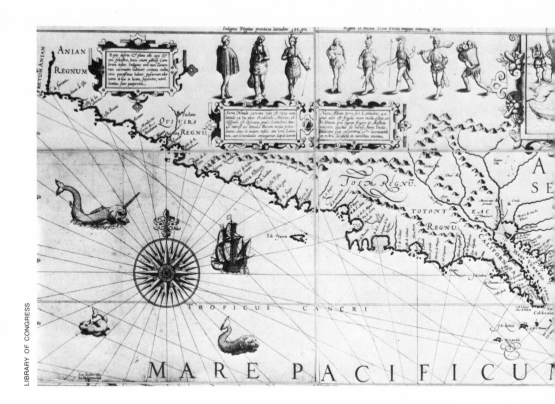

had on their prows pelicans made of gold and silver, and they thought they must be from Catayo or China, as they made signs that they had sailed thirty days."

Coast? Gold? China? The most renowned cartographers in Europe picked up on Gómara's displacement of Quivira, being very scrupulous with regard to his latitude. The Venetian mapmaker Giacomo Gastaldi placed Quivira at the proper forty degrees on his map of 1556, only three hundred miles from the Pacific coast, east of the "Sierra Nevada"—another of Gómara's inventions. The Flemish Abraham Ortélius also showed Quivira near the coast on his 1564 map, and in 1569 the famed Gerhardus Mercator moved Quivira all the way to the Pacific's edge, placing the city at forty degrees latitude and the Sierra Nevada on a westward-slanting littoral at about forty-one degrees; Cicuic and Tiguex—both Coronado place-names—had followed Quivira west, proof that Gómara was being read and improved upon.

This widespread belief that Quivira fronted the Pacific persisted

That problem of longitude—Europe's geographers gave to scarcely explored North America a girth that ranged from very thick to very thin. The unknown author of this map (circa 1600) was of the former persuasion.

in Europe through the eighteenth century, long after Spain had realized its mistake and was again sending expeditions northeast to the Great Plains, drawn there by more talk of gold. As late as 1786, "A New Map of the Whole Continent of America" was published in London showing the new post-Revolutionary War boundaries and Quivira as a district on the Pacific.

Quivira, then, was even more insubstantial than Cíbola—one part earth to ten of hot air. Lacking any mass to speak of, it blew freely like thistledown over a land that had about as many configurations as Europe had geographers. But it was not the only creation of errant ink.

ALTHOUGH SPAIN DID HER BEST to keep what she knew of the West from prying foreigners, occasionally some information, or misinformation, did slip out. In the typical pattern, a new south-flowing river would abruptly turn up on an Italian map, to be

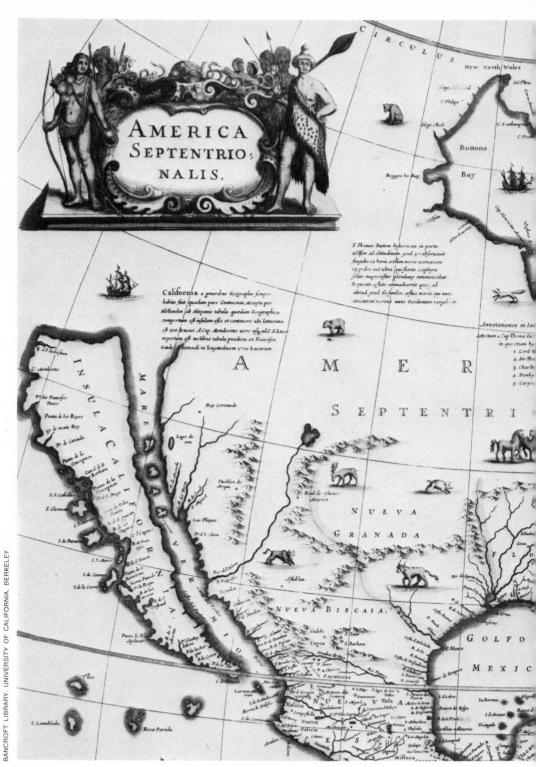

Somehow California came unstuck from the mainland in the seventeenth century. Henricus Hondius was but one to show it as an island.

adopted a few years later by French cartographers; it would then make its way to Holland, finally being incorporated by English mapmakers, who were almost always the last to get the word. Naturally, these geographers, who operated by guess and synthesis, and who plagiarized freely, got things muddled from time to time. Therefore, when Spain's information was wrong, all Europe's maps perpetuated the error.

California was such a case. Both Ulloa and Alarcón (in 1539 and 1540, respectively) had sailed up the Gulf of California to the mouth of the Colorado—Alarcón some distance inland—and had established that California was a peninsula, correcting Cortés, who had believed it to be an island. Somehow this was forgotten after their voyages even in Mexico, where reasons for remembering it would seem to have been considerable. Nevertheless, an island it had been and an island it became once more.

Those who believed it was anything but an island obviously had not read Garcí Ordoñez de Montalvo's *Las Sergas de Esplandián,* the chivalric romance in which the island of California was first described, in astonishing detail:

> Know ye that at the right hand of the Indies there is an island named California, very close to that part of the Terrestrial Paradise, which was inhabited by black women, without a single man among them, and that they lived in the manner of Amazons. They were robust of body, with strong and passionate hearts and great virtues. The island itself is one of the wildest in the world on account of the bold and craggy rocks. Their weapons were all made of gold. . . . The island everywhere abounds with gold and precious stones, and upon it no other metal was found. . . . They had many ships with which they sailed to other coasts to make forays, and the men whom they took as prisoners they killed. . . . In this island, named California, there are many griffins. . . . In no other part of the world can they be found. . . . [And] there ruled over that island of California a queen of majestic proportions, more beautiful than all others, and in the very vigor of her womanhood.

The queen's name was Calafia, and she had this itch to travel, so she collected some of her sisters and a herd of griffins and sailed to Constantinople, where a band of Crusaders was being besieged by a host of the infidel. She knew nothing about politics or religion, and that may account for her taking the part of the Turks in the original version. Anyway, she led her Amazons into the fray and released her cruel griffins on the hapless Christians, who were devoured wholesale in the beastly orgy or carried skyward and then dropped to splatter on the earth. Unfortunately, the griffins could not discriminate between the featherless bipeds, and they were soon doing the same thing to the Turks, with equally devastating effect. In time the valiant Calafia was captured and soon fell in love with Esplandián, the handsome hero of the piece. This chaste knight, however, was already spoken for by an emperor's daughter, so he arranged a match for the black queen with his cousin. Calafia was so grateful that she became a convert and ceded California, with all its gold and gems, to the Christians.

Montalvo's story appeared early in the sixteenth century and was known to Cortés and his followers, who undoubtedly gave the name to the land they found northwest of Mexico. It was just the kind of lowbrow literature to be carried in the duffel bags of the day. (Cervantes gleefully had Don Quixote's copy thrown on a bonfire with the rest of the knightly foolishness that had addled the poor don's brain.) Of course, very few of the fantastical features of Montalvo's California could have been transferred to New Spain's California. The *hispanos* may have been impressionable but they were not mad. On the other hand, the idea that California possessed gold and riches was an article of Spanish faith as long as they owned the land, and even non-Spaniards afterwards regarded it as a terrestrial paradise until the proliferation of the internal combustion engine.

There was a more plausible but equally erroneous reason for the seventeenth-century belief that California was an island. It fit in nicely with another myth of greater weight and longevity— the Strait of Anian, which was thought to cut through the North American landmass and emerge somewhere north of California. The voyage of Sebastián Vizcaíno in 1602 seemed to support both notions. Sailing out of Acapulco with two ships in order to locate likely harbors for reprovisioning the Manila galleons arriving from the Orient, the voyagers reached Cape Mendocino. One ship was then blown off course to a point where the crew said they saw a northeastward turn to the land and a large river issuing from it. Here was support for other seamen who claimed to have visited the Strait of Anian. The large river could not be just a river; it must be the strait, and California an island touching its southern waters. Among the members of Vizcaíno's "armada" was Father Ascensión, the Carmelite who had seen God's plan in putting gold and the unbaptized in the same places. Ascensión had a keen interest in the unknown lands and some university training in cosmography. It was his doubly informed opinion that California was clearly "separate and distinct from the lands of New Mexico . . . the sea between these two realms, which is the one called the Mediterranean Sea of California . . . must be about fifty leagues wide."

California's insularity got further confirmation when Don Juan de Oñate marched west from New Mexico to the Colorado and Gila rivers and conversed with the Indians there. According to one account of the journey, the Indians told the Spaniards that the Gulf of California was not closed, but that west of a mountain range beyond the Colorado was a sea, and in that sea an island ruled by a giantess—old, fat, and with outsized feet. The gulf, then, had to run farther north, probably connecting with the Strait of Anian. Thus did mere rumor, raised to respectability by the written word, cut California off from the mainland.

It only remained for the word to get around, and that was aided by the theft of a Spanish map (possibly of Ascensión's own authorship) by the Dutch. The English professor Henry Briggs claimed to have seen the purloined document, and his own map that appears in the 1625 edition of Purchas' *His Pilgrimes* bears this legend: "California, sometimes supposed to be a part of ye western continent, but scince by a Spanish chart taken by ye Hollanders it is founde to be a goodly Ilande; the length of the west shoare beeing about 500 leagues from Cape Mendocino to the South Cape thereof called Cape St. Lucas. . . ." California's island status had been authenticated, and an island it remained throughout the seventeenth century.

The man most responsible for putting things right was Father

Father Kino, drawing on his own explorations north from Sonora, put California and the mainland together again on his map of 1701.

Eusebio Kino. He had been taught in Germany that California was a peninsula; but when he arrived in Mexico, he found opinions overwhelmingly of the opposite persuasion, and for a time he accepted the common view. By 1700, however, his own explorations into Arizona convinced him that the others were wrong and that California had to be joined to the continent. Maps he sent to Rome with his writings became the basis for a change in thinking. The noted French cartographer Guillaume Delisle restored

California's peninsularity as early as 1701. Other mapmakers slowly fell into line, but Delisle's fellow Frenchman, Nicolas de Fer, "His Catholic Majesty's Geographer," continued to show its ill-defined shape positioned in the Pacific as late as 1720, and atlases of the time frequently contained old plates along with the new, which left one a choice in the matter.

Father Fernando Consag finally settled the question for good in 1746 when he followed the coast of Baja California all the way to the mouth of the Colorado River. The Amazon queen and her man-eating griffins did not dwell in a land apart after all.

THE MYTH OF A WATERWAY through North America was almost as old as Europe's knowledge of a stubborn continent interposed between home and China. It was a durable myth, destined to have adherents for three hundred years, and would sap the talents, energies, and treasuries of many nations as well as inspire some mighty fancy lies. The commercial and military value of a water route to the East in northern latitudes was as incalculable as it was obvious. Any nation that could find it and control it would put its rivals at a decided disadvantage, for the goods of the East had become necessary luxuries. There simply had to be a way to and from the East without circling those two distant capes in the wrong hemisphere.

During the sixteenth century Europeans were divided on whether America was an extension of the Asian mainland or separate. The Italians initially favored the former, and the nations of northern Europe the latter, as their respective maps would show. (The Spanish and Portuguese generally followed a policy of not showing anything on their maps that they had not actually seen.) Between 1530 and 1540 the idea of a Northwest Passage began to gain in popularity. A 1535 globe by Gemma Frisius shows a strait with a notation that the Portuguese had tried to navigate it. A 1538 map by Battista Agnese goes one better by claiming that the French had already sailed through it to China. Momentum was plainly shifting to the pro-strait scholars, who could cite as additional evidence the existence of Antarctica and the Strait of Magellan; according to the rule of symmetry, the

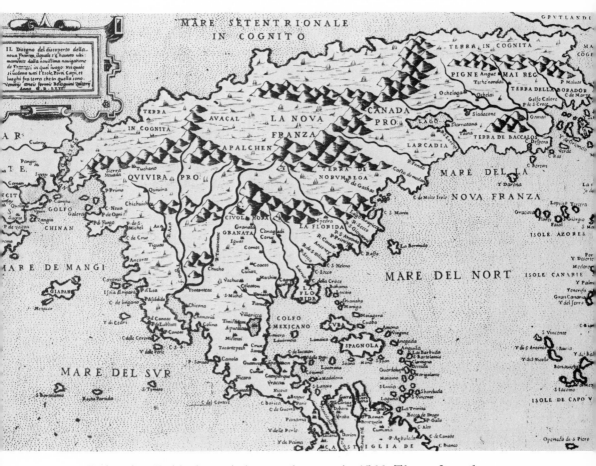

Bolognino Zaltieri put Anian on the map in 1566. Thereafter, the "Northwest Passage" roamed east from the Bering Strait.

northern antipodes could be expected to show similar features.

In a 1562 pamphlet entitled *La Universale Discrittione del Mundo,* Gastaldi first called the strait Anian, a name apparently gleaned from the writings of Marco Polo, which in a different spelling described a province near Siam. Four years later, Bolognino Zaltieri was the first to put the name on a map, and it subsequently became a fixture on world maps well into the eighteenth century. Zaltieri placed it roughly where the Bering Strait is today, but like Quivira, Anian would not stay put. It strayed generally from west to east—sometimes wide, sometimes narrow, sometimes straight, sometimes crooked, sometimes slicing through the shoulders of the continent, sometimes darting north into the Polar Ocean by way of Hudson Bay.

Of all those who sought the Strait of Anian, none wanted it more than the English. Being one of the last links in the medieval chain of trade with the Orient, they had the greatest need to find a new route westward; they were also the first to make a systematic effort to find the waterway and among the last to give up the search. During the reign of Elizabeth I, when England grew from a budding maritime power to mistress of the seas and a trading nation of the first rank, there clustered around the court a handful of influential men who were convinced a shortcut could be found to eliminate those endless unfriendly miles through Iberian-controlled seas. Among them were Sir Walter Raleigh, the intellectual John Dee, a London merchant named Michael Lok, the monied Earl of Warwick, Richard Hakluyt, England's dean of geographers, and Sir Humphrey Gilbert, a sometime soldier and an all-the-time dilettante. Gilbert petitioned the queen in 1565 for the privilege of finding the Northwest Passage at his own expense, in exchange for a monopoly on the trade through it while he was alive and 25 percent of the customs duties levied on what was brought back to England. Gilbert also wrote, and later published in 1576, *A Discourse of a Discoverie for a newe passage to Cataia,* a compilation of what was known or thought to be known about the legendary strait, from Plato's island Atlantis down to the testimony of sailors and scholars of his own day who happened to agree with him. Mention was even made of a priest named Antonio Urdaneta who had recently sailed the strait from west to east. The *Discourse* was hortatory and chauvinistic, and any Englishman, Gilbert promised, "that will give the attempt, may with smal danger passe in Cataia . . . in much shorter time than either the Spaniard or Portingale doth, or may do, from the neerest parte of any of their countreis." Gilbert included a heart-shaped map of the world showing a wide passage north of Canada that gradually narrowed as it ran southwest, emptying into a great ocean near Japan. From there it was a short trip to the gold, silver, precious stones, and spices of the East, which could be obtained in trade of exclusively English goods. A convenient way station, say "about the Sierra Nevada," might be built; or better yet, the

strait could be colonized with "suche needie people of our coun-
trie, which now trouble the common welth, and through want here
at home, are inforced to commit outragious offenses, whereby
they are dayly consumed with the Gallows." Here was a formula
that would be put into practice later, elsewhere.

Gilbert's *Discourse* influenced later Englishmen, but it served
the immediate purpose of promoting the trading company that
he and his colleagues were forming. Their man, Martin Frobisher,
an able seadog with a privateer's past, was commissioned in 1576
to find the Northwest Passage. He found instead Baffin Island and
proceeded up Frobisher Strait, where he had a costly run-in with
some Eskimos. Frobisher returned to London with some heavy
ore samples he had picked up, which caused a five-year-long
gold fever until the "black stones" were found to be of no value.
Frobisher tried again in 1577 and a final time in 1578, but without
success. He had to swallow his claim made before his maiden
voyage that the trip "was not onely possible by the Northwest"
but also, as he could prove, "easie to be performed."

Frobisher's failure did not deter England's Elizabethan master
mariners from future attempts to discover the passage, for which
twenty thousand pounds in prize money had been raised, with
Queen Elizabeth herself a contributor. The respected Hakluyt
encouraged his countrymen: "On the backside or west of
America, from 24 degrees of Northerly latitude to 43 degrees . . . ,
[the Spaniards] have not one foot of actual possession, much less
more northerly. And therefore in time to come they shall have no
pretense of cavillation against a north-west passage, if it shall
please God to lay open the same." John Davis made three more
voyages across the North Atlantic in the mid-1580s, but it did not
please God to lay open the strait to him.

The picture always looked rosier in London. It looked rosier,
too, in Venice in 1596. That year the London merchant Michael
Lok, partner of Gilbert in sponsoring Frobisher's passage, was in
the city of canals to settle a lawsuit. There, by his own account,
he met a man known as Juan de Fuca—a Greek, actually, whose
real name was Apostolos Valerianos—who had sailed under the
flag of Spain for forty years as a mariner and ship's pilot. Juan had
stories to tell. One recounted how he had been captured by the

English rover Cavendish off the coast of Baja California and robbed of sixty thousand ducats. Another, by far the more intriguing, concerned a voyage he had taken in 1592 at the direction of the viceroy to find the Strait of Anian. Find it he did, by sailing up the California coast with his caravel and a tiny pinnace to a latitude of between forty-seven and forty-eight degrees. There the coast bent northeast into an inlet of the sea through which he sailed for more than twenty days until, after passing many islands and heading in almost every direction of the compass, he reached a very much broader sea. De Fuca had gone ashore in several places and observed "some people on Land, clad in Beast skins; and that the Land is very fruitfull, and rich of gold, Silver, Pearle, and other things, like *Nova Spania*." De Fuca reasoned that he had reached the North Sea, but lacking arms to cope with the savages, he turned around and sailed to Acapulco that same year.

This humble servant of the Crown expected to be compensated for his feat; instead, the viceroy put him off for two years, then suggested he go to Spain and get his reward from the king. When de Fuca presented himself at court in Madrid, he got some flowery words but nothing for his purse. As shabbily as he had been treated, de Fuca was still willing to put what he knew to some good use. He had always thought well of the noble Queen Elizabeth, and if her majesty might be willing to make good his losses to Cavendish, he would gladly go to England and rediscover the Northwest Passage. All he needed was a ship of forty tons and a pinnace, and he would do it "in thirtie days time, from one end to the other of the Streights."

Juan must have been a charming fibber, and Lok either one of the more gullible men of his time or himself a skilled con artist. Lok sent letters to notables in England asking that one hundred pounds be raised to bring his "Greeke Pilot" to England. They thought it a splendid idea, but the money was "not readie." Two years later Lok tried to organize an expedition with de Fuca as its pilot. He was unsuccessful and later learned that Juan had apparently died in his native Greece.

The Juan de Fuca story entered print in 1625 when Samuel Purchas included it in *His Pilgrimes,* along with two treatises by Henry Briggs on the probability of a Northwest Passage. Its appearance aroused little interest. By then, Henry Hudson had tried four times to find the strait, and William Baffin twice. All were failures. Perhaps England's investors and merchants, who had borne much of the expense to find the Strait of Anian, were out of patience — not to mention gambling stakes. So English enthusiasm for a Northwest Passage cooled for a time. Though sailors had known waters above eighty degrees in latitude, the turbulent weather, contrary winds, hazardous ice, and clashes with hostile natives made life miserable, to say the least. And while England's knowledge of arctic geography was being expanded, its trade with Cathay was not.

The Spaniards now kept the legend alive. Pearl fishermen after concessions in the Gulf of California used it as bait. One of them, Pedro Porter Casanate, promised the Crown he would find the Strait of Anian if his petition was approved. It was, in 1640, but there is no evidence he kept his word. Francisco de Seyxas y Lovera, in his *Theatro Naval Hydrographico* published in Madrid in 1688, included a story of an English captain, Thomas Peche, who in order to save time on a Philippines-to-London run, sailed 120 leagues up the Strait of Anian before adverse currents and the coming winter turned him back. When he finally reached England by way of Magellan's strait, so the account went, he had left behind 150 crewmen in watery graves.

The choice of an Englishman as protagonist did not hurt the story's credibility. The existence of the strait was always primarily an English obsession, and in the eighteenth century, when competition between England, France, and Spain for possession of North America sharpened, Anian with all its promise again sent mostly Englishmen down to the sea in ships. It all started, or was restarted, with a brazen fraud perpetrated in London in 1708 by (one has every reason to suspect) a magazine editor named James Petiver. His *Monthly Miscellany or Memoirs for the Curious* carried that year a two-part account of yet another voyage through the Strait of Anian, which was to have a dramatic, if delayed, effect. This time the daring sailor was Bartholomew de Fonte, with the grand title of Admiral of New Spain and Peru. According to the *Monthly Miscellany,* de Fonte departed Peru in 1640 commanding four ships on orders of the king and viceroy to find the

Northwest Passage the English were so diligently seeking. The admiral took his fleet northwest to California, where he dispatched his vice-admiral—none other than the future intriguer and self-proclaimed discoverer of Teguayo, Don Diego de Peñalosa—to determine whether it was an island or not. The admiral's main force proceeded north, finding at fifty-three degrees a river he named Los Reyes, up which he eventually sailed, after first sending one of his captains into the Arctic Ocean to discover whether it connected with the Atlantic. (It did not, the captain reported.)

The northeast-flowing Los Reyes took de Fonte to a Lake Belle, which had an Indian town, Conosset, on its south side. Here the admiral rested before sailing on up another river he called Parmentiers (after his interpreter who was miraculously able to communicate with the Indians) to a lake he immodestly named de Fonte. On he went, up another connecting river and another lake, the countryside becoming more and more bleak. Then it happened. He encountered a ship "of New England, from a Town called Boston," that had arrived there from the other direction. De Fonte was gracious to its skipper, Captain Shapley: "I received him like a Gentleman, and told him, my Commission was to make Prize of any People seeking a North West or West Passage into the South Sea, but I would look upon them as Merchants trading with the Natives for Bevers, Otters, and other Furs and Skins." De Fonte was also generous. He presented Captain Shapley with his diamond ring, which had cost him twelve hundred pieces of eight, and sent along for the ship's owner, Scimor Gibbons of Boston, "a quarter Cask of good Peruan Wine." In late summer of 1640, de Fonte bade the north country farewell and sailed back to Peru, his mission accomplished.

There never was any Bartholomew de Fonte. There never was any Admiral of New Spain and Peru. (If there had been, the Spanish would probably have known about it.) And for all the account's detailed attention to tidal fluctuations, ships' provisions, and flora and fauna observed, it is hopelessly unintelligible and wretchedly written. Curiously, research did reveal that a Captain Shapely and a Seymour Gibbons lived in Massachusetts at approximately the time of de Fonte's alleged voyage. This, apparently, coupled with the reference to the notorious and conveniently dead Peñalosa, convinced many future believers, including an American named Benjamin Franklin.

The imaginary admiral might have sailed off into the sunset of memory had it not been for an Irish engineer named Arthur Dobbs, who more than two decades later resurrected the de Fonte fantasy and determined it had "throughout the air of truth." Though its geography bore no resemblance to Juan de Fuca's, the two were paired as mutually supportive. Dobbs knew there was a Northwest Passage. What is more, he knew that Hudson's Bay Company knew there was a Northwest Passage, and that the monopolists were deliberately suppressing knowledge of it out of selfishness. Disgraceful conduct! It deprived the very nation that had granted its charter—a charter that stipulated the company was to search for the passage—of trading opportunities that were beyond imagining. Dobbs entered into a lengthy and bitter

This placement of the nonexistent "western sea" was based on a voyage of a nonexistent Admiral Fonte up the nonexistent Strait of Anian.

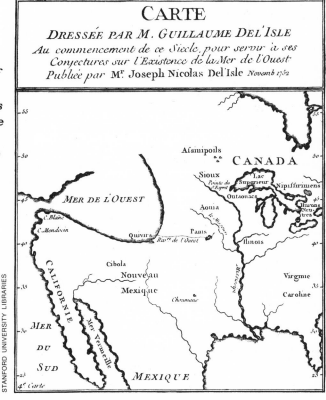

wrangle with the company trading in Hudson's Bay, and in 1741 he succeeded in having Capt. Christopher Middleton sent on an independent voyage of discovery. Middleton probed the western shores of Hudson Bay for an opening, but in vain. After Middleton returned, Dobbs became furious. Obviously the man had been bribed by the monopolists. All England had been duped!

Everything pointed to a passage. There was the news from Russia (an occasional dark horse in the race for the American West and employed by some expansionists as a stalking-horse) that Vitus Bering and Alexi Chirikov had departed Kamchatka in 1741 and from their separate ships had sighted the Alaskan mainland. There was, indeed, a strait between Asia and America. Further corroboration had just arrived from France. It was a garbled report from a half-breed named Joseph La France, who had spent the years 1739 to 1742 in the Hudson Bay area, that an Indian war party had reached the western sea and had found there a strait running east to west, which they followed by canoe and on foot for three months.

Dobbs went public with his cause and Parliament raised another twenty thousand pounds in prize money in 1745. Because Anian had to exist and was not found where men had looked, it therefore had to be where they had not looked, or had not looked very closely. Shares were sold to finance an expedition and the purchase of two vessels, one of which bore the sanguine name, *California*. Two reliable captains were chosen, and on May 31, 1746, the great adventure got under way. The ships were gone more than a year, the time spent mostly in exploring the western indentations in Hudson Bay for a linkage with de Fonte's discoveries. None was found, and in 1750 even Dobbs called it quits.

By then the will-o'-the-wisp was glowing in France, where a pair of geographers, Joseph Nicholas Delisle (the younger brother of Guillaume) and Philippe Buache, served up a cartographical stew with few equals. It was a map, based only in part on the discoveries of Bering and Chirikov, published in 1752 with the long-winded title of *Carte Générale des Descouvertes de l'Amiral de Fonte et autres Navigateurs Espagnols, Anglais et Russes, pour la recherch du Passage à la Mer du Sud*. It drew hoots from some English and Spanish scholars, but by then the whole legend had gotten so out of hand that it would not fade away.

In 1776 the Parliament of England put up another twenty thousand pounds. That same year, while rebellion was becoming revolution on the east coast of North America, Capt. James Cook set off on his third and final voyage of discovery to see if from the west coast there was not a water connection to Hudson Bay or Baffin Bay. Whether out of confidence in the navigator or merely to cover all bets, the Admiralty actually dispatched two ships to Baffin Bay to meet Cook, should he be successful. Neither Cook nor his successors found the passage, the search for which historian Nellis Crouse has described as no longer having any practical commercial value, but one that "lingered as a sort of scientific sporting event."

It also lingered, with a progressively fewer number of die-hards and academicians, as still the shortest way to China. In 1775, a French *abbé* gave a Spanish duke an account written in about 1609 of a 1588 voyage by a Spanish adventurer named Lorenzo Ferrer Maldonado. Yes indeed, Maldonado had been through the Strait of Anian, though east to west this time. Maldonado, as expected, had much to say. The strait was in sixty degrees of latitude, only 1,710 leagues from Spain, and a mere 15 leagues long. Easily negotiated in six hours with the right tide, it had anchorage space for five hundred ships at its southern mouth. Though the waters could be rough, the weather was surprisingly mild, given the latitude, and the land abounded in partridges and in wild pigs whose umbilical cords were attached to their backs. While there, Maldonado saw a ship of eight hundred tons pull in, manned, he guessed, by German Lutherans returning from China with a shipload of brocades, porcelains, silks, and (naturally) gold. But Spain had no reason to fear such free use of the waterway in the future. The strait's topography was such that it could easily be defended. Detailed drawings were provided, showing where lookouts and gun batteries should be placed.

There really was a Lorenzo Ferrer Maldonado alive in Spain in 1609. He was an opportunist of the more unsavory type, and his alleged adventure, surfacing from the archives so long after the fact, must have sent many in Europe into fits of mirth, but not all. Spain stopped laughing when Philippe Buache de la Neuville (son of the geographer Philippe Buache of the infamous 1752 map) embraced the story enthusiastically before an assembly of the Academy of Sciences. Buache was a man of considerable reputation, and if he gave it his imprimatur, well then, had something been missed? Alejandro Malaspina, on a round-the-world scientific voyage, was sent from Acapulco in 1791 to find out. He searched the west coast at sixty degrees and found nothing.

Anian had finally lost its hold on men's imaginations. Of course, there had been a Northwest Passage all along, not where most explorers had looked for it, but farther to the north, above seventy-five degrees, through the ice-clogged Arctic Ocean. The Norwegian Roald Amundsen proved that fact in 1905, long after the contest for North America had been settled.

Chapter 3

Grand Liars
in a Grand Land

FRANCE WANTED A SHORTCUT to the Orient every bit as much as her rivals did. While England and Spain were searching for a Northwest Passage by water, the French sought the western sea, the Pacific, by land.

As fur traders and missionaries moved inland up the Saint Lawrence toward the Great Lakes, they met Indians who said that to the west — one moon, three moons, six moons away — were both a great river and a large sea. The French learned soon enough that the river found by Marquette and Jolliet was not the one; the Mississippi flowed south into the Gulf of Mexico. So then the River of the West had to be beyond, toward the yellow horizon, where the trees stopped and the endless sea of grass began. In time the French would add another geographical invention of their own, a large, landlocked body of water that, more often than not, had a river outlet to the distant ocean.

La Salle's exploration and the follow-up French occupation of the Mississippi gave to eighteenth-century Europe's greatest land power the possession of the heartland of America. Understandably, interest in the western sea and the River of the West was greater than ever. Yet France was ill-prepared to find whatever was out there. She had already overextended herself. As brave and hardy as those French *voyageurs* were, their numbers in the vast river valley were woefully few. The birchbark canoe so perfectly suited to Canada's deep rivers and the usually placid Great Lakes was useless in the West. The Missouri and the Platte and the Arkansas and the other streams branching west from the Mississippi did not behave like any known rivers; they were

The bison (depicted here by Johan de Laet, 1630) shared the Great Plains with the less plentiful tiger, leopard, and griffin.

seasonally angry brown torrents or shallow, snag-filled trickles; always the currents were contrary.

And yet, the ideas of a large river and lake in the uncharted West were so beguiling that for two centuries the French would move them freely over a plastic landmass. At times the lake was said to be on the central plains near the Pawnees, or farther west and north in what we call Wyoming. Sometimes it would be fresh water, sometimes salt. It joined with an east-flowing river, with a west-flowing river, with both. At other times the lake evaporated, leaving only a single river or a pair of connecting rivers that emptied into the western sea.

If the natives they met had not fostered a widespread belief in a River of the West, it would have been advisable for the French frontiersman to have invented one. He was dependent on Montreal for provisions and a market for his furs, and the last thing he wanted was to be abandoned in the middle of a hostile nowhere. Montreal was equally dependent on the good opinion of Paris for survival, and glad tidings sent home were always preferable. For its part, Paris eventually came to greet the good news with perfunctory pleasure and a firm no to whomever it was that wanted money to find "it" this time.

"There is no country in the world where more lying is done than in Canada," concluded one Father Nau after a particularly encouraging report came from the West. He went on to echo another observation that officials in New France were not looking for the western sea "but for the sea of beaver."

New France had a goodly number of liars, as Father Nau believed. One might also add that most of them, or at least the best of them, were in the West. If Louis XIV was so ignorant of his distant and neglected holdings, then why not dress the place up a little, particularly if it stood to boost one in estate or reputation? France would supply the western mystery her own fair share of truth-benders.

A MAN CALLING HIMSELF MATHIEU SAGEAN turned up in France in 1699 with a story that was beyond believing, though a few influential Frenchmen tried. He was a Creole born in Montreal and said he had accompanied La Salle down the Mississippi. Later, with the blessing of Henri de Tonty, La Salle's second-in-command, he claimed he had gone upstream with eleven countrymen and two Indians to forty leagues above a cataract, where he saw a river as large as the Mississippi that ran southwesterly. It looked so promising that he made a portage, thinking it might lead to the south sea. Through a country alive with tigers and leopards, he coasted two hundred fifty leagues to the kingdom of the Acaanibas, a populous people whose splendiferous King Hagaazen traced his descent from Montezuma, the Aztec man-god.

The land of the Acaanibas was unlike any previously reported. The climate was mild all the year round, and the ground was so fertile it yielded an encyclopedic variety of foods in abundance. Disease was unknown, death the consequence of ripe old age. This, of course, produced a large population of Acaanibas, and, indeed, King Hagaazen was able to keep nearly a hundred thousand men under arms in case the hated Spaniards should come. In their past these gentle people had suffered cruelly at the hands of the *conquistadores,* those unpleasant memories being kept alive in the songs sung by the children. Acaanibas ate continu-

73

ally, drank palm wine in moderation, and worshiped huge black apes, which were believed to house the souls of their ancestors. The men were lucky fellows. They took as many wives as they wished, and as for Acaaniban women—ah, monsieur!—not only were they many and willing, but they were white and beautiful, just as white and beautiful as European women! Sagean could only fault them for their ears, which were enormous. This disfigurement resulted from their custom of piercing their ears and weighing them down with gold ornaments. Yes, gold. The Acaanibas had much gold. It came from the nearby mines, which were really not mines at all, but dry streambeds where nuggets could be gathered like eggs in a henhouse.

Montezuma could not have lived in more opulent surroundings than King Hagaazen. His palace was of gold, with walls eighteen feet high. They were not gold-plated either, but of solid gold bricks held together by a mortar of the same element. Gold being a surplus commodity, the Acaanibas not only made their tools from it, but used it in trade with a distant people—possibly the Japanese, because it took their caravans six months to make the journey to the Acaanibas.

After a five-month stay among this hospitable people, Sagean decided he ought to be getting back home. But before he left, King Hagaazen urged him and his men to take all the gold they could carry and made them promise to return and trade for more. (The Acaanibas happened to have a critical shortage of beads and trinkets.) Unfortunately, much of the gold had to be discarded on the return trip up the "River Milly" lest it sink Sagean's three small canoes. And then, back in Canada, at the mouth of the Saint Lawrence River, an English pirate robbed them of the rest and butchered six of Sagean's companions. As for other survivors of his party, Sagean thought two might still be alive in a New York jail, from which he had escaped before wandering half the world on his way back to France.

Upon the instructions of Minister of Marine Jerôme Phélypeaux Pontchartrain, Sagean was sequestered in a Brest jail and questioned closely. He really had nothing to add to what he had already said, and he could only remember the Indian names of those Frenchmen who had been with him. Nevertheless, the story

The great La Salle, once dead, became the "friend" of such worthy truth-benders as Mathieu Sagean and Louis Hennepin.

was not taken lightly. A French sea captain home from the West Indies had while there met a Canadian gentleman who had also told of this tribe living approximately where Sagean said, with a king dwelling in a palace of gold. This Canadian gentleman, too, said he had been with La Salle. The minister of marine put one and one together and got two, when it probably added up to one. Sagean had been in the West Indies at about the time of the sea captain's visit there.

The Sagean story became hush-hush among a small circle of officials that included Pontchartrain and a few highly regarded scholars, who found some intriguing parallels between what Sagean reported and what old accounts of Spanish explorers had to say. Maybe it was all true. Maybe France was at last to get some of the New World gold that had been denied her — that is, if she could get there before the English, who, rumor had it, were already out there trading in Acaanibaland. Pontchartrain ordered that this other Canadian should be watched for and, if seen, held and interrogated.

In New France, Sagean's fable caused not a stir. The explorer Pierre Le Sueur said he knew the man by another name and that he had not been with La Salle. What is more, the man could not have found the river he claimed because he, Le Sueur, had explored that section of the Mississippi and had seen no such stream. When Sagean arrived in Biloxi in 1701, sent there by Pontchartrain to lead an expedition to the land of gold, he was greeted with jeers and indifference, and was very soon swallowed up in the great river valley, forgotten, not even immortalized with a place-name.

Sagean had reached too far. He had also been preempted by a far abler liar who had been exploring in the Upper Mississippi before him, and who forsook the well-worn way to El Dorado for a fresher path to glory.

Father Louis Hennepin also claimed intimacy with La Salle. He actually was with the great explorer for a short time on a journey through the Illinois country toward the Mississippi, where the two would part and take different directions on the river. The Belgian-born Recollect friar had a knack for exaggerating his own first-hand experiences and stealing the unpublicized experiences of

Father Hennepin's lively potboilers kept Europe's armchair travelers "informed" about North America's Wild West.

others. To judge from the remarks of contemporaries (confirmed by a reading of the friar's pompous prose), Hennepin was a fraud, a plagiarist, a braggart, and a toady. There was no end to his posturings, which earned him more enemies than an ordinary man could afford in three lifetimes. Yet it is a tribute to his storytelling skills that his three books on the North American wilderness were must-reading for Europe's armchair travelers for three generations.

La Salle was aboard the same vessel that brought Louis Hennepin to New France in 1675, and the two had an immediate falling-out. The gray-gowned friar, ever a prude, objected to the rowdiness of some women colonists aboard. La Salle objected to Hennepin and told him so. When the pair reached Canada, Hennepin went about his priestly duties in the Quebec area for four years while La Salle was preparing to establish his western fief. When La Salle was at last ready to move, Hennepin was selected to accompany an advance party west. The choice may seem strange. But La Salle was feuding with the Jesuits, whom he saw as a threat to his designs, and preferred some harmless Recollect for the *pro forma* fulfillment of the religious side of the expedition. La Salle was hardly impressed with the man. "It is necessary to know him somewhat," La Salle cautioned his men, "for he will not fail to exaggerate everything; it is his character . . . and he speaks more in keeping with what he wishes than with what he knows."

In the late winter of 1680, La Salle dispatched Hennepin and two *voyageurs,* Michael Accau and Picard du Gay, down the Illinois River from Fort Crevecoeur to take a look at the Upper Mississippi and learn whether sailing vessels could be used on it. In mid-March the trio paddled up the big river and straight into a waterborne fleet of Sioux on the warpath. They were taken prisoner by these Issatis (Hennepin's name for the particular tribe) and removed farther upriver to modern Minnesota. There they were shifted from place to place as curiosities by a people who had had very little contact with white men. The lives of the captive Frenchmen were probably almost as harrowing as Hennepin described. The Sioux were a fierce and rugged people surviving in a harsh land, and the thirty-seven-year-old gray-gown may have suffered as much as he claimed. Their deliverance came in July of the same year when Sieur Greysolon Dulhut and a contingent of soldiers arrived and took them away—not without the thanks, it has been suggested, of the Sioux, whose patience with the complaining priest must have worn thin.

In 1682, Hennepin was back in France, cloistered and busily writing. The next year *A Description of Louisiana, newly discovered to the South-West of New France,* with a fawning dedication to Louis XIV, appeared as an instant popular success, with equally popular translations to follow. No matter that the work was roundly criticized, by the knowledgeable in New France and by his fellow clergymen, as a hash of half-truth and invention. The book was precisely what his readers wanted: a rip-roaring adventure story in a setting that was made to order for escape readers everywhere. Hennepin was at his best in describing what he saw among the wild Sioux. He told of their games and how they gambled, of how they went naked and rolled in the snow, of their

An after-the-fact drawing of Hennepin (the heroic bearer of the light) being captured by the Sioux on the Upper Mississippi in 1680.

deplorable toilet habits, their shameless belching, and how they "mated grossly." These strange people seemed not to value riches and were brutish in every other respect. Hennepin knew his audience, and European civility got a healthy lift at the expense of the savages, who nevertheless made interesting subjects for study.

Distortions and all, *A Description of Louisiana* would have been a valuable contribution to geography and ethnology if Hennepin had just stopped there. He did not. Criticism within and without his own Recollect order had damaged his already shaky reputation in France, and he was financially hard put to survive. From Utrecht the Spanish subject who served France now threw his fortunes to England — and any claim he had to respectability to the winds. In 1697 he published *A New Discovery of a Vast*

Country in America, extending above four thousand miles be-tween New France and New Mexico, and the following year *A New Voyage in a Country Larger than Europe.* Each contained a groveling dedication to William III of Orange that was excessive even for those days of abject flattery. The good father was eager to lead the English across the North American continent to find the passage to China that they had unsuccessfully sought in the frozen waters of the North. As for those who criticized a Catholic priest for his willingness to serve a Protestant monarch, he pleaded a lofty, ecumenical Christianity that made little of rifts within the true religion. William and the English seem to have humored Hennepin, possibly just for the nuisance value it had with the Sun King. Hennepin, however, was serious. He wanted to return to the New World, and if his own order would not send him, then maybe the king so renowned for his magnanimity, valor, justice, equity, sincerity, and piety would. There could be no doubt that the wilderness-wise friar was the right man, "having liv'd Eleven Years in Northern America." In fact, Hennepin had only spent six years there—less than six months west of the Mississippi—but that was the least of the lies he told.

A few years after La Salle had met his ignominious death in Texas, a Frenchman named Chrétien Le Clercq had published a work entitled *Établissement de la Foi,* which contained an ac-count by Father Zénobe Membré, who had accompanied La Salle on his famous expedition down the Mississippi to its mouth. The book was almost immediately suppressed for political reasons, and few knew of it. Hennepin was one who did. Appearing in his second book, *A New Discovery,* was the startling revelation that he and Accau and du Gay had in that chilly March of 1680 dis-obeyed orders and had not gone up the Mississippi until they had first gone down it—all the way to its mouth! Their journey had upstaged La Salle by two years. As proof, the missionary said he had erected a cross and left a letter informing the wayfarer of what they had done.

Hennepin, of course, had stolen Membré's account of La Salle's trip and reworded it to describe his own apocryphal voyage. There was no way he could have covered the 3,260 river miles and still been taken prisoner by the Sioux within a month. Skeptics also

Looking slightly more pious than in his portrait on page 77, Father Hennepin "poses" for Europe's readers at the Falls of Saint Anthony.

wanted to know why he had waited until La Salle was dead ten years before making public this remarkable achievement. Why indeed? Because he feared La Salle and his men would exact vengeance on the humble father, who deserved the real honor for having been first to run the Father of Waters. He knew, too, of La Salle's secret plan to wrest away by force the Spanish mines down Mexico way.

It was as big and as bald a lie as Hennepin could have told. While those who knew better reviled it for what it was, *A New Discovery,* and then *A New Voyage,* became big sellers and increased his public reputation as the reigning authority on North America's wild West. The later books were really only magnifications of the first, even more boastful and self-promoting. With La Salle dead, Hennepin elevated himself to the status of partner to the great explorer. He became La Salle's confidant. He encouraged the moody man in his moments of self-doubt. Together

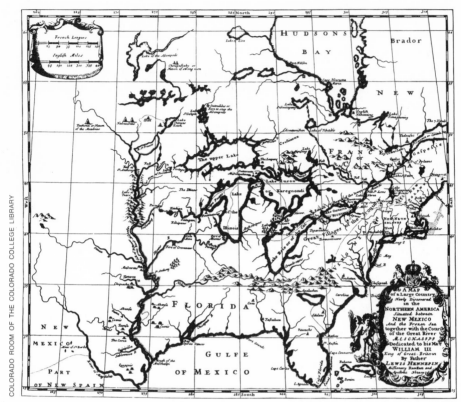

Hennepin's map of North America had a case of the splits: Hudson Bay came east, the Mississippi went west—toward nearby Japan.

they planned their grand strategy for the Mississippi Valley.

The self-professed discoverer of "two hundred nations" also included learned opinions on a wide range of subjects that engaged Europe's speculative thinkers. Hennepin did not favor Asia as the original homeland of the American Indians but thought they might be descended from a lost tribe of Jews because they dwelt in tents, anointed themselves with oils, and were given to great lamentations over the dead. As for the Strait of Anian, he doubted its existence as such, because while he was among the Sioux, "an Embassy of Savages from a very remote Nation to the Westward" traveled three months overland without having seen any likely seas. The thoughtful friar was confident, however, that a great river did exist that ran to the Pacific, and therefore to Japan, which, both he and the wise German geographer Joannes

G. Graef were in accord, was contiguous with North America and not an island as thought. Inserted in the last two books were also more horrors and mayhem for the *canaille:* savage beasts, crocodiles, a bumper crop of poisonous serpents, details of Indian tortures and ritual cannibalism. As a kind of afterthought that must have seemed odd to some, he expressed the view that the American Indian was so rude and barbaric that he might very well resist forever all Christianizing and civilizing efforts—a strange admission for one who professed a longing to return to North America and accomplish that very thing.

Hennepin is last known as having gone to Rome in 1701 to gain support for a final fling of proselytizing in North America. There is no evidence he was successful. In spite of his many loyal readers, whom he entertained superbly with his lively prose and the liberties he took with the truth, this fastidious man, a prisoner of his own vanity, could not impress either those who knew him or those who could do him some good.

LOUIS HENNEPIN FOOLED the many but not the few. Louis-Armand, the third Baron de Lahontan et Heslèche, fooled them all. Louis's father was a distinguished civil engineer who died when the boy was eight, leaving him a title and an estate hopelessly entangled in lawsuits and chicanery. Louis-Armand, already bright, was soon broke and bitter, so he did what many another nobleman short of means did: he joined the army as an officer and went off in 1683 to New France.

This Lahontan was a complex man—a cynic, an acid wit, a freethinker who had no use for the Church and who deplored both the religious wars that had long embroiled Europe and the fripperies of Montreal and Paris life. He preferred the wilderness, hunting parties, and Indians and rough *coureurs de bois* for companions. His military career in Canada was spotty. At times he performed well enough against the English or the Iroquois; at others his conduct seems to have bordered on cowardice. Initially he was a favorite of Louis de Baude, Comte de Frontenac, but after a match had been arranged for him with a beautiful young girl of New France and he belatedly backed out, even the powerful

A Map drawn upon Stag skins by ỹ Gnacsitares who gave me to know ỹ Latitudes of all ỹ places mark'd in it, by pointing to ỹ respective places of ỹ heavens that one or t'other corresponded to; for by this means I could adjust ỹ Lat: to half a Degree or little more; having first receiv'd from 'em a computation of ỹ distances in Tazous each of wich I compute to be ỹ Long French Leagues:

Lahontan's Long River led west, conveniently filling a void. His Gnacsitares, Tahuglahuks, and Mozeemleks were complete fantasy, too.

MOZEEMLEK
Many Villages of ỹ Mozeemlek
High Mountains
The Canows us'd by ỹ Gnacsitares & ỹ Esana
COUNTRY.
Land Mark
COUNTRY of the GNACS
Villages on ỹ Islands
TARES
Villages on ỹ Islands
High Mountains
MORTE or
The upper face of the Medal
Lim
A MEDAL of the TAHUGLAHU
made of a certain sort of metal of a Red colour unlike C
The Reverse of the Medal
New M
H. Moll S.

252   257   261

governor of the French colony seems to have cooled toward him.

In 1688, Lahontan wrote to a friend that he intended to go west. In October of that same year he reached the Mississippi (or so he claimed), went upriver to the intersecting *Rivière Longue* with some of his own men and several Fox Indian guides, and set out by canoe (which he certainly did not do). The account of what Lahontan saw between November 2, 1688, and March 2, 1689, on his Long River, which ran nearly due west at forty-seven degrees of latitude, was to please sophisticated readers in Europe and delight geographers with empty space on their hands.

Lahontan made quick time up the Long, "notwithstanding the great calm that always prevails upon this . . . least rapid River in the World." He met the Eokoros tribe and their "Great Gover-

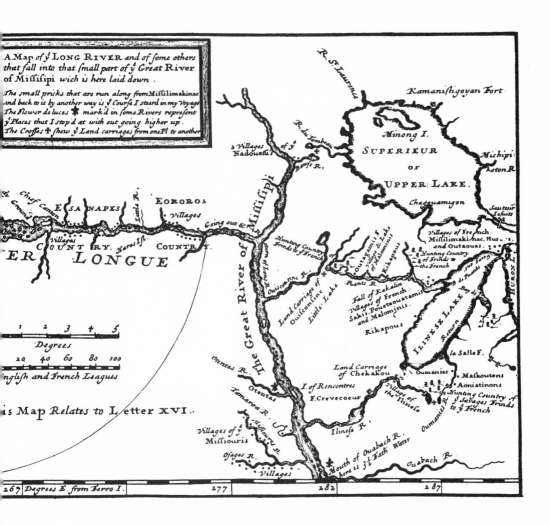

A Map of $\bar{y}$ LONG RIVER and of some others that fall into that small part of $\bar{y}$ Great River of Missisipi wich is here laid down.

The small pricks that are run along from Missilimakinac and back to it by another way is $\bar{y}$ Course I steerd in my Voyage. The Flower de luces ✱ mark'd in some Rivers represent $\bar{y}$ Places that I stop'd at with out going higher up. The Crosses ✚ shew $\bar{y}$ Land carriages from one Pl. to another

Degrees

English and French Leagues

is Map Relates to Letter XVI.

267 Degrees E. from Ferro I.   277   282   287

nour," an obliging old gentleman. When Lahontan distributed gifts, the governor reciprocated with six Essanapes slaves to assist him in his journey west to the country of Essenapes, with whom they were in continual war. The Eokoros were "very civil, and so far from a wild Savage temper, they have an Air of Humanity and Sweetness." Their women, though, were not as handsome as those in Canada, observed Lahontan, a Frenchman to the core. Farther west he went on the Long River through dangerous driftwood to the Essanapes, who prostrated themselves before the strangers with their hands on their foreheads, so happy were they to see them. Their chief, or "generalissimo," informed the baron that he would give him a couple of hundred men as escort on his visit to the Gnacsitares, the next tribe upstream, who were their allies against the Mozeemleks, "a turbulent and warlike Nation" beyond. Lahontan immediately ordered his men to improve on some borrowed pirogues, and the song of axes soon rang out in the virgin land. Every stroke caused the Indians to cry out, "as if they had seen some Prodigy; nay the firing of pistols could not divert 'em from that Amazement, though they were equally strangers to both the Pistol and the Axe."

Lahontan concluded that these people must be Pythagoreans when he saw some women rushing "to receive the soul" of a dying old man. But when he asked them why they ate animals into which departed souls might have migrated, a fine point of metaphysics was explained: "They made answer, that the Transmigration of Souls is always confin'd to the respective Species, so that the Soul of Man cannot enter a Fowl, as that of a Fowl cannot be lodg'd in a quadraped, and so on." No fools, these Essenapes.

The baron pressed on farther up the stream, surviving the cold of December and hunger in what was becoming a barren and unfruitful land. At last he reached an island and the Gnacsitares. The natives were alarmed, mistaking the visitors for Spaniards. Lahontan protested that he and his men were enemies of the Spanish, but emissaries were sent south to bring back some Indians who would be able to judge. The verdict was that Lahontan's party were not the hated Spanish, who were 80 *tazons* (240 leagues) south in New Mexico. His fears allayed, the chief of the Gnacsitares was hospitable. "He requested me to accept a great House that was prepar'd for me: and his first piece of Civility consisted in calling in a great many Girls, and pressing me and my Retinue to serve our selves. Had this Temptation been thrown in our way at a more seasonable time, it had prov'd irresistible: but 'twas not an agreeable Mess for Passengers that were infeebled by Labour and Want.'

Lahontan writes that he did not actually go farther up the Long River, but by interviewing four captive Mozeemleks he was able to learn more of the land beyond. The Mozeemlek nation was some 150 leagues west, on the other side of a mountain range ("so high that one must cast an infinity of Windings and Turnings before he can cross 'em") and on a westward-winding river that drained into a "Salt Lake of three hundred Leagues in Circumference." Yet another tribe, the numerous Tahuglauks, lived around this lake. The Tahuglauks were a powerful people who lived in six cities and more than a hundred towns under a despotic government. They were excellent artisans and worked in leather and a reddish metal resembling copper that became heavier upon melting. All this was elicited from the Mozeemlek slaves, for whom Lahontan had taken a special liking. He found them quite different from his Gnacsitare hosts, "of a greater measure of Reason" and so courteous that he had thought at first they might be Europeans. Oh yes, they also had thick bushy beards.

When Lahontan decided it prudent to thread back down the Long River, he tried to entice the Mozeemleks to return with him to Canada, but they would have none of it: "The love they had for their Country stifled all Perswasion; so true it is, that Nature reduc'd to its just Limits cares but little for Riches." Before setting out on January 26, 1689, the baron planted a pole and affixed a lead plate bearing the arms of France, thus extending French influence into a wondrous land easily reached by a river that would take barques of up to fifty tons.

One wonders in what frigid hut Lahontan whiled away a long winter contriving it all, or whether it had not perhaps been concocted many years later in some European capital when he was facing starvation. Though the account of his trip up the Long River was contained in one letter of the more than twenty finally published in Holland in 1703 describing his adventures in North America, it was understandably the most engaging, particularly with the detailed, illustrated map executed in the baron's own hand. *New Voyages to North America* appeared in French and English editions in 1703, with numerous French editions to follow. In 1709 it was translated into German and the year afterwards into Dutch. The book sold quite well, treading a middle ground between Hennepin's performance for the gallery and the pious comprehensiveness of the Jesuit *Relations*. Elegantly written, ironic, arch, it had special appeal to court-weary effetes and anticlerical liberals; it extolled the Indian-as-innocent living a natural life in a bountiful wilderness, free of civilization with its corrupt officialdom, pleasure-dashing priests, and grasping merchants. Rousseau and Voltaire would come to some of the same conclusions many years later without making any on-the-spot comparisons.

By the time *Voyages* appeared, Lahontan's fortunes had long since suffered too drastic a plunge. In 1692 he had a falling-out with the governor of Newfoundland, to whom he had been promoted to second-in-command and whom he loathed with a passion. His witty libels of the governor brought a violent reaction, and the baron decided to make a run for it, abandoning his post in an unsoldierly fashion. He secretly shipped out of Canada to Portugal, traveling later to Holland, Hamburg, and Denmark, and writing a forgery about the survivors of La Salle's Texas expedition to curry French favor. When he did return to France, he was exiled to his native province, his barony already confiscated. Soon he was fleeing arrest again, to Spain. Finally, he settled at the court of the Elector of Hanover, where he became a friend of the philosopher Leibnitz and is believed to have died about 1715.

Lahontan's fame lived a while after him. His imaginary Long River and the Salt Lake became familiar to those interested enough to consult an atlas. Doubt was cast on the baron's reliability by Pierre Charlevoix, the learned cleric sent to New France to inquire officially about routes to the western sea, in his 1721 *Journal Historique,* but many continued to believe in Mozeemleks and Gnacsitares. Only later in the eighteenth century did Lahontan's reputation sink to the level of his luck, and then he slipped into such disrepute that all the fine reporting he did on life in New France was neglected because of the one infamous letter, Number XVI.

ANTOINE SIMON LE PAGE DU PRATZ was a perfect foil to Lahontan. Born a Dutchman but a veteran of the French army, du Pratz went to Louisiana in 1718 as a French colonist, spending sixteen years there as a planter. He was a continent, practical sort, given to the close study of Louisiana's plants and animals and native peoples. Though he took part in some punitive campaigns against them, he had a humanitarian's concern over the

Typical winter attire for an Indian, according to du Pratz. Europeans found the damp chill along the Mississippi called for something more substantial.

treatment of the Indians, whom he saw being corrupted by loose French morals and sharp practice.

Du Pratz did not go into rapture as did his fellow colonists when it came to the metallic wealth widely supposed to be west of them awaiting discovery. A good silver mine did exist on the Red River, he asserted, and he had heard that many other, richer mines were located northwest of the Mississippi-Missouri river junction. But gold for him had no allure: "To what purpose serves this beautiful metal, but to make people vain and idle among whom it is so common, and to make them neglect the culture of the earth, which constitutes true riches. . . ?"

Such sentiments were typical of this rational, steady, honest man, who eventually returned to Paris and published *Histoire de la Louisiane* in 1758, a personal memoir of his years in the Louisiana territory. Du Pratz meant to tell it like it was and regretted "that the first travelers had the impudence to publish to the world a thousand false stories, which were easily believed because they were new." He probably had Lahontan, among others, in mind.

Unwittingly, du Pratz would add to the world's lore a false story of his own. He had collected it while among the Yazoo Indians in the Natchez area from a wise old man whom the French had relied upon as an interpreter. The Indian's name was Moncacht-Apé, which translated as "the killer of pain and fatigue" (to which might also be added, truth). The usually wary du Pratz was dazzled by this Indian so "remarkable for his solid under-standing and elevation of sentiments." His accomplishment was the more remarkable. Moncacht-Apé, well advanced in age, had taken several years off to do the continent, ocean to ocean, on foot with no other purpose than to satisfy his own curiosity. What he had observed, he freely and modestly passed on to du Pratz, who likened the old man to the great Greeks of the Golden Age who traveled deep into the East purely for the sake of knowledge.

Moncacht-Apé first walked to the Great Water in the direc-tion of "the sun-rising," visiting Niagara Falls enroute, making friends of other nations he passed among. It only teased his curiosity about the other way: the direction of the sun-setting, from whence the ancients had said the red man had first come. So he followed the northern bank of the Missouri River beyond the Kansa tribe, where he met a hunting party of Otters, a nation that more or less adopted him and took him home. Home was reached by traveling a distance up the Missouri after it assumed a northern course to the Fine River, which flowed west; a day's journey on the Fine brought the old man to the Otter village, where he wintered. The following spring, Moncacht-Apé grew restless to see the Great Water and accordingly traveled down the Fine through many nations to the coast. The Indians he found there lived in great fear of white men who came from the west in floating villages to make slaves of their children. They also came searching for "a yellow stinking wood, which dyes a fine yellow colour," which they harvested and took with them.

Moncacht-Apé later had the opportunity to see them for himself when he joined in an ambush of a landing party, in which eleven of the hated raiders were slain. "Upon examining those whom we had killed, we found them much smaller than ourselves and very white; they had a large head, and in the middle of the crown the hair was very long, their head was wrapt in a great many folds of stuff; and their cloaths seemed to be made neither of wool nor silk; they were very soft, and of different colours."

The aged pilgrim resumed his journey, traveling northwestward along the coast of the Great Water until the days grew short and the nights long and cold. He was advised by his companions to go back, for game grew scarcer and the land only continued farther to the northwest before turning due west where it was cut north to south by the Great Water; indeed, there was a very old man still alive who had been there before the land was eaten up by the water. Whereupon the wanderer did the sensible thing and returned to the Natchez country.

Excepting the strangely-garbed pale dwarfs, Moncacht-Apé's account sparkles with verisimilitude, and du Pratz must be forgiven for letting his guard drop. A check of the actual distances involved, however, and the time Moncacht-Apé reports it took him to travel from point to point simply do not mesh. We can picture a wise old man, probably a revered storyteller among his people, mentally collecting others' tales of where they had been and what they had seen, and blending them in with his own circumscribed knowledge of the world. He then passed them along to his rapt interlocutor around, say, a dying lodge-fire while the calumet made the rounds. He might have been amused, and even flattered, to know his story achieved a small but permanent place in the literature of two continents. The nation of the Otters and the Fine River even made it onto some of Europe's maps.

Chapter 4

English Envy and Bardic Blather

MORE OR LESS CAN BE MADE of the kind of phantom truth lurking in the many legends and fables about the West. Many, not all, were later found to have had at least a kernel of substance. The Bering Strait and the Arctic Ocean did constitute a seasonal Northwest Passage, albeit useless for commercial purposes. There was the Great Salt Lake of present day Utah, which partly fitted Spanish and French notions of an inland lake of salt. There was also a Great River of the West in the Columbia-Snake system, which, if it didn't connect with that lake of salt, at least reached the "shining mountains" that Lahontan and other Frenchmen had been told about or had seen from afar; the Rockies just happened to be a lot higher and a lot wider than anyone could have guessed. The gold and silver that Spain was seeking (and that France and England believed had been found) had been there in abundance all along, awaiting a discoverer with the technology to extract it. The southern Paiutes of Utah and Nevada even had rudimentary beards.

The Indian was the crucial agent in the dissemination of knowledge about the West. He, after all, lived there—for how long the European could only wonder, but it had been a long time. When he was unhappy with the white invader and had had his fill of sharing his cornfields and streams with those who dishonored his religion and all but enslaved his children, he naturally spoke of the spoils to be had elsewhere—anywhere—just to get the white man off his back. But there were other times when he wanted to please, when relations were cordial and the trade items the white man brought were appreciated. Questions of what lay beyond might be answered honestly with all he knew, but what he knew was chiefly what had been passed from mouth to mouth, through translation after translation, over great distances. Distortions were inevitable.

The European frontier must have had its gainsayers, those who winked at each other whenever rumor of another mountain of gold started making the rounds. *Plus ça change, la plus de la même chose.* There were also skeptics in Paris and Madrid who issued the often conservative colonial policies regarding stepped-up explorations of the trans-Mississippi West. Any adventurer who came to court with another scheme had better make it good; those quick returns that were promised had a way of showing up in red ink. Of course, it was fine if the petitioner was willing to finance the venture himself, but if royal funds were needed— well, they had already been earmarked for the war. (The Continent never lacked for wars.)

England was the exception. The English had no frontier in the trans-Mississippi West until the 1760s. It is possible that a few drifters and traders may have wandered out that way, but if they had they had not provided much in the way of first-hand information. So England borrowed. Spanish documents were translated, as were the works of Hennepin, Lahontan, du Pratz, and Jean-Bernard Bossu. Often, these translations might begin with a preface that demeaned the achievements of France or Spain and speculated that if England had those western lands (the recommendation to take them by force was implied if not stated), she would manage them a lot better. Between the lines shows a peculiar racial pride that afflicted the English—not just during their eighteenth-century rise to imperial eminence, but with origins at least as far back as Elizabethan times. The Spanish were a benighted people and the French lewd and frivolous. It was the English who were destiny's chosen.

But the English also had a nagging obsession with law and rights. There had to be a legal foundation for their claims on the West. Drake's 1579 voyage to the California coast was therefore cited periodically; New Albion predated any Spanish presence there—wherever "there" was. Prior discovery took precedence over occupation.

Drake's 1579 landing on the California coast had given England vague claims on the unknown West—and a justification for aggression.

By 1698, Daniel Coxe, a London physician, had bought what he thought was the proprietorship of Carolana, a province-on-paper that extended westward from central Virginia on the north and Florida on the south to the Mississippi River valley. Coxe actually outfitted an expedition to take possession of his Carolana, but it was driven off by the French at the mouth of the Mississippi.

Doctor Coxe, who never saw the New World, had a son, also named Daniel, who did—spending fourteen years in New Jersey before getting in hot water with the colonial government and hurrying back to England. Coxe Junior tried to make good his father's title. He published in 1722 *A Description of the English Province of Carolana*, which not only verified his just claim on the territory as his father's heir but made an appeal to the patriotism of the English to take what was rightfully theirs, or, more accurately, his. He had it on good authority that English mariners had beaten the French to the West. One of two unnamed vessels "discovered the mouths of the great and famous river Meschacebe, or, as term'd by the French, Mississippi, entere'd and ascended at above one hundred miles, and had perfected a settlement therein, if the captain of the other ship had done his duty and not deserted them." But at least that crew of river-runners had taken possession in the king's name, "and left, in several places, the arms of Great-Britain affix'd on Boards and trees for a memorial thereof." It was the first ship to enter the Mississippi from the sea, Coxe insisted, and the "boasts and falsities of the French" were at last exposed.

Daniel Coxe the Younger had a lot more to say about his country's unoccupied territory, most of it cribbed from Lahontan and other Frenchmen, but some of it fresh from the obscure journals of English sea captains. There was an easy access from the Gulf Coast to northern New Mexico up the Meschacebe and the southern branch of the Yellow River, which rose in the hills dividing New Mexico from Carolana and made the English and Spanish neighbors. The wise policy might just be to unite with the despised Spanish for the moment and throw the bloody French out!

The northwestern branch of the Yellow was called the Massorites (Missouri) and flowed from a great fresh or saltwater lake or sea many thousands of miles in circumference. There was another, easier way to this great inland sea: up a river that spilled from the sea's southwest shore and flowed into the Pacific at forty-four degrees north latitude. This was known to the "proprietor" and England's own Privy Council. After all, the English had "discover'd the said Lake from the South-Sea" and sailed thereto. As for gold, Coxe knew from an English "gentleman admirably well skill'd in geography" of the Gold Islands, which lay between Japan and California at approximately forty degrees latitude, whose inhabitants paid gold by the pound for Europe's commodities when the greedy Nipponese, their steady customers, were not looking.

When England, the borrower, stooped to her own storytelling, the results in pure old humbug were the equal of any fables of Aztec caves and lakes of gold.

IN THE YEAR 1170 OR 1171, the Welsh Prince Madoc, one of King Owain Gwynedd's eighteen or nineteen children, weary of a bloody civil war that would decide his father's successor, sailed in one, two, seven, ten, or eleven vessels from the port of Aberwli or Abergele or Lundy either north or south of Ireland and landed in Newfoundland or Mexico or Rhode Island or the Antilles or Massachusetts or Virginia or Nova Scotia or Yucatan or Florida or Panama or Alabama. This Madoc, possibly legitimate but more likely baseborn, not only sailed across the Atlantic to the New World more than three hundred years before the Italian Columbus did the same, but deposited 120 countrymen there. He then went back to Wales and picked up another shipload of dissatisfied Welshmen (and Welshwomen, we must assume). It was a lucky thing he did return, too, or otherwise nobody would have known that he had made the first crossing.

Madoc may or may not have gone to Mexico first as Quetzalcoatl, the plumed serpent god-incarnate who came from the direction of the rising sun and taught the Toltecs and Aztecs all they knew that was worth knowing, and who was unkindly repaid for his generosity by the Aztec's forgetting every word of Welsh that Madoc ever taught them. More likely Madoc first landed in Alabama. We have as an authority on this no less than the Daughters of the American Revolution, who have erected in Mobile Bay a marker that reads "In Memory of Prince Madoc, a Welsh explorer, who landed on the shores of Mobile Bay in 1170 and left behind, with the Indians, the Welsh language."

Others have gone further in acknowledging Madoc's gifts to the New World. They say he brought good old-fashioned Welsh know-how to the savages and printed Welsh Bibles that his descendants preserved and revered centuries after they had forgotten how to read them. Evidence of a Welsh presence has been found in the remnants of fortifications in Tennessee, which showed such a sophistication of military science that they could not possibly have been erected by the lowly Indian. They were built strictly for defense, we can be sure, for Madoc's people were peace-loving, albeit buffeted about by warlike tribes who resented their presence and their airs. In time their fierce neighbors drove them west, up the wide Missouri, where the living was, if not easy, at least a little less crowded.

This is a brief composite of the Madoc stories, which had as many variants as there were Welsh bards with embellishments to add. Over the centuries, as the English slowly moved west, the Welsh Indians likewise fell back in that direction. Several witnesses, though, claimed to have spoken Welsh with these Indians of lordly bearing in the east. A couple had even seen the Bibles. Of course, this testimony was often given in taverns, where Welshmen gathered to fortify themselves against the winter cold and sing the praises of their ancient race.

Opinions differed, and differ still, on whether the Welsh retained their racial purity and ultimately died out, or whether through miscegenation they gradually became Welsh Indians. The latter view gained more support as westward-moving frontiersmen failed to find the blue eyes and blond hair attributed to that peripatetic colony. Among the tribes variously said to be Welsh descendants were the Navajo, Seneca, Osage, Hopi, Shawnee, Creek, Tuscarora, Modoc, and the yet-to-be-located Doeg. The smart money, however, shifted to the Padoucas (Comanches) and the Mandans. The Comanches had their backers, including one who pointed out that "Padoucas was a corruption of their original name of Madawgwys." (Some corruption!) Another gentleman, who had seen a Comanche with his own eyes, inexplicably commented on their fair complexion, all-around nobility, courtesy, and honesty—not the best description of a short, dark Shoshonean people who, once they got the horse, descended from the Rockies and by their ferocity became known as the Tartars of the southern Plains.

Then it had to be the Mandans. French traders who visited the tribe at their Dakota homes on the banks of the Missouri River were impressed by their dissimilarities with other red men. They had fair skin. Some had blue eyes. They were on the tall side, robust, and muscular. In their language were words that seemed European, possibly Welsh. Their food was superbly prepared and would have done credit to a French table; their villages were laid out in streets and squares, and were spotlessly clean. Cleanliness, of course, was next to godliness; no news of Welsh Bibles, though.

From the 1730s on, these French reports excited Welshmen back home, and at last a London literary society sent John Evans, a pious young Methodist, across the ocean to lead the Mandans back to their old-time religion. Young Evans had his problems. The financial assistance he counted on from interested Welshmen in the "colonies" was not forthcoming. Undaunted, he proceeded in 1793 to the Mississippi Valley, which at the time was Spanish and unfriendly toward British subjects. Evans was quickly jailed in Saint Louis, eventually released, and subsequently employed by a Spanish-controlled company run by a freewheeling Scotsman named James Mackay, who sent the young man to the Mandans on a trading mission. In 1797 Evans reported his conclusions in a letter to Dr. Samuel Jones of Philadelphia: "In respect to the Welsh Indians, I have only to inform you that I could not meet such a people, and from intercourse I have had with Indians from latitudes 35 to 49, I think you may safely inform our friends they have no existence."

Evans' revelations should have put an end to the Madoc myth, but they did not. It was so old, and so many Welsh poets had written about it that it could not be dropped on one man's word — particularly one who was later said to have become a common drunk. Besides, it has been pointed out, Evans was in Spanish territory in the employ of the Spanish. He had probably become a turncoat and a spy, like Mackay. The Spaniards would naturally suppress the truth to keep the English from snooping around their lands, which, since Madoc had been there first, were not rightly their lands at all.

The Madoc legend survived Evans and later damaging scholarship, and survives today. Every so often a new book appears in support of one or more of the many versions of the Welsh prince's career in the New World and the legacy he left. It does not seem to matter that linguistic scholars have found nothing in American Indian languages to suggest a Welsh influence, or that the occasional incidence of light pigmentation and blondness in the Indian has been explained by anthropologists as resulting from previous contacts, direct or indirect, with whites (French *coureurs de bois*, not known for their chastity, had reached the Mandans well in advance of any Welshman).

The part about the printed Welsh Bibles does seem to have been abandoned by Madoc boosters. Bernard DeVoto, among others, has remarked that Gutenberg did not come along until the fifteenth century and that the Bible was not translated into Welsh until three centuries after Madoc shipped out of Wales a second time. It is also curious that the story of Madoc was not generally known in England until the sixteenth century, when the Tudors (who just happened to be Welsh) had an uncertain hold on the English throne, and English envy of other nations was peaking.

Of course, all things are possible, but that a small band of peace-loving Welshmen under a Prince Madoc could have crossed the Atlantic in small boats and that their descendants could survive as an identifiable people for five-hundred-odd years in so threatening an environment is highly improbable. The first Spanish, French, and English colonizing attempts in North America seldom lasted long, and those colonists came more than four centuries after Madoc, in greater numbers and with more amenities obtained in the years that bridged the high Middle Ages and the post-Renaissance. That Madoc did what he is said to have done is about as plausible as Moncacht-Apé having plunked a canoe down in the waters of the Gulf Stream and sailed to London where he established the premier grand lodge of Freemasonry.

THE FRENCH AND INDIAN WAR came to an end in 1763, with England victorious and France divested of her North American properties. Frenchmen in Canada and eastern Louisiana and the upper Mississippi region now had their traditional enemy, England, for a master. It must have been both shocking and galling to any self-respecting French frontiersman to suddenly have to answer to an Englishman for his actions; he could only take

Captain Carver of Connecticut had dreams of empire not unlike La Salle's. They would come to even less.

heart that things would probably get back to normal with a French triumph in the next war, which could not be far off.

The English did not go pouring into their newly-won far-western lands. They barely trickled in. This bothered Jonathan Carver, a well-to-do resident of Connecticut and a veteran of the recent war who was mustered out of the militia with the rank of captain. While in the conflict Carver had developed a taste for adventure, and now he felt the patriotic urge to inspect the new territory for its commercial possibilities and its future place in England's ever-expanding empire. He felt strongly that it had to be secured against threats from both the French and the Spanish, and he took it upon himself to report truthfully for once on the lands that the French, as was commonly known by Englishmen everywhere, had deliberately kept secret or lied about to serve their own wicked ends. Poor Carver! Before all was said and done, he would be an accessory to even more lying and obfuscation.

The captain left Boston in June of 1766 to join an old army

buddy at faraway Fort Michilimackinac, strategically placed at the strait connecting Lake Huron and Lake Michigan, the north-western limit of British occupation. This friend was none other than Robert Rogers, the commander there, a hero of the just-over French and Indian War, and the hit-and-run leader of Rogers' Rangers. The pair had previously discussed exploring the West. Carver was now ready to do just that. Rogers, however, was having his difficulties. British authorities had reason to suspect the man of financial irregularities and, worse, treasonable activities. So the determined Carver, who had come this far on his own funds, was obliged to pay out of his pocket the additional expenses necessary to take him to the Mississippi and the West he felt compelled to see. Rogers promised him credits; supplies would also be sent on to him later at the Falls of Saint Anthony.

The Falls of Saint Anthony, where Carver's promised supplies did not arrive. Later he went to London, there to die of malnutrition.

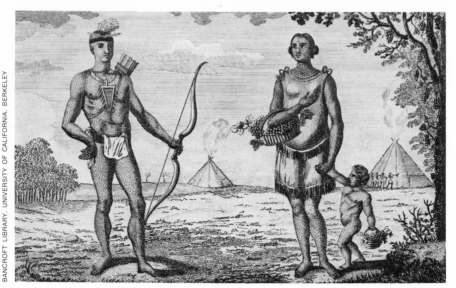

A family of Carver's beloved Sioux, as pictured in his "expanded"
Travels Through the Interior Parts of North America.

First, Carver wandered the country east of the Mississippi to familiarize himself with its geography and people; then he traveled west to Lake Pepin, where Hennepin had been nearly a century before him and had written what was for Carver almost a Baedeker guide to the region. From there he proceeded northwest to the Falls of Saint Anthony and then another two hundred miles west to where the Dakota Sioux were encamped on the plains. Here Carver was in his glory, wintering six months with this noble warrior people still not corrupted (as the more eastern tribes were) by contact with the French. He kept a journal of his adventures among his hosts. They treated him with cordiality, and he reciprocated, on the spot and later in print.

In the spring of 1767 he left these newest English subjects with assurances of a quick return with trading goods. But there was none awaiting him at the Falls of Saint Anthony, nor did he get any when he returned to Fort Michilimackinac. The original shipment had been somehow misdirected, and Rogers was not in any position now to make good his earlier promises. It was a heavy blow to Carver. He could not very well return to the Sioux empty-handed, so his hopes of traveling farther west beyond their country were shattered. He took what consolation he could in the fact that at least he had a story to tell, and when he returned to Boston in 1768, he tried to raise funds for its publication, his own resources having been depleted by his long journey. He failed. The last thing the colonists wanted to read was a book about those mangy redskins, who had long proved uncooperative in vacating their lands for English settlement.

Capt. Jonathan Carver then did the logical next thing for a man with a dream not unlike La Salle's. He would go to grateful England and tell all of what he saw and how a rich empire could be made of the lands taken from the French. John Coakley Lettsom, in a biographical foreword to the third edition of *Travels Through the Interior Parts of North America* (1781), describes Carver as wellborn, courageous, and enterprising. But he also makes much of the captain's diffidence and modesty, which "kept him in general reserved in company." Lettsom might have been blunter and said that this agreeable man from the boondocks fell into the "company" of connivers and highbinders—a mackerel in a school of sharks.

Back in London and virtually penniless, Carver petitioned the lords commissioners of trade and plantations for reimbursement for the money he had spent in the interest of his country. He would, of course, prepare a document on what he had seen. But "in a large, free, and widely extended government, where every motion depends upon a variety of springs, the lesser and subordinate movements must be acted upon by the greater, and consequently the more inferior operations of state will be so distant, as not to be perceived in the grand machine." The words are Lettsom's and, boiled down, read "bureaucratic red tape." Carver was destitute and could stand no delay, so he took a copy to a publisher. When the government got around to paying him eleven hundred pounds for his account, Carver had to renege and buy the copy back from his publisher. He stayed on in London to encourage people's interest in joining an expedition across North America. He succeeded in mustering support, but only after the impending war with the colonies rendered the plan out of the question. Meanwhile, he had gone deeply into debt to the money lenders. In 1778 he again took his copy to a publisher, where strange things were done to it including quadrupling its length with material appropriated from Hennepin, Lahontan, and other nameless liars. The book sold out quickly and went into a second printing. It is plain that Carver, who had taken a lowly position of clerk to try to feed himself, shared in none of the profits. When the third edition appeared in 1781, Jonathan Carver, Esquire, who had performed "many important services to his country," was already dead a year, the victim of dysentery and malnutrition.

Travels Through the Interior Parts of North America went on to see more than forty editions and several translations, which for the first time reversed the pattern: an Englishman had finally gone west and written something that could be exported to the Continent. The book became a standard, until later scholarship exposed its fabrications, at which time Carver was widely condemned as just one more damned liar who had probably never gotten west of the Appalachians.

Carver really did go as far as he said he did, and a reading of the *Travels* now evokes sympathy. His descriptions of his beloved Sioux are perceptive, sound, and highly readable. His judgments of them—that they were neither odious barbarians nor perfect models of the "natural man"—reveal a deep understanding not shared by his contemporaries. Even some of the sections that his grasping publishers added (and to which the desperate man must have agreed) are informative. Yet the deed was done, and Carver had his own misconceptions about the dark side of the continent that, when added to those of his editors, only confounded the world more. He believed in the Strait of Anian, "which having been first discovered by Sir Francis Drake, of course, belong[s] to the English." Moreover, he knew where it was and how to reach it without getting lost in some frosty arctic bight. Four great rivers rose in the Sioux country; one of them, the "River Oregon, or the River of the West," connected with both the Pacific Ocean and the elusive strait. He placed the Rocky Mountains just west of his Sioux friends. For whatever reason, he lauded the climate of the northern plains as more temperate than that of the east coast. He was also guilty of passing along to his readers without comment some Indian claims that were at the least fantastic, including one from the Winnebago Indians of Wisconsin of how they went west across the plains and massacred some "black people" (Spaniards) who had horses laden with "white stone" (silver). Carver himself claimed to have discovered "several mines of virgin copper."

The great mistake made by the Connecticut captain was to generalize about the West from the little corner of Minnesota that he had seen. Though he locates Indian origins north of China, he breaks all their languages down into four groups and, lacking any real knowledge, has all tribes west of the Mississippi speaking the Siouan stock. There is no doubt that the English could have cleared up some of the confusion produced by the published version of Carver's travels simply by consulting his original manuscript, which was submitted to the lords commissioners and now reposes in the British Museum. But they did not. Probably it was filed in the wrong pigeonhole.

In 1768, the same year Carver trekked back to Boston, Thomas Jeffrey, geographer to the king, published in London a general map for the edification of the realm. It featured New Albion, a "River of the West according to Russian maps," a "River of the West according to the French," Quivira moved back inland from the Pacific, de Fonte's mythical waterways, and large islands in the "Tartarian Sea" where lived the "Ye-Que or the Nation of the Dwarfs." On the eve of rebellion the intelligence available to George III was not the best, either in the East or out West.

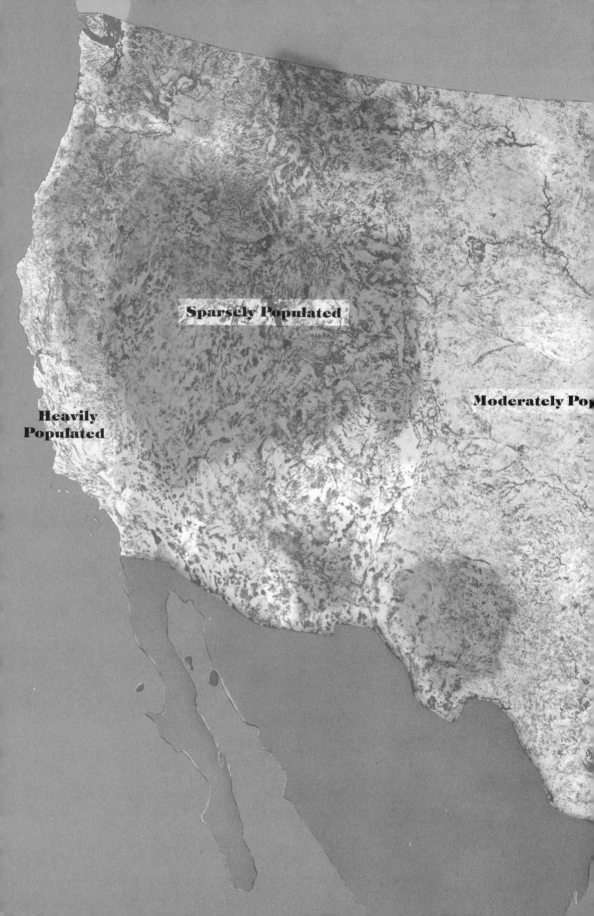

PART II: AN INDIAN SUMMER

Sparsely
Populated
(because of
white settlement)

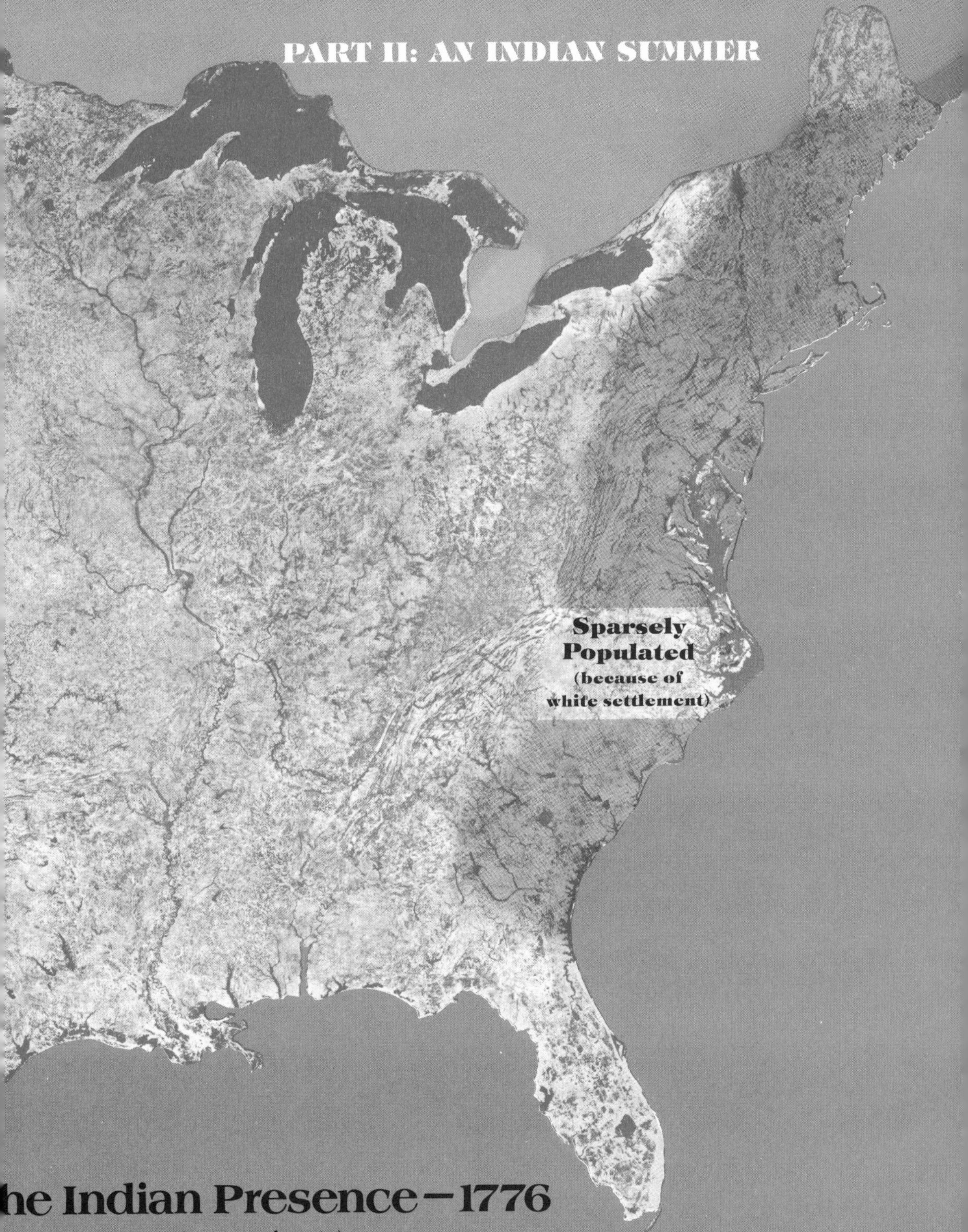

he Indian Presence—1776
(Approximate)

PART II
AN INDIAN SUMMER

July 4, 1776. The stranger squatted alone and fearful in the morning sun as the *Hópitu-shínumu* in great numbers gathered about him.

Drums and flutes mixed rhythm with wail as the People of Peace stopped at the street corner where the man in gray had slept the night. Then there was silence, and a tense expectation among those who had left their storied houses to see what the *Castillo* would do. He did nothing. At last, four honored men stepped toward him. The tallest frowned and spoke. "¿Por qué has venido aquí? Begone without delay—back to thy land."

The visitor made a sign for all to sit and talk. But the Hopis did not sit and they did not wish to talk. Everything had been said before—by the old one who came only the summer last from the east, and by those many who had come and were sent away for more than a hundred summers before this one. It would only be more talk of the sky god, and the stranger would then ask leave to splash water on the heads of the children. The Peaceful Ones had their own gods to please for the gift of corn, worshiped since the war gods first led the ancients up from the underground world. Could he not see he was unwelcome? Had not the white shells he brought as gifts been returned to him? Had not lodging for two nights and the food he desired been denied him? Had he not seen that some men had painted their bodies the color of blood?

The stranger rose to his feet with the image of Christ in his hand and told in a mixed tongue of the nations he had seen in the west and how he loved the Hopis. He wanted the People of Peace to press their lips to the figure of El *Cristo*.

"No! No!" cried an old man with a scornful grin.

The man in gray with the wild look in his eyes hesitated, then called for his mule. The beast was brought and the stranger smiled, then briskly he led his animal down the rocky path from the Third Mesa and the place of the rock called Oraibi toward the resting place of the sun, where the Yumas and other enemies of the *Hópitu-shínumu* lived. The People of Peace watched the padre become small on the dry earth below them. They were pleased.

Father Francisco Garcés, as dedicated a man as ever served his God and a veteran of the sage-and-sand circuit, was admittedly disappointed on that long-ago Arizona morning. He could not have been surprised, however. The apostate Hopis had resisted all Spanish missionaries who came to them after the Revolt of 1680. The zeal, courage, and kindness of the padre made no difference. Furthermore, what was true of the Hopis was also true of other natives who rejected the True Faith; even the tribes who received it did not revere it as they should, and could be expected to practice the old pagan worship in secret. Souls were hard to come by in the West, as hard as gold itself.

But even gold is where you find it only if you find it, and islands of dwarfs are yet to be found off the Pacific coast. For all the white man's fantasizing about the West, when he did arrive, he was confronted with one hard and often painful reality: the land was already spoken for. Those who spoke did so in strange and varied tongues that might or might not bear similarities to one another, but actions, then as now, spoke louder than words. The Indian was simply there, in situ, occupying space that in time the white man had to have. Exactly how long he had been there could only be guessed, but rights of prior discovery could not be extended to him anyway because he was barbaric, a worshiper of false gods, and therefore not a party to any gentlemen's compact.

If the European newcomer was Renaissance man on his way to becoming modern existential man, the American Indian was in virtually every way his opposite. He needed no abstruse logic to prove his existence. He was not given to worrisome reflection on the state of his soul. He did not believe himself an alien on earth, marking time until the Day of Judgment, when he would be consigned to some other-worldly realm of pain or pleasure. Rather, when he thought about it at all, he saw himself as one with the deer and the wind and the buffalo — just another breath in the scheme of things. Usually his prayers to the Great Spirit were about such simple matters as providing rain for his maize or courage for himself against his enemies. He was tradition-directed, one of a family, band, or tribe with taboos and prescriptions for conduct that were seldom questioned.

Nothing separated the thinking of the Indian and the white man more than their contrary attitudes toward the land and its ownership. With a few exceptions, Indian land was not something that could be bought — won from another tribe in war and occupied by a kind of earthly caretaker, yes, but not passed like a commodity from hand to hand for a payment in specie or a promise of the same. Said the great Shawnee chief Tecumseh when informed that his people had welshed on a purchase agreement: "Sell a country! Why not sell the air, the clouds, and the great sea . . . ? Did not the Great Spirit make them all for the use of his children?"

The Indian's limited notion of private property especially confounded the Anglo-Saxon, who either owned or rented his land or was indentured to it. A man's home was his castle and the land around it his fief; by a set of mind, his thoughts were also his own, and all fostered a self-centeredness and belief in abstract rights that were beyond the red man's ken.

Other pulls of culture divided the peoples to a greater or lesser degree. Indians tended to be seminomadic, while the majority of Europeans were static, rooted in soil. Indian economies rested on hunting and gathering and seldom more than a marginal agriculture; barter was for necessities and a few luxuries. Europeans were in the act of industrializing; they were mature in the art of trade and were importers and consumers of luxuries. War for most Indians was ritualized—an occasion to pilfer a horse or two, to prove a man's worth and acquire esteem within his nation. War for the white was a down-to-earth business, often total and almost always territorial, fought for economic advantage or national honor. Lacking a written language, the Indian's knowledge was transmitted orally from generation to generation, and his arts were wedded to what was functional in domestic and ceremonial life. The European had literatures and schools, arts and sciences that were already academic, and a sense of the purely aesthetic.

All this may have created a gulf between white man and red. It did not, however, mean all red men were brothers, or even distant cousins. "Indian" is a white man's misnomer that has the effect of lumping together diverse peoples who probably came not as a group across the Asian land bridge before rising waters created the strait called Bering, but in distinct waves that may have been thousands of years apart. The Amerind was not one man but many, and his lives were as plural as his adjustments to the varied circumstances in which he found himself. He spoke Algonkin or Siouan or Athapascan or another of sixty linguistic stocks with hundreds of different dialects. He could be a woodland hunter or a plains stalker of the bison. Some tribes planted maize and squash and beans. Some fished. Others gathered acorns or grubs. Some, like the Dakotas and Apaches, were committed to warfare as a way of life, while at the opposite end were the Pimas and Papagos who considered violence abhorrent and made a man who killed, even in self-defense, undergo a decontamination rite to restore his "sanity." Some were culturally impoverished like the Gosiutes of northwestern Utah, near-naked eaters of insects; others were rich in art and artifact, like the Pawnees of the central plains—a Caddoan people thought by some to have descended from the prehistoric mound-builders of the Southeast.

A tribe would adapt to the fickleness of a geography that might provide rain and cold aplenty on the northwest side of a mountain and arid mildness a few leeward miles away. As nature bequeathed, so a man and his clan or tribe dwelt, unless drought or the pressure of a more powerful people sent them searching for a more congenial elsewhere. If there were buffalo, the people wore the hides and had dogs to drag their belongings in the wake of the migrating herd. If corn was the crop and the sun dominant, the people stayed put, built sturdy ceremonial lodges in which to worship fertility gods, and, in the Southwest, wore cotton. The Cheyennes of the northern plains lived in movable tipis; the Salish of the Oregon coast, in rectangular communal houses of planks; the Chumash of the mild California coast, in conical brush huts; the Tewas of New Mexico, in sunbaked apartments. There was no end to the differences.

The Amerind knew change before the coming of the European, but he had not until then known it in its most jarring form. A tribe need never have seen a white man to be affected by him: his influence preceded him in the items of material culture that found their way over the beaten paths that hugged watercourses and crossed mountain passes to reach peoples far removed from the advancing edge of an alien civilization. An elaborate trading system long predated the white man in North America. Trading habits and decorum, established routes, and perhaps the most comprehensive sign language in the world went back to prehistory, and the itinerant Indian trader, a skilled and valued man, was welcome wherever he went. He brought grain from the river valleys to the drier plains, and the best dyes and pigments from the Pacific Coast and the Southwest; he brought red pipestone from Minnesota and obsidian from present-day Wyoming; he took eagle feathers from the Rockies to the pueblos, carried dentalium from the far Northwest, and wampum from the shore of the eastern ocean.

But when the white man's goods reached the trade veins, they did not flow so freely. Acquiring native pottery that made daily life easier, or earthen cosmetics to cut a fancy figure at an upcoming ceremonial, was all very well. But as things started circulating that when possessed made one strong or when lacked made one vulnerable, barter took on a new quality of competition and urgency. Perhaps the old men who gathered round the council fires reflected on these changes and how the old ways were vanishing and how the lives of their children would never be the same. We can only guess.

Had there been an Indian blessed with supra-consciousness in 1776 — say a wise chief miraculously endowed with the vision to see the trans-Mississippi West in overview—he might very well have judged it an excellent year for his people. For most it was a kind of Indian summer, with the greater tragedies either past or on time's horizon. The best of what the white man had to offer—the horse, the gun, metal knives and hatchets and cooking pots—had arrived. His worst bequests—insatiable land hunger, spirits in ruinous quantities, and the further spread of deadly poxes—were yet to come.

The fateful year fell almost midway between the two greatest-seeming victories the red man won on the western battlefield against the white. The Pueblo uprising of 1680 had swept the entire Spanish population out of New Mexico all the way south to El Paso (though twelve years later the foreigners would return in force to stay). In the summer of 1876, Lt. Col. George A. Custer and more than 260 bluecoats engaged a superior force of Sioux and Cheyennes on the Little Bighorn, and half did not survive the June day. Again, the victory was but a defeat in disguise, coming as it did at the height of a proud nation's centennial festivities. Retribution was swift and crushing; Custer's debacle in reality a starburst of red man's America.

In 1776 there was no such Pyrrhic victory. History had paused to look elsewhere. In the East the white men were busy fighting each other for reasons of their own. To the south others had long been stalled, but the tide seemed at last to have turned against them. True, in the far Southwest, new white men had recently come to change the ways of the red men; but they were few in number, and perhaps the high mountains with the crowns of snow would keep them there. Besides, in the dry basin of the West's core, and the highlands above, and along the salmon waters of the Northwest, the whites were not.

Chapter 5

The Wild Bunch

THE HOLLYWOOD STEREOTYPE of the Indian is a Plains Indian, and the image is familiar: flowing bonnets of eagle feathers, lathered ponies, sun dances, tipis, painted war parties thundering over a treeless and limitless range. The choice is a natural one. Not only was he exciting, active, fascinating in his gaudy contrariety to the white man, but the Plains Indian was in large part a white man's creation.

Some scholars have said the culture of the Plains was the only one to rise after the European reached the New World. They have further marked the beginning of that culture about the year 1775 and have assigned it a full century of vitality. The idea and the time have been hotly disputed by others who say the culture was not new but had its origins long before the nomadic peoples got the horse or the gun or anything else the European had to give or to have stolen from him. But whether it was a flowering of the new or whether it sprang from dormant seeds long of the soil is truly academic. What can be safely said is that the thirty tribes who lived on the grassland west of the Mississippi and east of the Rockies were living far richer and more complex lives than their ancestors, thanks to the European. And while the "white eyes" destroyed one another for possession of the eastern woodlands, the Plains Indian ruled the white man's West—not in any united front, but tribally, controlling greater or lesser pieces of it. It was the dawn of his brief but glorious season.

The Plains Indian had the advantage of knowing the white man by reputation before he met him face to face. The Spanish,

the "bearded ones," had been in the south for nearly two hundred years. The French, the "heavy eyebrows," had been among them in small numbers for almost a century, trading for furs they sent east or south by the rivers. Beyond them were the English, the "blond ones," rarely seen west of the Mississippi but with the best goods of all to exchange. Maybe the lot of them were not to be trusted, but they had to be tolerated for what they could bring.

By 1776 the Plains Indian had looked over what the white man could bring and had shown a preference for the horse over the dog, for metal over pottery and flint, and for Venetian glass beads over quills. Already, before the visitors became intruders, before they moved into his domain in large numbers with their wagons and cattle and plows, he had become dependent on them. But through his dependence, he had become the stronger, not the weaker, for it—at least in the short run. His old warring instincts were intensified by an imported weaponry, to the point where he constituted a formidable, if fractured, barrier to any immediate ideas of westward expansion by the outsiders.

It was the horse, captured in the wild, won in a raid, or stolen from the Spaniards, that made the Plains Indians so formidable a force.

By temperament the Plains Indian was ill-suited to become a menial or a junior partner to the white man in hewing out an empire in the West, as was the naive dream of Jonathan Carver and others. He was as rugged an individualist as the West would ever know, lacking any small ruling class that could be easily overthrown and replaced by a new master, as had happened with the Aztecs in civilized Mexico. He was, in short, a volatile, unruly force whom the white man was obliged to court and placate and set against Indian neighbors and his own European enemies whenever he could.

The new life started with the horse: the god-dog of the Comanches, the elk-dog of the Blackfeet, the medicine-dog of the Sioux. The miraculous beast made it by hook or by crook out of New Mexico and Spanish husbandry with the rapidity of a prairie fire. First it appeared on the southern plains, to spread north. The Apaches had it by 1650; the Pawnees of Nebraska, before 1700. Meanwhile, along the second major avenue of distribution, the horse was traded among the Shoshonean peoples of the Rockies

Buffalo, an estimated thirty million of them, provided food, clothing, and lodging for the tribes living on the short-grass flatlands.

until it emerged on the northern plains in the early 1700s. By 1750 it had been mastered by Montana's Blackfeet, and by 1770 even the Sauks and Foxes of the western Great Lakes were riding. For buffalo hunters and fighting men everywhere, it was heaven-sent.

The gun came later and from the opposite direction: from the north by way of the French and the English (rarely from the south and the Spanish, who early forbade all traffic in firearms and wisely bought themselves some much-needed time). Though of more use on the open range than in the eastern forests, where an enemy with a tomahawk behind a tree neutralized its effectiveness, the gun was never quite the talisman that the horse was. Even with the best piece available in the eighteenth century, discharging and reloading for a single shot took thirty seconds to a minute — time enough to launch more than a dozen arrows. It was eagerly traded for and killed for, nonetheless. Its very noisiness was music to a young brave's ear — bravura that heightened an already exalted image of self.

There were times when the horse and the gun met in classic face-off. In the 1730s, so one story goes, the northern Shoshonis acquired the horse from the Utes about the same time the Blackfeet got the gun from the Crees. Sagging Blackfoot fortunes were reversed when the reports of weapons spaced along the battle line threw the Shoshonis into utter panic. The Blackfeet soon became full-fledged members of the horse-and-gun club, then did their damnedest to see that no firearms were traded to their enemies, who, given the ill temper of the Blackfeet, numbered many indeed.

The horse and the gun and the expansive pressures of the white man in the East all worked to make the Plains a more crowded place in the eighteenth century. For original occupants and immigrants alike, it was *the* place to be, a platter of plenty whose entrée was buffalo. To mounted hunters, the shaggy beasts were easy marks. One week's hunt could supply a band with enough food for a season and with skins for many winters' clothing and tipis (which the women could set up in fifteen minutes and strike in even less time). In addition, the ease of it all meant more time for the deadliest sport: raiding old enemies, counting coups, garnering glory.

The horse brought the Comanches out of the Rockies about

1700, onto the Plains in a steady southerly direction, away from the tribes with the guns the Comanches did not have. *Comanche* was a Spanish corruption of a Ute term meaning "he who wants to fight me all the time," and between 1727 and 1786 Comanche belligerence was almost constant. The Utes were not alone in their appraisal of this Shoshonean people, who loved fighting and plunder and, above all, their horses. The Pawnees of the central Plains knew their enmity, as did the poor Tonkawas of central Texas and the Spaniards when they showed themselves. But the big losers were the Apache tribes of eastern New Mexico and Texas whom the Comanches drove west and south in the eighteenth century into the lap of the Spaniards.

The Comanches, the lords of the southern Plains, roamed in several bands and in their heyday probably numbered twenty thousand. The noted artist George Catlin later gave this eyewitness description of them: "In their movements they are heavy and ungraceful; and on their feet one of the most unattractive and slovenly looking races of Indians I have ever seen; but the moment they mount their horses, they seem at once metamorphosed, and surprise the spectator with the ease and grace of their movements."

The horse did for the Comanches what it did, more or less, for the Kiowas and the Arapahos and the other Indians of the Plains: it lifted them up off the earth, expanded their vision, gave them the speed of the wind and the power of demigods.

The northern Plains were likewise in flux. The Blackfeet—fierce, sulky, with a deserved reputation as one of the few spoilers of trade—moved south from Canada into northern Montana and sent the Shoshonis, Flatheads, and Kutenais into the mountains for cover. The Crows were being pushed to the south. But the greatest agents of change were the Dakota Sioux, tribes with a woodland habitat east of the Mississippi that had been displaced by the white man and gun-toting Chippewas. When the Dakota Sioux reached the buffalo lands, they liked what they saw, put horse and gun together, and took what they wanted, becoming as dominant in the north as the Comanches were in the south.

A Yankee trader named Peter Pond left this vintage description of a Dakota band he dealt with west of the upper Mississippi in the 1770s: "Ye Yantonese [Yanktons] are faroshas and Rude in thar Maners Perhap Oaeing in Sum masher to thare Leadi[n]g an Obsquer life in the Planes. Thay are not Convarsant with Evrey other tribe. Th[ey seldom] Sea thare Nighbers. Thay Leade a wandering Life in that Exstensive Plane Betwene the Miseura & Missicippey. . . . Thay Have a Grate Number of Horses and Dogs which Carres thare Bageag when thay Move from Plase to Plase. . . . Thay are continuely on the Watch for feare of Beaing Sarprised By thare Enemise who are all Round them. Thare war Implements are Sum fire armes — Boses and arroes & Spear which they have Continuely in thare hands. . . . In Order to have thare Horseis Long Winded they slit thair Noses up the Grissel of thare head which Make them Breath Verey freely."

About 1775 the Dakotas reached the Black Hills, running the Kiowas south, where the latter clashed with the Caddoan-speaking Wichitas. They then joined the Comanches in a common effort that pushed the Lipan and Mescalero Apaches deep down into Texas. The Plains had become a billiard table with all balls

The Mandans of the Upper Missouri were an exception to Plains life. They planted crops and dwelt in semipermanent earth lodges.

in motion. Despite the never-ending hostilities, there were com-
pensations, not the least of them being an estimated thirty million
buffalo. Freed from the old drudgery of the hunt, there was time
for working hides into tipis and circular shields, time for decorat-
ing them with an art that was both geometric and symbolic, and
time for forming male military societies, going to the sweathouse,
and perfecting the sun dance and the scalp dance.

Not all Plains tribes shared all the attributes of the Plains culture. The gifted Mandans and the Hidatsas and the more southerly Arikaras chose to continue living in semipermanent villages
along the upper Missouri, contenting themselves as traders of
horses rather than raiders. They grew corn and beans, which they
traded to the nomads who came from all points of the compass for
supplies. Unfortunately, the Sioux also came with more than
trade on their minds, and the Mandans eventually found themselves besieged in their earth-covered lodges. Then, in a sorry
irony, when the white man's poxes came, it was the sedentary
people in the closeness of a village who suffered the full ravages
of the disease—not the centaurs galloping over the grasslands.

Armed conflict was ever a condition of life on the Plains. It was
before the eighteenth century and it was in the century after the
eighteenth, when the internecine war of the Plains Indian was to
be both a bother and a benefit to the white man. During the last
half of the eighteenth century, the situation was reversed somewhat; the white man's wars in the East were both a benefit and a
bother to the Plains Indian. He could not have guessed that the
noisy battles between formally uniformed men marching in rank
and file were for the mastery of a continent that included his buffalo grounds. But he was aware of some short-term inconveniences
they caused.

Prior to 1740, for example, the French had built up a mutually
profitable and orderly trade with the Osage and Kansa Indians on
the Lower Missouri: guns and knives and trinkets for pelts and
buffalo wool. Then King George's war intervened; French boats
on the Mississippi bound for New Orleans were prey to English
pirates, and those that made it found the prices for trade goods in
the port city raised—an increase that had to be passed on to the
Osages and the Kansas. A brief peace intervened, then hostilities

were resumed in 1756 with the French and Indian War, which proved disastrous for the French and disruptive to the Indian. Almost overnight the Frenchmen became subjects of Spain, in accordance with the Treaty of Versailles in 1763, acting as agents for a European nation that was never comfortable on the Plains. For the Plains Indian, things were not the same. The Spanish were insulting and the merchandise inferior and more expensive—nothing like the good old days when the joyous, dancing "heavy eyebrows" came among the tribes and were their own men.

As French strength ebbed, the English tried to fill the void, using French middlemen or their own traders to obtain furs from the Indian in exchange for superior wares at cheaper prices. But the traffic was hit-and-miss, especially after western Louisiana became Spanish and the English had to cross the Mississippi furtively from Canada, where the new English governor, Guy Carleton, encouraged French *coureurs de bois* to do what the Spanish were doing so poorly. That was fine, if the Spanish did not catch on. But they did, and in the winter of 1772–73 they confiscated boatloads of furs that Jean-Marie Ducharme, acting for England, had acquired among the Osages. The outbreak of the Revolutionary War put a squeeze on the Indian supply of powder and shot and metal tools, which was all but shut off when Governor Carleton in 1777 closed the Great Lakes to all craft except those in royal service. Commerce with the Plains had come to a temporary standstill.

When the war ended, the victors were not the English, whose primary interest in the West was its potential as a fur supplier and a market, and who were therefore preferred by the Indian, but the resident splinter group—the "dirt eaters," so called for their land-hungry ways (many a mutilated corpse of a settler had been found with dirt packed in its mouth).

The Europeans may have created the Plains culture; the Americans would be the ones to destroy it. Yet that would take a century, and they would not do it alone. For all its pageantry and earthy splendor, the Plains culture was self-consuming, self-destructive. Before the Americans ever came, some tribes, including the Paloma and Carlana Apaches, had been exterminated—by red men. Other tribes, among them the Tonkawas of central

An Indian camp on the great grassland. Tepees of buffalo hides could be struck quickly in order to follow the migrating herds.

Texas, the Caddoan confederacy of northeast Texas, and even the once-mighty Kansas of the lower Missouri, had been reduced to a pitiful few—by red men.

The doom of the Plains Indian came from within as well as from without. Economically, he was always more a consumer than a producer, and his over-reliance on the buffalo (his harvest of which could be wasteful) made his future precarious to say the least. Politically, his organization was so weak as to border on anarchy. What he did, and what he had, derived from what he was: the embodiment of all that was masculine and predatory, a Dionysian votary committed to excess, which led not to Blake's palace of wisdom but, in time, to his own destruction.

Chapter 6

Corn Farmers, Thieves, and Borrowers

THE PUEBLO INDIANS living along the life-sustaining floodplain of what the Spanish called the Rio Grande del Norte are considered exceptions among the aboriginal peoples of North America. Even in 1776 they were exceptions, in matters of circumstance as well as culture. Far from enjoying any Indian summer, their metaphor might have described an unusually harsh and early winter spilling down upon them from the white heights of the Sangre de Cristo Mountains. Ushering in that winter of the spirit were fierce Comanches, more of them than had come before, with pillage on their minds.

Still, there had been worse times: the years before the revolt of their ancestors in 1680, when the *encomiendas* were in full force, and the grasping and arrogant *gentes de razón* (a description of those who were blessed with at least some Spanish blood) violated venerable taboos and desecrated the gods who had come from *Shipapu* to teach the people the methods and the ceremonies for planting corn. There were also, for that matter, the twelve years when they were free of the Spanish yoke but when the Tewa medicine man, Popé, mystic co-instigator of the rebellion, had himself become a tyrant. The pueblos quarreled with one another, and the people, displaying an uncharacteristic fury to be rid of alien ways, had allowed wheatfields and fruit orchards and vineyards to go to ruin. The Revolt was a time remembered, a touchstone for reckoning changes, good, bad, and neutral.

The peoples of the pueblos dwelt not only along the Rio Grande. There was a western spur that ran to the sky city of Ácoma, through the mountain of Zuñi, and far west onto the bald mesas of the Hopis. On a map it showed like a bent cross with the left transverse beam shorn away. The peoples east and west were not united by language; if anything, they were divided by it. Those of the river valley spoke various dialects of Keresan and Tanoan tongues, the Zuñis a language unique unto themselves, and the Hopis a Shoshonean dialect. What united them was a common view of the world—and corn, the cultivation of which in a remote past had kept hunters home and made farmers of them.

There was a harmony in this horizontal world of mesas and mountains and volcanic badlands and the deep-blue closeness of the sky, if one but looked. The Pueblos did look and saw proportion, a command for moderation in all things. Religion was life itself, and ritual owned each mundane act of everyday life. Earthen homes were of earth colors and alike, as the people were supposed to be alike—serene, forbearing, and vaguely uptight. Grief and joy were private and should remain that way in the communal interest. Growing corn was preferable to waging war, for it kept one close to home and to the women around whom life focused. The corn planter lived with the family of his wife; children of the union belonged to the clan of the wife—squash people of summer, or turquoise people of winter, or whatever divisions the pueblo had. Women's work might never be done, but it was the important work, keeping house and hearth and a continuity through the rhythms of days and seasons and generations. Going away to war might be necessary. It was, however, appraised as sadly necessary.

In the latter part of the eighteenth century, it was necessary for the Rio Grande Pueblos to go to war again. When they did, they acquitted themselves well, not only against Comanches from the north but also against Apaches from the east and west and south. From any direction, there might resound without warning spine-chilling shrieks of raiders, whose horses kicked up swirling dust devils on a dun landscape both coming and going. With them were only the Spaniards. The Spaniards! Those were strange bedfellows for the Pueblos, and no longer the best of allies either. Through their greedy traders, the Hispanos had helped to arm the enemy, who now had more and better horses than the Pueblos, who in their turn had certainly more horses than the

Ácoma, the "Sky City," was typical of the defensible high ground settled by the maize-growers of New Mexico's mesa tops.

Spaniards. Moreover, the Spanish soldiers were neither as numerous nor as valiant as they once had been. It was an odd alliance, indeed. Yet together they stood for the nebulous idea of civilization against what the Spaniards called the *Indios barbaros.* Civilization—yes, there was something in that. But whose civilization was it? In 1776 there were an estimated 6,000 Spaniards compared to some 11,000 Indians; in 1680 there had been 2,500 Spaniards and 25,000 Pueblos.

After the Revolt and the reconquest by the man-of-his-word, Don Diego de Vargas, conditions had gradually worsened. The old arrogance of the *Españoles* showed itself in different guises. True, the priests could no longer force their religion on the red men as they once had, with whippings for failure to attend Mass; nor did the priests have easy access to their homes. Now the padres were their friends—defending them against the secular officials who corrupted their young women, made field hands of their men, and cheated them all at the marketplace. Yet the

*Long before the Spaniards came to conquer, the peaceful corn-planters
had to be watchful for the approach of fierce nomadic raiders.*

people could now retire behind their own adobe walls and, in the
secrecy of their dim chambers, practice ancient rites to propitiate
fertility gods and thwart sorcerers who brought disease. What the
fathers preached need only be paid lip service and made a lesser
part of what they believed — or pretended to believe.

But while passive resistance might work in coping with the
Spaniards, it was no way to combat the nomads who had hounded
the Pueblos since long before the Spaniards arrived. Those with
the reverence and patience to grow corn in surplus had always
had to be on guard against the wanderers who would not grow it
but would kill for it. Had not their ancestors, the Anasazis of the
rumpled red canyon country to the north and west, learned that?
Why else had they lived high up in the recesses of sheer canyon
walls? Yet it could not be denied that at this time there were
more of the marauders, and they were closer. From the mid-
eighteenth century on, Pueblo and Spaniard stood side by side
against the disruptive forces of the outside world. Even though

the thin green line of riverside farms possessed more spiritual than material riches, wealth was relative, and the restless horsemen had come to get what they could.

In August of 1760, the Comanches in force attacked Taos, the northernmost of the Rio Grande pueblos and the place of the annual trade fair. Before the attack and after it, the summer fair was the commercial highlight of the year, where Comanche, Ute, Navajo, Apache, Spaniard, and Pueblo could meet in momentary peace to swap horses, slaves, guns, corn, hides, blankets, jewelry, feathers, and dyes. The raid was an outrage, but only a foretaste of what was to come.

In the 1770s the Comanche chief Cuerno Verde and his horde rode in from the northeast to terrorize the Rio Grande Valley. To the northwest, the Utes were leaving their mountain homes to get their share of plunder, and in 1778 the Spaniards would issue an empty retaliatory decree forbidding trade with them. Then there were the Apaches, more bold and far-ranging than ever, uniting the corn people with the Spaniard and anybody else who would join the common cause of defense.

THE WESTERN PUEBLOS of the Zuñis and Hopis knew much less of the Spaniards than their eastern counterparts. There, too, lived sedentary agricultural peoples, worshipers of the Corn Mother, and even more peace-loving than those in the river valley. After the 1680 Revolt, when they killed the Christian priests sent among them, Spanish visits were infrequent. Both Zuñis and Hopis were exempted from Spanish taxes; both were Spanish subjects only in Spanish minds. The Zuñis, two hundred miles west of the Rio Grande, did receive occasional missionaries, whom they treated kindly. The Hopis, about one hundred miles northwest of Zuñi, received them and then gently but firmly sent them away. Yet neither of these staid, independent tribes was immune to the new troubles. Navajo raids on Zuñi were stepped up from the west, and in the 1770s they faced a new threat from Apaches. As for the proud Hopis, also familiar with Apache and Navajo raiders but with superb defensive positions atop their three mesas, 1777 was the culminating year of a period of drought that forced many to come down from their desiccate high ground. Some agreed to be relocated on the Rio Grande by the Spanish, some went west to live on the floor of the Grand Canyon with the Havasupais, and others stayed to see the dry years through. In 1781 the rains came, and so did the smallpox.

Some three hundred dry miles south of Hopi, in a land of thick saguaro stands and other Sonoran Desert flora, the tip of a feeble Spanish finger protruded up from Mexico into present-day Arizona. It was part of what New Spain called Pimería Alta, so named after the Pima Indian bands living there, who were united by speaking dialects of a single language. The countryside south of the future border looked exactly as it did to the north: sable-hued and broken by jagged upthrusts of a darkish color, with succulents growing where rainfall allowed, and cut through by a few life-sustaining rivers. Two of these were the Santa Cruz and the San Pedro, which ran northwest into the Gila. Bordering the Santa Cruz and the San Pedro there was vegetation—not all of it put there randomly by nature. Some of it had been planted and some of it was maize, tended by the Sobaipuris, the northeastern branch of the Pimas. Like most corn people, they were peaceful, and like most corn people, they drew Spanish padres. The seed of faith always did better where maize also grew.

Father Eusebio Kino was the first to envision a Catholic harvest in Pimería Alta back in the 1690s. In his usual fearless fashion he went among the *rancherias* of the Sobaipuris and their western neighbors and fellow Pimas, the Papagos (who lived by reaping seasonal harvests from their irrigated gardens and by gathering what they could from the desert), as well as the Pimas south of the future border. Kino brought with him cattle and practical advice on improving life in the here and now, as well as spiritual uplift. Skillfully and successfully, he protected his new flock from the greed of Sonora's mine owners and *hacendados,* who were in need of forced labor for their pits and their farms and did what they could to poison the Jesuit's reputation in New Spain. He even mediated misunderstanding-become-atrocity to the point where he was trusted by the Pimas, if not by the entrepreneurs of Sonora. The Pimas actually wanted missions and wanted Spaniards to live with them. But Kino was, alas, mortal, and after he

Early in the eighteenth century, Father Eusebio Kino brought both cattle and the Word of God to the Indians of Pimería Alta.

died in 1711 the rim of Christendom slid southward again.

In 1732 the Jesuits did send more missionaries north to recoup what, if ever won, had been lost. The missions of San Xavier del Bac and San Miguel de Guevavi were manned, a modest achievement undone in 1751 by a Piman uprising. The following year the missions were reoccupied, but the Jesuits never recovered their strength before they were banished by royal decree in 1767. The Franciscans came in their stead, and as Hubert H. Bancroft suggests, the year 1776 can be taken as marking the Spanish occupation of Tucson. The Sobaipuris and the Papagos did not see much of the newcomers they were prepared to welcome, and that was not attributable solely to Spanish weakness or indifference. The new cry in the land was no more than a magnified echo of a very old cry familiar to the ear of Piman and Pueblo and Spaniard. It spelled terror in a single word—*Apache!*

WITH THE CORN PEOPLE in the Southwest long before Coronado and his bearded countrymen came looking for Cíbola were a pair of Athapascan-speaking groups related by language but showing a widening cleavage in habits in the eighteenth century. We know them today as the Navajos and the Apaches, convenient handles for what were neither nations nor tribes but many roaming bands fending for themselves. How long they had inhabited the Southwest is a matter of conjecture still. They are believed to have descended from the last prehistoric migrants across the Asian landbridge, some of them leaving many relatives in upper Canada to wander down the east side of the Rockies. Once in the Southwest they scattered, with those known as Apaches not really settling but by the eighteenth century living both east and west of the Rio Grande. Those east of the river, in the New Mexico hill country and on the southern Plains, the "eastern Apaches," were either pliant farmers facing annihilation at the hands of the Comanches, or warriors in southwesterly retreat — a people being tempered between a Comanche hammer and a Spanish anvil.

Apache is a Zuñi word for "enemy" that stuck for these savage, fugitive bands, who by fate and disposition became enemies to all. No one else was so begrudged a place under the ample southwestern sun or made the object of a common hunt by an alliance of Pueblos, Comanches, Spaniards, and even Navajos on occasion. They were the unwanted, the unclean, the pariahs of the Southwest. But to the chagrin of their enemies, they prospered in adversity and were never so prosperous as in the eighteenth century, when they became chronic disrupters of orderly business.

Historians and ethnographers have said there never were very many Apaches. One estimate puts their number west of the Rio Grande at not many more than six thousand. If this is correct, then each fought with the strength of ten, not out of any purity of heart, but out of the will to survive by grit and theft. In the eighteenth century their sphere of chaos extended from southern Texas and northern Chihuahua through Sonora all the way to the Yaqui River, north to central Arizona, and east to cover the southern half of New Mexico. Between the most southerly New Mexican pueblo and the most northerly Mexican stronghold, they controlled what has been called the "Apache Corridor" — an avenue wide enough to march twenty modern armies through.

Early Spanish reports from the seventeenth century make sparse mention of the "western Apaches," or bands that would later fit that description. We can picture them as dim figures on the far horizon, watching, from umber hilltops or in the mauve shadows of a desert wash, the arriving Spaniards and their baggage. They were interested in Spanish possessions as they had been and still were interested in Pueblo possessions. Above all, they were interested in the horse. The Apaches practiced a kind of haphazard agriculture around their brush shelters both before and after the coming of the horse, but they were not as comfortable in the stooped position as they were upright, mounted.

In the eighteenth century Spaniards saw more Apaches than they cared to see. The marauders came, they saw, and they stole, with growing regularity — hitting and running with what they could take, and killing but not for killing's sake. This fine moral distinction did not stay the Spaniards, who tried a variety of countermeasures: Christianizing them, which was a complete fizzle; ostracizing them, which only encouraged them; organizing punitive campaigns of pursuit, which too often ended in some empty blind canyon of broken rock; and making slaves of them, particularly their children, which only fired Apache ardor more.

The years between 1765 and 1785 were the height of Apache terror. The Rio Grande Valley was bleeding; the future of the Taos pueblo a cause of the greatest concern. The western pueblos all the way to Zuñi now felt Apache pressure, and the Sobaipuris were chased out of the San Pedro River Valley. The northeast portion of the rich mining and ranching province of Sonora had been abandoned, and the capital had been moved south from San Juan Bautista and away from the area of desolation. Even on the far southern Texas plains, the eastern Apaches were making living hazardous to health.

In 1786 the desperate Spaniards resorted to their "final solution" to the Apache question. It was a many-sided plan that aimed not at immediate extermination but at containing the menace and reducing it to manageability. The Cross was dropped from Cross and Sword. All hopes of Christianizing the Apaches were to be given up. Peace treaties were to be made with them whenever possible and fighting among the bands encouraged. Bribery was chosen as the best way to induce the Indians to settle near presidios, where, in a radical turn in Spanish practice, they were to be given, along with food, alcohol in generous amounts and poor-quality firearms. Such profound cynicism was not normal in Spanish Indian policy, but then the Apaches were not "normal" Indians. The plan actually worked reasonably well for about twenty-five years. Then all reverted to the old state of affairs, as the Mexicans and later the Americans were painfully to experience.

ABOUT 1696, THE PUEBLO INDIANS of Jémez, in the company of some unhappy neighbors on the Rio Grande, fled their homes and the reconquering army of Don Diego de Vargas, to whom they refused to knuckle under. They headed west from the river of life to settle with a people living north of Zuñi who called themselves *Dineh,* were called by the Tewa *Navahú,* later by the Spaniards *Apaches de Navajó,* and still later by Anglos the Navajos. The exiles brought with them pottery and weaving, stonemasonry, ceremonials, and a softening of manners. Intermarriage occurred and the coming together took on the characteristics of a Greco-Roman exchange. Then about 1764, the Jémez left the red canyon country as suddenly as they had come and returned to the Rio Grande, but their influence remained behind them among a people who were eager to learn and ready to better themselves.

Whereas the Apache shunned contact and gloried in his isolation, his fellow Athapascan (considered by some to be merely an Apache mutation) valued meetings with outsiders and the tangible gifts they brought. The Apache stole horses and relished war that was constant; the Navajo bred horses and went on intermittent raids to increase possessions. At the fork in the trail, the Apaches chose the way that led to the mentality of the Plains, while their deviant kin chose a path that led to cultivated fields and grazing herds.

The Navajos were borrowers who did not care from whom they borrowed. Supplementing what they got from living with corn people were the sheep, horses, and cattle they acquired by stealth from the Spaniards. Not that they were overly fond of the Spanish; the Jémez who arrived after the reconquest were not the best advance men for the "bearded ones." Yet the Spaniards were not rubbing elbows with the Navajos as they had with the Jémez, and anybody who had what the Spanish had could at least be learned from. Geography favored the Navajos in this. Canyon de Chelly and Chinle and Window Rock were on the periphery of northern New Spain, out of royal jurisdiction but close enough to the hub of activity and the popular trade fairs at Taos.

Harassment could come from only one direction; that was from the north, from the Utes, and it did so from time to time. Ute raids sent one group of Navajos begging for Spanish protection in the 1740s—an action that earned them the tag of "enemy people" among other Navajos. The Spaniards did what they could to accommodate their wards, resettling the harried Navajos near Ácoma and establishing Franciscan missions in the new pueblos of Ceboletta and Encinal in 1745. It was failed generosity; the practical-minded Navajos watched patiently as the missions became poorer and poorer through lack of funds, then they drifted off again, with no hard feelings, but convinced that Spanish gods were not Navajo gods, and Spanish goods might already be more plentiful in Navajo care.

By 1776 the borrowers had borrowed well and put together a culture of their own. Like the Plains Indian, the Navajo was on the brink of a new era, but unlike the Plains Indian he had diversified, becoming at once farmer, rancher, and shepherd to large flocks of sheep raised from Spanish foundation stock. Navajo population was higher than it had ever been, perhaps double or even triple what it was in 1700. New ideas and new skills and new crafts released an energy and an expansion westward toward the juniper- and piñon-covered canyonlands abutting the Colorado River. Raiding continued as a part-time occupation, but in 1781 a Spanish report gave the Navajos high marks for citizenship: they were industrious, stable, and wove fabrics that incorporated their own designs. For the Navajos, the year of the Revolution was more the solstice of summer than an Indian summer. Autumn was deferred until the nineteenth century, when raiding increased, warfare became more important, and the Anglo-Americans forced them to take a long walk into winter.

Chapter 7

Wakers from the Dream

OLLEYQUOTEQUIBE, KNOWN TO THE SPANIARDS by the less tongue-defying name of Salvador Palma, had every reason to be optimistic in the autumn of 1776. The Yuma chief had left his people in the fertile bottomlands where the Gila River joins the Colorado, to embark on a great journey in the company of new friends. His destination was none other than Mexico City, which would dazzle him with its splendors; and his traveling companion was none other than Juan Bautista de Anza, the illustrious Spanish frontier captain. Two and a half years before, Anza had personally bestowed on him the canes of office and the title of governor on behalf of a king whose lands were said to be vast and separated by several oceans. Anza was on his first visit to California at that time, but he had returned in 1776 with more gifts to distribute among the Yumas. Palma treasured his own eye-catching uniform of yellow and blue with gold braid, and he was taken with the Roman Catholic doctrine and rituals.

Salvador Palma and three countrymen, including his younger brother, Ygnacio, were regaled in the grand Spanish manner in Mexico City. His hosts impressed upon him how important the Yumas were in Spanish plans for the future, controlling as they did the overland way to Alta California, where the king's men were bringing a better way of life. Salvador and Ygnacio lingered and listened with pleasure, taking the sacrament of baptism during their stay. In a petition, Salvador asked for missionaries to be sent among his people (over whom he had less than absolute control) and for arms to be provided for protecting those same people from their enemies. To please the king, no doubt, he also forswore polygamy forever, both for himself and for his people. In turn, the chief received assurances of great things to come, and when he left the capital of New Spain in 1777 laden with personal gifts, he also took with him high hopes and memories of an opulence that was soon to spread northwest to the Yumas.

The history of Spanish contact on the lower Colorado was long but spotty, and for that reason rather a happy one through 1776. In 1540, Hernando de Alarcón had sailed up the Colorado River through Yuman territory, and in the same year Melchior Diaz arrived by land. Oñate had visited the Yumas in their settlements in 1604; Kino met some on the Gila in 1699 and 1700, and sent them wheat in 1702; and others no doubt reached them both before Kino and after. But it was not until the 1740s, when the Jesuit father Jacobo Sedelmayr went among them, that a permanent alliance with the Colorado River tribes became a goal of Spanish policy. This postdated an old slave trade that had Yumas sending enemy captives to Sonora and their enemies capturing Yumas to face the same unkind fate of hard labor.

In the early 1770s the Yumas had *gentes de razón* with them on what was to be a very temporary basis. Mutual respect was high but short-lived. The Indians admired Spanish pomp and panoply, and desired the horses and finery they brought. By 1776, partly through the diplomatic offices of Father Francisco Garcés, peace had been made between the Yumas and their traditional enemies, the Cocomaricopas east on the Gila and the Chemehuevis west of the Colorado; intertribal trading waxed as a result. For their part, the Spaniards found the Yumas a handsome people, tall, muscular, superb swimmers, of a disposition definitely inclined toward joy and gaiety, and by all outward signs generous and smitten with their new friends. Father Pedro Font did express some reservations in 1775 about their uninhibited attitudes toward bodily functions. They were abominably licentious and even given to allowing homosexuals to engage in "nefarious practices" with apparent sanction. This, he concluded, was certainly due to their being without religion, which rendered them "disorderly and beastlike." They were also, Font prophetically said in so many words a year later, of a proud and independent nature with a known reputation as warriors.

Salvador Palma returned home in 1777 with promises that *they* were coming soon—those padres and presents. But they did not come soon. Apache raids and a Seri uprising depleted Sonora, the logical supplier, that very year. It was a delay that neither his sponsors nor Palma were long to live with—not together. Palma made nervous inquiries in 1778 and 1779 to find out when the great day might be expected, and when Fathers Francisco Garcés and Juan Diaz arrived late in 1779 with a small contingent of soldiers, they noted that the Yumas were sullen and Palma's authority was slipping. Finally, late the following year, about one hundred sixty soldiers and settlers arrived to settle, not in missions, but in pueblos Concepción and Bicuñer, which were to secure the vital route to California. The settlers were a hungry, bumptious gang who meant to show the Yumas their place straightaway. They appropriated the choicer lands for themselves, and the new commandant, Alfárez Santiago Yslas, had the bad judgment to imprison a couple of tribal leaders, including Ygnacio Palma, and to allow the livestock the settlers had brought to forage without restraint in the fields bordering the rivers, devouring crops that were barely adequate that year to feed the natives. Overall, there was an on-site high-handedness toward the Indians (who in truth expected more gifts than visitors), and a foolish Hispanic presumption that the Yumas were timid souls who could be cowed into obedience with a minimum of force and vigilance. Unheeded went the counsel of Salvador's friend Anza that these freedom-loving natives not be pressured into the customary near-peonage of Indian "reduction." Unfollowed, too, was the 1777 order of Spain's Carlos III that Palma's people be treated gently and not "be injured in any way in their goods or their lands with a view to giving them to Spaniards."

Even before the greedy settlers came, there were signs of trouble. Salvador's brother, the baptized Ygnacio, had become a magnet for young male dissidents who had grown weary of waiting for *mañana*. For a while Salvador held the thankless role of mediator and double-dealing placator, trying to maintain authority with his own people and also to reassure the Spaniards who had placed their trust in him. Then in June of 1781 a group of soldiers under the command of Fernando Rivera y Moncada dropped in

137

on the Colorado River community for a layover before heading on to California. Without supplies, they took food from Yuman mouths. It proved to be the willow wand that broke the burro's back. On July 17, not long after most of the transients had moved on to California, the Yumas rose in bloody revolt, Salvador as much following as leading them. Bicuñer and Concepción were sacked and burned, and more than a hundred Spaniards slaughtered, including, on the following day, after some deliberation, Father Garcés.

For a year and a half the Spaniards tried with force of arms to reassert themselves among the Yumas, but even with the aid of Indian allies they failed. The strategic riverlands would never be theirs. What had begun as Salvador Palma's dream had ended as a Spanish nightmare.

FRIENDLY NEIGHBORS TO THE NORTH had joined the Yumas in their 1781 extirpation of the Spaniards. These were the Mojaves, a striking people physically, said to have been the tallest of all North American Indians, who had within their number a cult called the *kwanamis* dedicated to offensive warfare. (Defensive war was apparently unnecessary, there being no one with the temerity to attack the Mojaves in their Needles-area stronghold.) The *kwanamis* were Spartans to heat and cold and hunger, passing their time, not in turning the river soil, but rapt in dreams of spirits who taught them how to mete out death and accept the same in combat with manly indifference.

The Mojaves and the Yumas were but two of one hundred three "tribes," speaking twenty-one mutually unintelligible languages, who lived within the present boundaries of California. Usually the Mojaves and the Yumas are considered peoples apart from the rest of California Indians. Their lives were benefited by their nearness to the Colorado River and the "higher" maize cultures of the Southwest. Their political organization was more elaborate (tribal with the Mojaves and approaching nation status with the Yumas), and their warfare was more developed, thought-out, concerted — all those words that mean they could kill with greater efficiency and common purpose. The rest to the west — well, they were not really tribes but communities, sometimes

These not-quite-believable drawings of California Indians appeared in a geography book printed in London in the year 1779.

even a single extended family living by an oak-shaded stream, and their wars were little more than family feuds, short-lived and remarkable for the little blood that was spilled. The gulf separating the river tribes from most of their fellow Californians was of the mind, in ways of looking at a world that physically did not always appear that different. If there was a bridge between the two, it may have been in the dream-prone *kwanamis:* an otherworldliness of visions and spirits and death-thought touched many west of them as well.

For a time it was fashionable to think of the California Indian as a hopeless retardate, a dimwit skilled in basketry and nothing else, a "digger" — in short, low man on everyone's cultural totem pole, whose housing, clothing, religion, and art were distinctly substandard. The scholarly work of Alfred L. Kroeber, Robert F. Heizer, and others has brought about some rethinking in the twentieth century. A man is always more than he seems, and the California Indian seen in retrospect is no exception. Back in 1776, Father Pedro Font described some Diegueños living east of San Diego as the "most unhappy people in the world," living among bleak rocks and off tasteless roots and seeds, and owning no more than a bow and a few bad arrows. "In fine," Font summed up, "they are so savage, wild and dirty, disheveled, ugly, small and timid, that only because they have the human form is it possible to believe that they belong to mankind." Much the same was said about other California Indians, many times.

Yet a nagging fact divides appearance from reality. Estimates of how many Indians lived in North America at any given time have fluctuated wildly in academic circles, but whichever figures are accepted, California keeps a disproportionately high number for its land area. (Kroeber estimated 133,000 for the year 1770 against a total of 719,000 in the present United States, though new research suggests both figures should be proportionately much higher.) The only thing made perfectly clear is that California Indians were better off than Font and others believed.

The Indians of California may have been the most omnivorous men of their time. Wherever they were they could count on food in variety. On the coast there were fish and mollusks aplenty (among the Chumash even bear cubs were raised as the Europeans might raise pigs); inland there were deer, small game, migratory birds, and grubs and insects. Almost everywhere, except the desert, there were oaks and therefore acorns, ground by the women into a wholesome meal and then leached by a variety of ingenious methods to remove the bitter tannic acid. The desert also offered staples. There was the nourishing mesquite bean in inexhaustible supply, which was pounded to a meal and then eaten; the screw bean, which providentially matured a little later; the ubiquitous agave, which through burning could be reduced to a fibrous, delicious, and nutritious hot salad; the yucca fruit, the prickly pear "fig," piñon nuts, and *chia,* the seed of sagebrush ground and cooked into the famed porridge, *pinole.* The land of plenty could even allow most "tribes" a taboo food, one that could be easily come by but abstained from for reasons sacred. Without it there was enough, and the satisfied stomach gave the gift of leisure and time — time in which to ponder time or to try to make it stand still. The languor might only be disturbed by a sudden quake, caused by "the giant who moves in the earth."

Time slowed was a cadence for life that went back far before any European left his erasable footprint on the Pacific sands. A recent dating of a Del Mar skull find puts man in Southern California for 48,000 years. Burials unearthed in central California reveal the deceased of 4,000 years ago laid to rest face down and extended, accompanied with grave offerings useful in the after-life. Those departed may have known where they were going, but where had they come from? Had they taken the wrong migra-tional offramp? Were they then, as some suggest now, flotsam collecting in a sluggish eddy? Maybe. Their many linguistic families would seem to say so. There were Hokans and Penu-tians, Algonkins and Yukians, Athapascans and Shoshoneans. But all were lulled and softened on the Pacific slope, where, when things happened, they did not happen too wrenchingly fast.

Outside influences did creep in from the Northwest coast and the Anasazi Southwest, and perhaps even from Mexico between 500 B.C. and A.D. 500. Later, after 1200, life in California's north-west resembled life in the Pacific Northwest, and there evolved among the salmon-eaters a rich and a poor through the scramble for property. Pueblo influence in the south was less pronounced, and in central California nativism prevailed. What outside ways entered the Promised Land developed conservatively and might be ignored altogether by one people only a valley removed from another who, say, practiced ground painting derived from South-west sand painting. Everywhere there was diversity, privacy, and a lack of intrusiveness. The Pomos north of San Francisco Bay wove the most intricate and beautiful baskets of any North American tribe, perhaps of any people anywhere. The Chumash of the Santa Barbara region constructed plank canoes sealed with asphaltum that were superbly seaworthy and only found in one other place in the western hemisphere, on the coast of Chile.

Other fruits of culture were more widespread. There was the sweathouse, a kind of men's club where males gathered daily around a smoky central fire to gab about business or hunting before excusing themselves to plunge into a cold stream. The passage of a girl to womanhood was widely regarded as a great event, with rigid proscriptions for conduct on the part of the ado-lescent and a general attentiveness from the rest of her people. Mourning rites that might last a year were widely observed, especially in the south, though a preoccupation with death itself

Father Junípero Serra arrived in 1769, and the missionization of Alta California was soon begun. The languid aborigines did not take well to regimentation.

was conspicuous throughout California. In the north there were Kuksu cults with spirit impersonations and ghost contacts; in the south, Toloache cults, which used the narcotic jimsonweed to achieve transcendence.

Mediums, cults, drugs — little is ever new under the California sun, and life in California then as now had an unreality about it. What the Indians had, and therefore were thought to be, did not meet the eye. Time that could have been used in making pottery and weaponry and masonry edifices that were unnecessary was spent instead in mystic contemplation of good and evil, origins and destinations, death and dreams.

THE DREAMERS ON THE DREAMSCAPE awoke in 1769 to find guests. Father Junípero Serra and a suffering handful of Spaniards had arrived in San Diego, and on July 19, Serra dedi-

The visiting French Comte de la Pérouse, on a scientific expedition, received this orderly welcome at the Carmel mission in 1786.

cated a rude brush church as Mission San Diego de Alcalá. Five years later a more permanent structure was raised, which augured something else for the Indians, who had had only occasional visitors since Cabrillo brushed their shores in 1542. These brief encounters between European and aborigine were by and large cordial, even fraternally affectionate by the accounts of Drake's 1579 visit to what were probably the Miwoks. The same climate of goodwill existed in June of 1775, when two Spanish vessels returning from an exploration of the Northwest coast put into Trinidad Bay and were welcomed by Yurok Indians wearing feathers and flowers in their hair. Don Juan Francisco de la Bodega y Quadra, captain of the small schooner *Sonora,* included in his journal the visit to this "happy paradise" and had these revealing words to say of those who greeted him: "Consistent with the indolent situation in which Nature places them, they exert little more effort than that of Nature; hence there is less hostility toward their neighbors, fewer disputes about property, and less hate produced by ambition." One suspects that Quadra had a romantic streak in him and was something of an early-day "bleeding heart."

The hardheaded José Espinosa y Tello, writing later of the Costanoans of Monterey Bay, called them the most stupid and degraded of all Indians. He was in half agreement with an early clerical evaluation of the Indians of Baja California which faulted them for their "extraordinary slackness" and ingratitude but nevertheless praised them for their honesty and for the tenderness they showed their children. Pedro Fages, a military man and a constant thorn in Serra's side, gave a soldierly appraisal of the Chumash in the 1770s. He found them friendly toward the Spaniards, quarrelsome among themselves, able as traders ("the Chinese of California"), inclined to work when it was in their self-interest, but "idolators like the rest" and "much addicted to the abominable vice" of sodomy. A composite portrait takes resolution from all these reports: that of amiable sorts, given to lethargy and sensuality, on the surface tractable and responsive to paternalism, but in sum a fragile people.

The Spanish requisites for a mission were arable soil, a ready water supply, and a large Indian population both to provide labor and to receive the gifts of civilization. These Serra and his associates located. After San Diego de Alcalá there was San Carlos Borromeo del Carmelo on Monterey Bay in June 1770; San Antonio de Padua in an oak-sprinkled valley of the Santa Lucia Mountains in July 1771; San Gabriel Arcangel in September of the same year, on the plain below the mountains named for the same archangel; San Luís Obispo de Tolosa on a sunny hill inland from the sea in September 1772; in October 1776, San Francisco de Asís was dedicated on the peninsula named for the gentle saint who founded the Franciscan order; and in the following month San Juan Capistrano was founded on the south coast, for the second time. A second founding was necessary because the previous year the mission had been abandoned by the Spaniards when word reached them of a revolt at Mission San Diego de Alcalá to the south. Perhaps the most revealing statistic from the uprising of the coastal Kamias was that, with the destruction of the mission, a grand total of three Spanish lives had been taken, including that of a padre, Father Luís Jayme. As if in sympathy, resistance flickered in December of the following year when Indians attacked Mission San Francisco de Asís at the northern end of the mission chain. That insurrection accomplished even less than the first.

The missionaries Spain sent to Alta California were among the most enlightened and humane of their calling. Serra, Francisco Palóu, Fermín Lasuén, and Juan Crespí. It was simply that discipline, learning a trade, growing citrus, dates, figs, and olives held nothing for a people who had not yet been sufficiently disabused of the notion that they had everything, or at least as much as they wanted. So far apart were the two peoples that cultural syncretism did not have much of a chance. Some neophytes fled the missions to the dry interior. Many who did not flee lapsed into a greater torpor, and Mission Indian women were known to induce abortions. In the words of Alfred Kroeber: "It must have caused many of the fathers severe pain to realize, as they could not but do daily, that they were saving souls only at the inevitable cost of lives."

When Father Serra died in 1784, one year after the Treaty of Paris, which certified the autonomy of the thirteen former British colonies crowding the Atlantic Coast, there were nine functioning Spanish missions ministering to 5,800 converts close by the Pacific coast. The number of California Indians affected were decidedly a small minority of the total, for whom the greatest suffering was still many years off, long after the missions were gone. All the same, the long dream was decidedly ended.

Chapter 8

Isolation, Splendid and Otherwise

THAT ARID HEART OF THE WEST called the Great Basin—which embraces virtually all of Nevada, western Utah, much of southern Idaho, the southeastern corner of Oregon, and, in California, the dry leeward lands east of the Sierra Nevada and most of the Mojave Desert to the south—that land where the rivers when they run at all run inward, away from the seas to end in salt sinks, that intermontane realm of sage and mesquite and piñon, had not felt the weight of a white man's foot. Not until 1776. In March of that year Father Francisco Garcés became the first known outsider to have seen the Basin, and he only its far southwestern tip. After accompanying the second Anza expedition as far as Yuma, Garcés set out north on another of his peregrinations; from the Needles area of the Colorado River, he turned west with a few Mojave Indians and rode across the desert to Soda Lake, where the seasonal Mojave River disappears in an alkaline flat near modern Baker, California.

Ironically, it was cold and wet that early March in this Land of Little Rain, as Mary Austin would later call it, and the priest actually found pasturage for his mules and horses. On March 11 he entered a *rancheria* of a people he called the Beñemés, probably Panamints of Shoshonean stock. With them he exchanged a few items from his "little store" for tule roots, their staple, which failed to please the palates of his Mojave guides. The gentle padre found much to love and pity in the generous Beñemés: these "poor people manifested much concern at their inability to go hunting in order to supply me, inasmuch as it was raining and very cold, and they were entirely naked." Well, almost naked. In his diary Garcés describes their coats of rabbit hides and their "very curious snares" made of wild hemp used to catch their quarry. To him they were unclean, yet quiet and inoffensive; they heard "with attention that which is told them of God." Garcés shortly left his new friends to proceed west over Cajon Pass to Mission San Gabriel, but not before having to slaughter a horse enroute for him and his proud companions, who did not even waste a drop of its blood.

A second *entrada* into the Great Basin was made later that same year by other Spaniards, this one a deeper penetration and from the southeast, out of sunny Santa Fe in July. Led by Father Francisco Atanasio Domínguez and Father Silvestre Vélez de Escalante, the expedition of ten skirted the San Juan Mountains, crossed the Uncompahgre Plateau, and zigzagged up most of western Colorado before turning sharply west across the Green River, through the Wasatch Mountains, and down into Basin country. In his journal Escalante predictably praised the "plains" around Lake Timpanagos (Utah Lake) as fertile and a likely spot for missions. The Indians with whom Escalante and his party stayed near the lake's shore were not doing badly, the good father reported; besides being "fish-eaters" (as they were described by the Utes to the east), they apparently had a good supply of seeds and hares.

For nearly a month after leaving them, the Spaniards traveled south, obliquely west, then south again before angling east to find a ford of the cavernous Colorado gorge. The few natives encountered in the region south of Sevier Lake, in the cottonwood country that would have a Mormon future, were exceptionally timid. Their fear was not only of the strangely clad white men passing through their lands, but it also extended to Utes and Apaches and Comanches as well. Escalante and his companions learned this when, after much coaxing and many protestations of kindness delivered through a guide they had picked up at Utah Lake, the trembling aborigines approached them. They were not unlike the Panamints, whom Garcés had seen in the spring. They listened with pleasure to sermons on the white man's God (no doubt swayed by beads and ribbons passed out to prospective converts). They dressed in rabbit skins, and they

Spaniards first penetrated the Great Basin in 1776. Artist Keith Eddington recreates Fray Escalante's approach to Utah Lake.

made snares of twisted fibers to trap their game, which weighed out at very little, for Escalante's hungry company tried to trade for any flesh that would stick to the ribs but usually had to settle for grass seeds and dried prickly pear fruit, which at least once badly upset their stomachs.

By January of 1777, the expedition had returned safely to Santa Fe, with more than a thousand new miles of outback known. The second entry into the great bowl-of-little was history. Visitors would not come again for almost half a century, and when they did they would not describe its inhabitants as innocent heathen in need of God's Word but would contemptuously call them "diggers," who were so pathetic they were hardly worth shooting.

Many American Indians have rich, colorful, and even romantic pasts; not so those of the Great Basin. They were almost all physically short and dark, speakers of the Shoshonean tongue, living in a largely treeless land that received less than ten inches of rain a year—a land sucked dry by evaporation and ravaged by extremes of heat and cold. The deeper into the Basin they lived, the more materially and culturally impoverished were its people. For the Gosiutes of western Utah, the Shoshoni of central Nevada, and the Paiutes to the west and south of them, maize would not grow, nor were there any grasslands to speak of. This meant an absence of buffalo, that great lumbering meal-for-many that fed the peoples of the Great Plains. In its place was the only game animal of any size: the pronghorn antelope, nature's cruel substitution, as fleet as a winter's biting wind, and lean and stringy fare for chasers lucky enough to corral one. As for the horse, the Spanish gift which must have occasionally reached them from the main south-to-north traffic on the west side of the Rockies, there was only one thing to do with it: without pasturage and with concave bellies, they killed it and ate it.

By necessity, Basin Indians were mainly gatherers living in democratic poverty. Except during winter, when they retired to more protected spots where caches of food had been buried to tide them over to spring, they were always on the move to make the next season's scanty harvest. In early summer the seeds of herbaceous plants ripened in the lower hills and desert valleys. At the peak of summer other seeds were ready higher up, and late in summer edible roots and berries had to be found. For some, fall meant pinõn nuts, the windfall from *Pinus monophylla*, an erratic but crucial harvest of no longer than two weeks' duration, which had to be stored to see a family through the winter. In the best years, only four months' supply could be laid away, which made early spring the critical time, when those who had not died of starvation fought hunger-induced stupor by nibbling the first green shoots pushing up through the earth to ready themselves for another round of roaming with the seasons.

With the pickings so slim, survival became a family's only business. Occasionally, families would come together in communal purpose. It might be for a rabbit roundup, some men stretching their lengths of ingenious nets into a semicircle hundreds of yards across, while the rest—man, woman, and child—beat the bush to drive the jackrabbits into the entangling barrier. The five-and-a-half pounds of meat on an animal could be jerked, but kept no longer than two weeks before spoiling. For supplemental food in winter there was the cottontail, either taken with bow and arrow or snared. Yet always the hunger for protein was there, to be inadequately satisfied by digging up gophers, catching lizards, clubbing rats, or driving grasshoppers into a trench where they could be roasted and ground into meal.

Culture was low among these wanderers. Life was too stingy for band or tribal organizations and religion was primitive — little more than an awareness that the world was managed by two contending brothers, Wolf, who was good, and Coyote, who was a mischievous cutup. Ceremonies were therefore rare, though an annual mourning rite might bring the nomads together briefly, or in summer there might be a community sing of the songs of birds, perhaps even a dance. War was a luxury that had no place where life was stripped to fundamentals: getting and eating, procreating and dying. In the eighteenth century, Navajos, Apaches, and Utes were known to have entered the Great Basin, there to ride down hapless Paiutes and sell them to the Spanish as slaves. It must have been one of the few instances in human history, in man's alleged upward struggle for liberty, that bondage was preferable to freedom.

Indians living on the outer reaches of the Great Basin generally had it better than those at its core. In the west, the Paiutes of California's Owens Valley found a good variety of food within short range. Grass seeds were cultivated in family plots; there were pine nuts, streams that were clear and sustained fish, and other-than-brackish ponds or lakes where game could water and be taken. Here band organization was possible, and there were week-long festivals, sweathouses, and dormitories where young men had enough to gamble in games. On the eastern fringe, where the Utes ruled the southern Rockies and robbed the Rio Grande cornbasket, possession of the horse made a difference. Below the Gunnison River they were in charge, benefiting from the Hispano culture to the south but providing an armed deterrent to any Spanish notions about straying north. Above the Utes, spread across Colorado's northern Rockies into Wyoming and westward through Idaho's Snake River valley, were the northern

Shoshoni, distributors of the horse to the northern Plains. Like the Utes, they rode down from the Rockies to hunt buffalo and adopted tipis and clothes of hides, martial arts, and the sun dance. Both the Utes and the northern Shoshoni were border peoples, between the grasslands and the grassless lands, and on elevated ground physically and metaphorically.

North of the Great Basin, just north of the tortuous chasm of the Snake, where the earth begins to lift itself off the lava badlands and lodgepole and ponderosa pines grow in upland patches, were the Bannocks of south-central Idaho. They were a Shoshonean people who shared their prehistoric homeland with the northern Shoshoni and who lived in relative peace with the more northern Plateau tribes—Nez Perces, Kutenais, Flatheads—trading with them and sometimes accompanying them east up the valley of the Snake to trade on the Plains. Here the Bannocks hunted buffalo, learned the uses of the tipi, and affected the warbonnet. But they did not stay, nor did the people of the Plateau proper. When they had had what they wanted, they returned to their rivers, meadows, and forests between Montana's Bitterroot Range and the Cascades, on the watch for their common enemy, the Blackfeet. It was the horses that had reached them early in the 1700s that made such long trips possible. Yet the horse was of limited use in the broken, timbered country of the Idaho panhandle, and so it became a status symbol, an item of export trade and the object of thoughtful husbandry.

This was particularly true of the Nez Perces, the most numerous and in many ways the most remarkable people of the Plateau. Perhaps as many as six thousand of them lived where the Salmon joins the Snake, where the future states of Idaho, Oregon, and Washington now meet, and northeast from there along the Clearwater River. Long before the outbreak of the American Revolution, without ever having seen a white man, they had acquired this beast and worked wonders with it. Inferior males were gelded and traded away; the best stallions were kept and selectively bred to likely mares, until the Nez Perces had developed their own spotted breed, the Apaloosa, named after the rolling green hills of the nearby Palouse country.

NOOTKA

MAKAH

QUINAULT

KUTENAI

CHEHALIS

PUYALLUP

KALISPEL

BLACKFOOT

GROS VENTRE

ASSINIBOIN

SPOKANE

COEUR
d' ALENE

CHINOOK

YAKIMA

TILLAMOOK

UMATILLA

FLATHEAD

HIDAT
MAND

NEZ
PERCE

CAYUSE

ARIKAR

SUISLAW

NORTHERN
SHOSHONI

CROW

TETON SIOU

KLAMATH

YUROK

MODOC

BANNOCK

DAKOTA SIOU

WINTUN

NORTHERN
PAIUTE

KIOWA

YUKI

MAIDU

GOSIUTE

CHEYENNE

WASHO

SHOSHONI

MIWOK

MONO

UTE

ARAPAHO

COSTANOAN

YOKUT

PAIUTE

SOUTHERN
PAIUTE

UTE

PANAMINT

WESTERN
SHOSHONI

COMANCHE

CHUMASH

WALAPAI

COSNINA
(HAVASUPAI)

NAVAJO

COMANCHE

SERRANO

JICARILLA
APACHE

GABRIELEÑO

CHEMEHUEVI

HOPI

PUEBLO

LUISEÑO

ZUÑI

MOJAVE

DIEGUEÑO

CARLANA APACHE

YUMA

MARICOPA

FARAONE APACHE

NATAGÉ APACHE

GILA APACHE

COMANC

PAPAGO

PIMA

MESCALERO APACHE

LIPA

OPATA

**INDIAN COUNTRY
1776
(APPROXIMATE LOCATIONS)**

*Culture was richer with the Indians of the Northwest. Along with
wealth, there was more leisure to pursue the arts and play games.*

Some neighbors of the Nez Perces also got into the horse
trading business, especially the Cayuses of northeastern Oregon,
whose name became western jargon for a mount. The Nimapus,
the "Real People," as the Nez Perces referred to themselves,
had other neighbors — the Flatheads, the Palouse, the Walla
Wallas, and the Yakimas — with whom they lived harmoniously,
intermarrying freely and sharing a spring and fall dependence
on the miraculous salmon runs in the Columbia and the rivers
that fed it. The Nimapus and their friends were not so much
tribes as concentrations of independent villages that cooperated
in digging up camas roots in summer to be cooked or stored
away against the future. Game was also to be had; elk and deer
seasonally descended to the meadows, and mountain sheep
trod high on the ranges that crosshatch the central Plateau.

The Nez Perces remained nuclear to those around them.
As for religion, it was, more than anything, a reverence for
nature and an exaggerated fear of the dead, with individual
guiding spirits — their *wy-ya-kin* — to help them along. Personal
ethics were the thing: rectitude, rightness, probity, honor . . .
behaving well.

ISOLATION SPLENDID AND OTHERWISE

Three decades after England lost her Atlantic colonies, a party of white men led by William Clark and Meriwether Lewis would be the first of their race to pass through the Nez Perce country on their way to land's end and to be saved from starvation by the open-handed master horse-breeders. After that the Nez Perces would bestow their generosity on white migrants bound for Astoria on the Oregon coast. Eventually they would be repaid for their kindnesses with the hounding of Chief Joseph and his people by the U.S. Army in one of American history's most disgraceful episodes. But that was a century later. In 1776 the Nez Perces and their Plateau brothers had not even reached their camas root summer. Figuratively, it was more like spring, say May, when the coho made the Columbia, the Snake, and the Clearwater flash silver with their thrashing bodies.

B Y GREAT BASIN STANDARDS, the people of the Plateau were living a life of luxuriant ease with their well-stocked larders. But on a larger scale they were merely transitional, as their geography and cultures were transitional, for to the west of them beyond the Cascades upon which Pacific clouds piled high, lived those on top of the economic totem pole. To the Chinooks living near the Columbia River's mouth, any visiting Nez Perce who came trading hides for dentalia (the conical shells from Vancouver Island that served as the West's answer to Eastern wampum) was no doubt considered a provincial outlander. The northern Pacific slope was the center of the world.

If one word could describe life on the Northwest coast, it would be surplus. From the southern coast of Alaska to the northern coast of California dwelt Indians of several language families (Salishan, Penutian, Algonkin), tied by common threads of culture and a reliance on the bounty of the sea or inland waterways. They were all preoccupied with wealth, with getting and spending, but their mores were not exactly uniform, nor were their attitudes toward property once they had it. The richest lived north of Puget Sound—the Nootkas of Vancouver Island, the Kwakiutls, Bella Coolas, Tsimshians, Haidas, and Tlingits—on the soggy shelf that curled out toward the bleakness of Asia. This was the

land of many salmon runs. It was also the land of cedar, a wood malleable to rude splitting and chiseling tools and from which great oceangoing canoes could be fashioned; a wood that could be hewn into long plank lodges, in which people slept according to rank, and whose inner bark provided soft material from which clothes were made; a wood from which totem poles — the forceful literature of a proud man and his clan — might be carved and raised. This was the land of the potlatch, a lavish party marking some major or minor event that might take years in preparation, at which the host would give away blankets and canoes and coppers (sheets of hammered copper that he valued more than the white man did his gold) to show his superiority to his wealthy guests, who were then expected to outdo him if they could. Of these most conspicuous of consumers, the Kwakiutls went even further. They perverted the potlatch into an orgy of outright destruction, sacrificing those blankets, boats, and coppers, even household slaves, in a pompous show of expendable wealth.

A Spanish drawing of the late eighteenth century shows suitors wrestling for the hand of a Vancouver Island princess.

To the south, on California's northern coast, nature was not quite so generous. Here property was hoarded and shown off rather than given away or destroyed. Those in between, in western Oregon and Washington, were middlemen, in economic advantage and behavior as well as in fact. They were at the trading center, the yawning mouth of the Columbia, where the Chinook language peppered with Nootkanisms later became the patois of commerce. Yet in fundamental attitudes the Tlingits of the north and the Yuroks far to the south and those in the middle were one. Society had its rich and its poor, its haves and its have-nots. There were slaves (usually taken from nearby villages in the intermittent raids that passed for war), as a rule well-treated but the only people denied the opportunity to amass wealth and thereby better themselves. North to south there was a premium on ambition, on amounting to something: becoming wealthy enough to be visited in dreams by animal spirits; to join secret societies, which worshiped the bear (a cult that harked back to the dawn of man), or to practice ritual cannibalism; to become worthy, in short, through the accumulation of earthly goods, to know terror of supernatural origin. If the caricature of the modern upward-striving middle-class American is apt, then the Indians of the Northwest coast were, indeed, the first Americans.

No one knows for sure where the Northwest peoples came from, but the evidence suggests it was from inland—prehistoric migrants who happed on a coast to their liking. No one doubts why they would have liked it. The Japanese Current, which flowed down from the Aleutians, had a moderating effect on the climates of land it brushed. It brought fecundity to coastal waters in the dark, high latitudes, and damp, dripping forests that climaxed in Sitka spruce to the north and in redwood to the south. The gifts

A 1776 portrait of Captain James Cook. Two years later the famed mariner put into Nootka Sound on his final voyage.

of the sea were more than enough: whales, seals, otters, halibut of prodigious size, cod, crabs, bivalves, herring, and oily smelt that filled the seas. In the inland streams of Washington and Oregon, there were trout and salmon and hybrid trout-salmon. Game might not be anywhere near as plentiful as it was on the Plains, but there was compensation in roots and berries that ripened in biblical prolificacy—huckleberry, blueberry, cranberry, and the mineral-rich saskatoon berry—all in all, a well-balanced diet. Despite the dampness, health seems not to have suffered. Life, for all its strange turnings, was no more fleeting than elsewhere.

The same current that for eons softened and moistened the Northwest coast became a natural sea-lane for sailing ships, perhaps for primitive junks in the dim past as well. (Among the Haidas of Alaska's coastal islands, wounds were expertly sutured and certain herbal remedies were known, suggesting previous contact with the Chinese.) Spanish Manila galleons in the late sixteenth and throughout the seventeenth centuries regularly arced through the north Pacific on their way to Mexico, and though landfalls on the Northwest coast were not planned, there is evidence that one or more met their ends on that obscure shore. In the nineteenth century Indians were to bring white settlers mysterious blocks of beeswax. One was graven with the Latin initials IHS, and another fragment with the close-cropped numerals 67 (for 1679?), which has recently been carbon-14-dated to approximately when the ill-fated *San Francisco Xavier,* Acapulco-bound, left Manila for a voyage it would never complete.

Indian lore is rife with other tantalizing possibilities of early meetings: of visitors who landed on their shores and buried chests along with dead men who would tell no tales; of other strangers cast up on their sands, some of them killed on the spot, some slain later when they took to quarreling over women, some spared who rose to prominence in the tribes that adopted them; stories of red-haired, freckled Indians, one of them seen by Lewis and Clark. But the shadowy coast that often had fir and pine and hemlock growing right down to the high-tide line remained a bizarre twilight world of the Indians' own making.

In January of 1774, a month after white Bostonians dressed up like red men and threw tea into Atlantic waters, the Spanish

When Resolution *and* Discovery *dropped anchor off Nootka, Cook did a brisk trade with the metal-mad Indians.*

Cook returned to the Hawaiian Islands to winter in 1779, a year after he had discovered them. But cordiality turned to conflict, and on February 14 "the first mariner of the world" was stabbed to death in the surf.

frigate *Santiago* sailed quietly out of Mexico toward the Pacific's northern waters in reconnaissance for the king of Spain. Skipper Juan José Pérez Hernandez anchored off Vancouver Island's Nootka Sound in August and was welcomed by canoe-borne Indians eager for trade. A follow-up Spanish exploration of the Northwest coast a year later brought a decidedly more mixed reception. When a party was sent ashore on the Olympic Peninsula, it was promptly massacred, and its small boat smashed for the metal fittings.

In 1778, Capt. James Cook approached Nootka from the sea on his third and final voyage of discovery. He received the same friendly greeting Pérez had from the trade-anxious canoemen. Cook put into the sound and stayed a while, making repairs on his

two vessels, the *Resolution* and the *Discovery,* and taking on provisions. It gave him a month to observe the natives of the island: they showed no fear of his ships and willingly came aboard; they were friendly enough with his crew, but they quarreled with each other for the right to trade with the Englishmen; as for the wares they wanted, cloth and many of the usual baubles did not interest them, but metal items — iron, copper, brass — which they already had in some quantity, were so prized that Cook had a devil of a time controlling their petty theft. Significantly, when Cook prepared to leave, the Indians let him know they expected to be paid for the wood, water, and grass he had taken from their lands. Nowhere else in red man's America would that have occurred.

In April Cook sailed away from Nootka for the Sandwich Islands and his own tragic end. Aboard were sea-otter skins obtained in barter. After he was killed in a skirmish with Hawaiians, his crew would take those pelts to the Orient and, to their surprise, touch off one of history's great seller's markets. In the 1780s and 1790s the Northwest coast became a mecca for enterprising mariners, who arrived for furs to take on to China. One of geography's last and best-kept secrets was a secret no longer.

The splendid isolation of the Northwest was ended — at least the isolation was. For years after the first contacts, the splendor, economic and cultural, actually waxed with the receipt of metal tools and firearms. The caste-conscious tribes of the coast now had even more wealth to hoard and squander, more cause to display their worth in what they owned. It would not be until much later, well into the nineteenth century, that liquor, prostitution, and disease, with their usual disastrous results, caught up with the big spenders.

I N 1763 THE OTTAWA CHIEF PONTIAC, having seen his old friends the French deposed and the red men of the Ohio Valley now being fleeced by an influx of opportunistic Anglo-Saxons, forged an alliance that included Delawares and Shawnees and Miamis and others. He tried to enlist more to war as one against the common peril, even sending emissaries among the Osage west of the Mississippi. For a while Pontiac's coalition gave the British a case of the frontier miseries, until the British broke the alliance with bribes and diplomatic pledges that would not be kept. Pontiac was not able to convince the more western tribes, the Crees, the Chippewas, and the Sioux, that the white man had to go and that the old ways should be restored. The westerners wanted traders and the things only the white man had. In the end the Ottawa chief retired to the Illinois country, a celebrated failure. A dark cloud had passed over the face of the sun, slightly before noon, on a western summer's day.

The Pontiac rebellion was the most concerted show of resistance the white man would meet in North America, but it failed, as it had to fail. In truth, the Indian's cultural inheritance was simply weaker than the white man's; the gadgets and corruptions of Europe proved irresistible and the new life irreversible. The very independence of spirit that often led the red man to war against his neighbors was the same trait that shut his ears to the warnings of a few seers that only in unity was there hope. In the West, as in the East, his summer could not last.

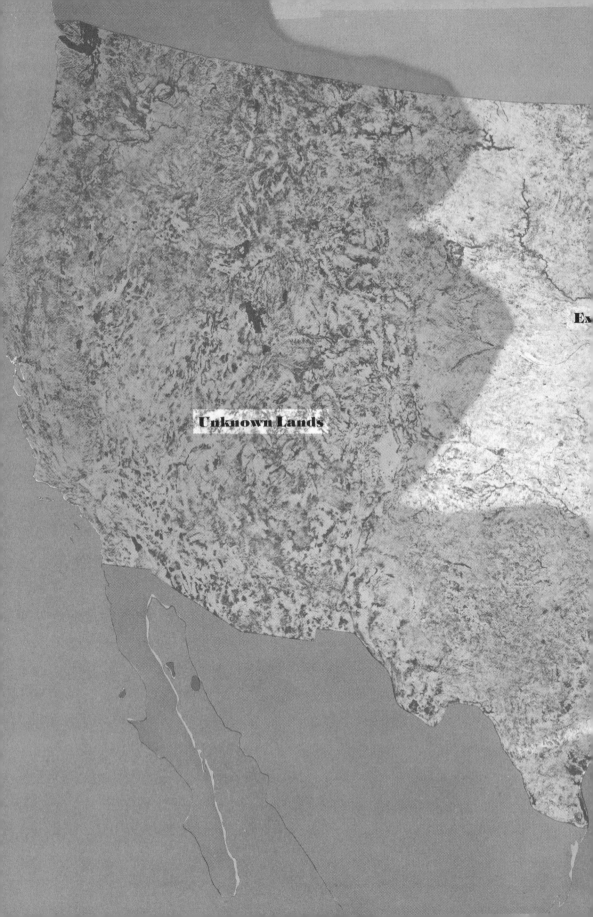

Unknown Lands

Ex

Known Lands
(Settled)

Lands

e French Presence – 1776

PART III
THE FAILURE OF FRANCE

June 10, 1776. Barely able to contain his excitement, the forty-four-year-old toast of Paris halted his carriage at 26 rue de Condé, got out, and hurriedly started toting mysterious canvas bags into his elegant reception room. When it was done, Pierre Augustin Caron de Beaumarchais—Protestant watchmaker's son, literary lion, inventor, sometime secret agent, and scarred veteran of many court intrigues and lawsuits—summoned his household. His mistress, two sisters, two nephews, a niece, and sundry servants looked on in astonishment as the *maître de maison*, with a flash of his huge diamond ring (a gift from the Austrian queen, Maria Theresa, mother of Marie Antoinette), loosened the bags and noisily emptied their contents onto the floor. Out spilled coins, gold coins, piles of them—one million *livres'* worth, until that very day stored in the French treasury.

How had Beaumarchais come by them? His request for the monies, spelled out in a secret plan submitted to the Crown on May 24, had been enthusiastically approved by the foreign minister, the Comte de Vergennes, and somewhat reluctantly by King Louis XVI. It was a good plan, one that could conceivably change history.

In 1775, Beaumarchais's *The Barber of Seville* had been a smash comedy hit in Paris; in 1777 he would write the equally popular *Marriage of Figaro*. But in 1776 he was deeply involved in a nonliterary effort that absorbed his boundless energies: that of supplying the American revolutionaries with war matériel shipped out of France's Atlantic ports. True, the plan he had submitted called for an outright gift of one million *livres* to back the colonists' flimsy paper money and give them hard currency to purchase what they had to have. But he was pleased enough with the compromise. The money was to be considered a loan to buy surplus guns and muskets from the French arsenal, as well as new gunpowder, shoes, clothing, and blankets; it would have to be repaid in shipments of tobacco and rice. Yet the details of the plan were his: the dummy corporation funded by a cool million from the coffers of France, a matching amount from ally Spain, and a third million easily raised from private

166

sources. *Roderique Hortalez et Cie* would be the name of the firm, and he himself would manage it, clandestinely channeling provisions to the needy American rebels. The motives of the foreign minister and the king may have been reducible to unadorned hatred of England. As for himself, Beaumarchais believed in "those brave people who defend their liberty" and, well, he just liked to be in the thick of things.

In 1776 there were Frenchmen in the West, but no France. The nation that La Salle had put in the Mississippi Valley with a dream of a new empire, the nation that knew more about the North American wilderness than any other, was gone—*sans* dream, *sans* empire.

The immediate cause was the Seven Years' War (known in North America as the French and Indian War), one of the most disastrous conflicts ever for France. It started as just one more of the imperial wars that had, for more than a century, involved France, England, Spain, and other European nations in shifting alignments. The clashes that had come before—the War of the League of Augsburg, the War of the Spanish Succession, and the War of the Austrian Succession—were each brought to a close when the parties were sufficiently exhausted and courting bankruptcy, at which time a peace parley would be held where one nation might give up a sugar island here, another might gain fishing rights there, or yet another obtain trading concessions at some distant post in a rival's far-flung empire.

Not so the Seven Years' War. This time France ran smack into an English haymaker thrown by First Minister William Pitt the Elder, whose aim was to reduce France permanently to a second-rate power, imperially and commercially, which were to his thinking but two sides of the same coin. Pitt got his chance when he came to power in a war that had seen a complete reshuffling of all traditional alliances on the Continent. Chiefly through Austrian statecraft, France found herself allied with Sweden, Russia, and old-enemy Austria against old-friend Prussia, while England was uneasily in bed with old-foe Prussia. At first glance the match-ups seem grossly uneven. But England's new ally was Prussia rising, the Prussia of Frederick the Great, the brilliant militarist and freethinker who was quite able to hold his own against the numerically superior forces aligned against him.

England maintained only a token force in Germany, sending Frederick money while allowing her own navy and armies to spread out in the colonial world in a grand strategy that included, as Pitt put it, "conquering America in Germany." The French coast was blockaded, the French fleet was trounced decisively, and one by one the French overseas possessions were peeled away. Clive took most of India. Canada and Montcalm fell on the Plains of Abraham. The West Indies sugar islands of Guadeloupe and Martinique surrendered. The island of Gorée that secured the Senegal slave trade was temporarily seized. And all the while France floundered on the Continent in a war against Prussia that made no sense.

When the Duc de Choiseul became France's foreign minister in December of 1758, he inherited the unhappy duty of presiding over the impending dissolution of the French empire. Desperately he sought help. But that could come from only one quarter: neutral Spain. With the ascension of Carlos III to the Spanish throne in 1759, Choiseul applied himself to that task. Charles was a Bourbon. So was Louis XV. Logic as well as blood dictated that they unite against rampaging England if they were to save their colonies and the commerce that sustained them both as nations of the first rank. So, in August of 1761, France and Spain signed another Family Compact, and Carlos started to mobilize for war with England.

Choiseul must have winced at each news report that followed the opening of those hostilities in January of 1762. The ill-prepared Spaniards took a shellacking from the juggernaut that Pitt had put together. The English stopped a Spanish attempt to seize Portugal, conquered Cuba, and later took Manila by sea. For Choiseul personally and for France, it had become a double disaster, and the shrewd duke went to the peace table with a hand hardly worth playing. He now had an added liability in Carlos III, who was smarting under the British humiliations and wanted to continue a war that could not be won. Only one favorable change occurred, and Choiseul resolved to make the most of it. William Pitt, the hard-nosed genius of English imperialism, had fallen from power in England, replaced by a bunch of political mediocrities who seemed, strangely, to want peace as much as did prostrate France — providing Spain would be a party to the settlement.

The Peace of Paris was signed on February 10, 1763, in Choiseul's city on the best terms he could get under the circumstances. Today they appear harsher than they did to the duke. France ceded Canada, all lands east of the Mississippi (save New Orleans), and navigation rights on the river proper to England. France also gave her Senegal and French claims in India, save for five small trading stations. But — coup of coups! — Choiseul managed to restore to France the sugar islands of Martinique and Guadeloupe. As for Spain, in order to get Cuba back, she had to give up the Floridas to the English. When Carlos III balked, Choiseul secretly agreed to give him Louisiana west of the Mississippi and the city of New Orleans. Carlos hardly needed to be told that, with the English now in possession of the river's east bank, he could use a larger buffer to guard those precious mines of Mexico.

Looking back, it is hard to appreciate Choiseul's amusement at the "good joke" he had played on the English in concluding the Treaty of Paris. The retention of the two tiny but commercially profitable sugar islands no doubt seemed a master stroke at the time, while the loss of Canada — those "few acres of snow" that Voltaire wished sunk "at the

bottom of the Arctic Sea together with the reverend Jesuit fathers"—
also fit French policy in 1763. Let England administer it and spread herself thin. Choiseul reflected the widespread cynicism in France when he
wrote Voltaire, "Don't count on me for furs this winter. You are hereby
notified to address yourself to England." The eighty thousand former
French subjects abandoned in Canada could scarcely have been amused.

The loss of Louisiana was not such a laughing matter, even in France.
Because its southernmost part was tropical and therefore fit the mercantile theory that colonies should produce what Europe lacked, there were
misgivings. Even Voltaire, without of course ever having seen Louisiana,
put in a few good words for the enormous land that still lacked a definite
western or northern boundary. Choiseul kept his mouth shut on the subject, but there is no question he considered the Seven Years' War just a
prelude to another that would have to be fought with England for imperial
dominance. Immediately he secretly set to rebuilding the French war machine, particularly its navy. The Family Compact was still in force, and
he held a marker from Carlos III. Louisiana might be redeemable one day.
Those living at the gates of the American West were still overwhelmingly
French—perhaps La Salle's dream had not died with the stroke of a pen.

Chapter 9

The River People

FOUR CANADIAN BROTHERS named LeMoyne served France with distinction in the lower Mississippi Valley. Antoine LeMoyne de Chateaugué put in many years in Louisiana; Joseph LeMoyne de Serigny only two. Better remembered, however, were Pierre LeMoyne, Sieur d'Iberville, and Jean-Baptiste LeMoyne, Sieur de Bienville. It was Iberville who commanded the French ship that entered the birdfoot muck of the Mississippi River in March of 1699, sailing perilously through the blue-black mounds of hardened ooze that had hidden the river's mouth from Spanish mariners. And it was Bienville who a year later, twenty-three leagues upriver beneath towering trees that one awed Frenchman later speculated were as old as the earth, turned back an English sea captain who had come to take possession of the Mississippi. France had won the race for the great river that commanded the heart of the continent and the eastern entrances to the West.

Louisiana in the south, in the subdelta, could not have lived up to La Salle's advertisement of a land that was both beautiful and fertile, "so full of meadows, brooks and rivers; so abounding in fish, game and venison, that one can find there in plenty . . . that which is needful for the support of flourishing colonies." But he had come downriver from the north and had seen the diversity in the vast territory to which he had given the name Louisiana. Now it was up to Iberville and Bienville to give it an existence, and starting as they did in the deltalands, that was to prove anything but easy.

An eighteenth-century Parisian phrase-maker said that what-

Jean-Baptiste LeMoyne, Sieur de Bienville, governed Louisiana.

Brother Paul, Sieur d'Iberville, had seized the heartland in 1699.

ever was found by Europeans, the French would have "constructed a fort there; the Spaniards would have built a church; the English a tavern." The French were first and they built forts, though the first two of any significance were not on the Mississippi proper but to the east of it: Fort Maurepas at Biloxi in 1699 and Fort Saint Louis at Mobile Bay in 1702. No doubt the locations made good sense. The swampy labyrinth through which half a continent emptied its burden of waters was not the best place to settle, let alone navigate, and coastal fortifications facing the Gulf of Mexico were easier to man and to supply, and they guarded the three entrances to the river better than any interior fastness. The main thing was that, from both the Canadian north and the delta south, wedges had been driven between rivals Spain and England in North America. By carefully cultivating the friendship of the river valley tribes, England could be contained in the east and the Spanish mines to the west made vulnerable to bold Frenchmen, of whom there was never a lack.

The strategy seemed sound enough, but the feeble colony established at Biloxi boded ill for the future of Louisiana. The War of the Spanish Succession distracted what initial interest France might have had in settling the heartland in strength. A few hundred soldiers and assorted vagrants vegetated at the Gulf Coast posts under the frustrated governor Bienville, far from the furs they were supposed to be gathering for the Crown, desultorily turning a sandy soil that yielded little.

Louis XIV was not pleased with the progress of the colony, and his minister of marine, the Comte de Pontchartrain, was suspicious of the LeMoyne brothers' ambitions. So, in 1712, the Crown turned over Louisiana to the Paris financier Antoine Crozat as his private monopoly for fifteen years. He was required to bring in colonists and permitted to import African slaves at his own expense to work the land for his own profit. Until the colony got on its feet, the king would pay for troops to defend it and for the new governor, Antoine de la Mothe Cadillac, sent to Louisiana from the north, where he had founded Detroit.

Cadillac was far from smitten with his duty in Biloxi. "This country is not worth a straw," he bluntly informed his superiors. "The inhabitants are eager to be taken out of it. The soldiers are always grumbling, and with reason." The unhappy official governed with a harsh and heavy hand, which was probably necessary, given the quality of colonists whom M. Crozat chose to send — beggars, vagabonds, whores, and scamps in the main, folks who could be had at minimal expense and were expected to toil gladly for Crozat and spend the little they earned in the company store.

In 1717, Crozat called it quits and, with his purse considerably lightened, handed over his patent and some seven hundred unhappy colonists to a vacant throne. Louis XIV had died in 1715, and the Duc d'Orléans, serving as regent for the young Louis XV, now called on the financial wizard John Law for a solution. The Scotsman had it. His public stock venture, the Company of the West (reorganized two years later as the Company of the Indies), would beef up the colony's numbers and move it off the unhealthful and unproductive Gulf strand into the fertile interior. There Law envisioned a great empire resting on the harvests of

Paris hucksters painted a dazzling picture of the "Port of Mississippi" in 1717. Investors who bit were soon to lose their shirts.

tropical plantations and on the ores of rich mines that, all Spain's experience foretold, had to be there. A successful gambler who was wanted for murder in England, Law convinced the regent that a strong injection of paper money would promote a lively trade between home and the colony, and the duke let his wonder-worker organize the *Banque Générale de France* to issue it.

Law's strong suit was promotion. In Parisian store-fronts there quickly appeared posters showing an Indian trading a gold ingot for a Frenchman's knife, and others depicting bejeweled ladies and gentlemen riding in carriages through a lush land of Canaan abundance, where slaves answered the gentry's beck and call. Prices in the stock soared to dizzy heights, and with the front money Law started peopling his empire. Titles of nobility were peddled along with land grants to interested buyers, a few of whom actually sailed for Louisiana and began working the land. Germans were recruited to the number of two thousand. Many of those who survived starvation when they debarked in impover-

Part Barnum, part Baruch, the Scotsman John Law peopled Louisiana with slaves from Africa, refugees from Germany, and the cream of French gutters.

ished Biloxi settled on the west side of the Mississippi, on the Côte des Allemands above the brand-new settlement of New Orleans; there with their customary diligence they transformed the dark delta soil into blooming gardens. Also brought in were black slaves; the first consignment, arriving in 1719, numbered four hundred fifty, and in the following two years, almost four times that number. For other warm bodies, Law resorted to what was fancifully entertained as the successful English colonial formula: cleansing the realm of undesirables to secure overseas lands. Once again the flotsam of the French urban gutters and prisons was collected and transported to the humbling new world of primeval forests and swamps and prairies and sky.

New Orleans was founded in 1718 under Bienville, reappointed to the post of governor for want of an experienced hand. That very year French newspapers complimented the city for having "eight hundred fine houses." But when the French Jesuit Pierre François de Charlevoix visited New Orleans in 1722, he described it with Gallic irony as being "reduced at present to a hundred barracks, placed in no very great order; to a great-store house, built of wood; [and] to two or three houses, which would be no ornament to a village of France." Elsewhere along the lower river, oaks were felled and canes burned to clear fields for planting. Law established a major post on the Arkansas, just north and west of that river's confluence with the Mississippi. And then, in 1720, the speculative bubble burst. The French bourgeoisie lost its chemise and Louisiana was branded a canard, stuck with a reputation it would never completely live down.

Law gave the colony a half-life that France would never allow to be a full life. Still it grew, two forts forward and one fort back, up and down the immense river that took about three months to ascend by pirogue and a mere ten or twelve days to come down in spring flood. In time the plantations did begin to produce, but the value of their exports failed to match French expenditures, and the colony struggled on with yearly deficits that exceeded 800,000 *livres* by 1750, subsidized for geo-political reasons.

It need not have been that way. The land was as fertile as advertised, yielding precisely those crops the mother country lacked. Tobacco — the much-sought commodity that France had been importing from the English colonies to the great distress of its mercantile theorists — was found to grow there and be of decent quality. Indigo, native and imported varieties, did even better. In lower Louisiana, near the river's mouth, trees were cut for ship timbers and bled of pitch for caulking. Mulberry trees supported a fledgling silk culture, and rice did well. Sugarcane cuttings were later brought from Santo Domingo and planted, while cotton grew in the wild. Its cultivation was not popular with the settlers, however, because the seeds stuck to everything, making the picking not worth the trouble. For many Louisianans the drudgery of plantation farming itself was too much trouble, fit only for the man who could afford slaves that frequently died in the malarial heat. Soldiers garrisoned in the dreary forts strung up the river were fighters, not farmers. The derelicts brought over in the cleansing of French towns found idleness was something you could take with you.

Some men of more enterprise discovered it preferable and profitable to get furs, hides, and buffalo wool from the Indians in trade, which too often meant chiseling and cheating the red man. One story tells of a French sharpie who visited the Missouri tribe early in the century to trade gunpowder for furs. The chief said no, they already had enough for their needs. But did they have enough to plant for next year's crop? the nimble-witted trader wanted to know. He explained to the credulous Missouri that the powder could be sown and harvested just like millet. He got his furs. Later the same trader sent his partner among the Missouris with another load of merchandise. The Indians, who had watched carefully over their gunpowder fields until they realized they had been taken, recognized the man as an associate of the dishonest trader. Without a word of complaint they invited the partner to unload his packages in the public cabin. No sooner was it done than some of the powder farmers grabbed the wares and ran. Furious, the trader went to the chief and bitterly complained. Yes, the chief agreed, a great injustice had been done. And it would be righted — just as soon as the tribe was done with harvesting its gunpowder crop.

For all its early promise, Louisiana under France never lived up to expectations, partly because they were false expectations. Besides Crozat and Law, there were many other Frenchmen who were convinced that gold and silver could be found in the colony west of the river. That was, after all, the direction in which the Spaniards, the erroneous belief persisted, were doing handsomely with their mines in Santa Fe. While he was governor, even Cadillac wasted much time and energy prospecting in the incalculably large and trackless land. Gold, copper, iron, manganese, lead, zinc, antimony, and other minerals were later mined within what was then called Louisiana, but all that the French found in any amounts were salt and lead. Salt springs and flats near the Saline Creek of Missouri were worked from as early as 1700, as were surface deposits of lead found in a three-thousand-square-mile tract from the headwaters of the San Francois River to the Meramec River — again, west of the Mississippi. Lead from this district, variously labeled "Regio Metallorum," "Endroit rempli de Mines," and "Country Full of Mines" on eighteenth-century maps, was melted and molded into horse-collar bars to satisfy local needs, with some left over for export to New Orleans and occasionally to France.

The lead weighed more than gold but lacked its luster. Given a coat of paint, the bars might have passed for one of Mr. Law's ingots shown in the infamous store-front posters, but after thirty years of promises, vain scratchings, and samples sent back home that failed assayers' tests, cynical Parisians refused to be gulled. The abuse heaped upon promoters of Louisiana's mineral wealth led Antoine Simon Le Page du Pratz, for sixteen years a planter in Louisiana and a man who felt deeply that the colony's true riches were agricultural, to answer the critics after his return to France. There were, indeed, precious metals there, he wrote. He had even seen gold dust with his own eyes in tributaries of the Arkansas River. Then why had no Frenchmen brought back gold? A man traveling in a country of "immense woods and deserts" peopled by savages had enough to do getting back unscathed without gathering riches, he explained. Furthermore, it was commonly known that mining ventures required enormous capitalization before any profits could be realized—capital that the colonists did not have and that the tightfisted stay-at-homes were too timid to advance. Finally, du Pratz admitted, the French colonists simply did not know very much about mining, and the "Spaniards, their neighbors, are too discreet to teach them."

Other ills beset the faltering colony. Contrary to the testimonials of returning Frenchmen on the "healthfulness" of Louisiana's climate, it was anything but that, particularly in the southern lowlands, the mosquito lands where, in addition to being nuisances, *Aëdes aegypti* brought the lethal yellow fever and *Anopheles* the even more prevalent malaria. Epidemics of mumps and smallpox regularly took their toll of white men and red men in a colony short of doctors. Upriver, the grippe and pleurisies were chronic, and venereal disease was freely distributed by men of casual morals. Terse notarial records tell the true story of life in eighteenth-century Louisiana: early deaths, estates in legal tangles, the names of three-time widows and widowers.

Despite the high mortality rate, Louisianans did grow slowly in numbers. In 1731, when the colony once again became an exclusively royal responsibility, there were about 5,200 non-Indian residents. At mid-century there were some 8,000, and when the Spanish took over in the 1760s, there were as many as 12,000. Yet, the figures are misleading. Half of those "Frenchmen" were black slaves brought from Guinea and Senegal by the flesh-dealers of Nantes to work the soil for their often cruel French masters. Inevitably, there were runaways, and time spent chasing down runaways; and on more than one occasion those runaways congregated in the wilds and threatened the colony with insurrection. The existence of a nascent fifth column could only have worried the French, especially in view of the widespread discontent within their guardian garrison, which in 1745 flared up in what was called the Bad Bread Mutiny.

There were other complications. It was the French custom to divide authority in its colonies between a governor and an intendant (called a *commissaire ordonnateur* in Louisiana). Both were the king's men, on a par with each other in power but with different administrative responsibilities. The royal intent was to check each man's meaner ambitions with this watchdog arrangement, but in practice the two frequently quarreled and, with their respective favorites lining up behind them, brought more division to the colony. On one occasion in the late 1750s, it was necessary to recall both governor and intendant to Paris for a cooling-off stint in the Bastille.

As in most colonial systems, high administrative offices most often went to homebred gentlemen with connections at court. With the exception of Bienville and Pierre François de Rigaud de Cavagnol, Marquis de Vaudreuil, Louisiana's governors came from across the sea. Even in lesser posts the talented Creole who meant to stay in the land of his birth was often passed over in favor of short-timers, who were understandably less interested in Louisiana's welfare than in their own. No wonder the Creole was not averse to gouging the Crown or to padding his own expense account for services rendered; a Louisianan's loyalty to mother France was apt to be less than absolute. Paramount among his complaints was the currency he had or, more accurately, the currency he lacked. Fearing shipwreck and English interception, France withheld shipments of hard money to New France. In-

**FRANCE
IN THE HEARTLAND
1763**

Lake of the Woods

• GRAND PORTAGE

• LA POINTE

SAULT STE. MARIE
• MICHILIMACKINAC

☐ FORT ST. ANTOINE
☐ FORT BEAUHARNOIS   ☐ FORT LA BAYE

PRAIRIE
DU CHIEN

MISSISSIPPI RIVER

DETROIT •

Des Moines River

Missouri River

Illinois River

Kaskaskia River

Wabash River

• VINCENNES

Ohio River

CAHOKIA •
ST. PHILIPPE •   • PRAIRIE DU ROCHER
FORT DE CHARTRES ☐ • KASKASKIA

STE. GENEVIÈVE •

☐ FORT MASSAC

River

Cumberland

Arkansas River

FORT ASSUMPTION ☐
CHICKASAW
BLUFFS

Tennessee River

ARKANSAS POST •

Yazoo River

Tom Bigbee River

Alabama River

FORT ST. PIERRE ☐

☐ FORT TOULOUSE

FORT TOMBECHE ☐

Red River

NATCHITOCHES •

• NATCHEZ
☐ FORT ROSALIE

MOBILE
•

OPELOUSAS •   POINTE COUPÉE •
BATON ROUGE •   • BILOXI   ☐ FORT MAUREPAS
• MANCHAC   • NEW ORLEANS

ATTACAPAS POST •
CÔTE DES
ALLEMANDS   • BALIZE

stead, the settlers had to make do with bills of exchange and "card money," which, like most such paper tender, was greatly discounted. So desperate were the colonists for specie in the 1740s that Spanish silver *pistoles* became the coin of this neglected corner of the realm.

With so much wrong in Louisiana, there had to be something right. The colony did, if not thrive, at least survive. Why? For one thing, neither England nor Spain was in much of a position or of a mind to seriously contest the French presence between them. This was partly due to the French Indian policy. By comparison with the Spaniard, who attempted to convert the red man to his religion and to integrate him into his society (usually as a bottom-rung menial), and the Anglo, who as a rule viewed the New World aborigine as an obstacle to his land lust and bereft of a soul worth saving, the Frenchman's attitude was enlightened, at times almost humanitarian. He approached the Indian as a near-equal, a trading partner, the bringer of furs, a worthy ally against his imperial rivals. Be he illiterate *voyageur* paddling up an unknown river toward the backside of nowhere or witty master of the *bon mot* in Parisian intellectual circles, he had a romantic admiration for this personification of *l'homme naturel* who lived life free of the day-to-day petty deceptions and corruptions so familiar to a Frenchman.

From the very first, Iberville's scheme for mastery of the river necessitated winning its Indians over to the side of the French. When he built Fort Saint Louis at Mobile, he called a great council of tribes to cement the Indian nations in alliance against the English, and with a few notable exceptions he succeeded. The scheme also called for the construction of forts (the nation that gave Vauban to military science knew precisely how to build forts and where to place them), the introduction of missionaries, and the annual distribution of presents among the friendly tribes.

No design for human relations, however noble or fundamentally sound, is ever applied according to the blueprint; greed and error will attend. A certain M. de Chepart, commandant of Fort Rosalie near the Natchez post on the east side of the Mississippi, decided he wanted the site of the Natchez Indian village burial ground for his own plantation and promised to put chains on any

THE RIVER PEOPLE

Indian who opposed him. Thus was the seed planted for a secret rebellion that broke out on November 28, 1729, and in one bloody day several hundred French subjects lost their lives. For almost two years the whole future of the colony teetered over a red abyss. Then, after many battles and brutalities, the French with Indian auxiliaries finally subdued the Natchez. Those not slain were sold into slavery or, in the case of a few, fled to join the Chickasaws. The extermination of the Natchez, an influential and gifted people, left a crucial vacuum in Lower Louisiana that was never truly filled again. The war had another loser: under its strain the Company of the Indies collapsed, and the colony again returned to royal control.

The alienation of the potent Chickasaws was not so much a case

Faith and flag came to the Mississippi with Father Marquette,
though neither was to prosper in the immense river valley.

of French blundering as of the English getting to them first, and the futility of trying to please all the people all the time. At Iberville's Mobile confab they were in attendance, along with the Choctaws, their hereditary enemies. Abetted by English bribes from the Carolinas (English goods were both better and cheaper than French goods), the Chickasaws became a permanent thorn in the French side. It was as though history were repeating itself with another version of the Iroquois story that had stunted the growth of Canada. As the French readily conceded, the Chickasaws were "a well-built people of unequalled bravery" who had good reason to side with the "blond men," as the Indians differentiated the English from the French. In 1739, after two expensive and disastrous campaigns against the Chickasaws, even Governor Bienville was discouraged, and submitted his resignation, though his replacement would not arrive until four years later.

There were other, lesser setbacks to French diplomacy in the lower Mississippi Valley—local instances of dishonest trading, Frenchmen seducing and abducting Indian girls, the debilitating traffic in brandy that robbed the red man of the manly virtues the Frenchmen respected. Yet, overall, the first French policy survived much: the debaucheries, the steadily deteriorating "mutual trust," and the annual presents, which inflation gradually made a Frenchman's burden and which were interpreted by some tribes not as gifts but as tribute.

THE FRENCH HAD FOUND THE MISSISSIPPI, not from the sandbanks and cyprus groves and canebrakes of the south, but from the north, out of Canada, old New France. After Marquette and La Salle, a sprinkling of hardy northerners began arriving in the river valley, long before there was a New Orleans or an Arkansas post. They had little in common with the effluvia pumped into the continent from the south. To have got this far south and west from the stony realities of the Laurentian Shield, to have reached by paddle and portage the first waterway of the West, they were equal to the rigors of frontier life. They spoke French because their ancestors were French, but their ties to the France of the Bourbons had worn exceedingly thin.

The gradual exhaustion of furs in eastern Canada brought the

A French Canadian of the Iberville party (from La Potherie's Histoire of 1722). It was a case of the strong being too few.

STANFORD UNIVERSITY LIBRARIES

Canadians westward — that, along with the impulse to adventure and the chimera of the western sea. Though they were to be found up and down the length of the Mississippi, they tended to collect in what the French called the Illinois Country, the easterly-tilted V between the Mississippi and Ohio rivers, where the deciduous woodlands backed off from the rich chernozem prairie. The nearness to the more and better pelts of the north was only one reason why the Canadians were drawn there. The goodness of the earth was another. A third was that the Illinois Country lay about halfway between the capitals of Louisiana and Canada — pretty much a no-man's-land until 1718, when the midlands were given to Law's Company of the Indies, to the chagrin of Quebec. The upriver residents did not mind whose jurisdiction they were under so long as the laws were not enforced.

The French fur trade was never free but always subject to some regulatory system that granted monopolies and licenses to the few and excluded the many enterprising free-lancers. Enforcing the *ordonnances* was something else. Officials comfortably settled in Montreal or Quebec seldom had a taste for tracking down errant *coureurs de bois* in the western wilds; and Montreal's fur merchants asked no questions, providing the price was right. So, early on, the Illinois Country became a sanctuary for fugitive field runners, a prototype of the American West's more celebrated outlaw territories where bad men and free men ruled and roistered to their heart's content. "License, laxity of conduct and vice are the characteristics of its inhabitants," read a shocked Spanish report on one settlement in 1769, after France had given western Louisiana over to its ally. "Religion is given but scant respect, or to speak more correctly, is totally neglected." This would have come as no news to the French. They had known that fact all along and probably would have been less scandalized anyway. All the same, in 1747 the Governor of Canada, the Comte de la Galissonière, tried to crack down on the Illinois Country's "lawless elements," which attracted army deserters. He prepared "wanted" lists for outpost commanders and even facetiously suggested licensing the rogues as privateers instead of traders, since they were by temperament suited to such a life.

Unlike the English (and to a lesser extent the Spanish), the French were not squeamish about cohabiting with Indian women. Indeed, such prior architects of French colonial policy as Richelieu and Colbert saw miscegenation as a way to win North America. Nevertheless, officials in France believed the *habitants* were going a bit far when they spurned French women specially imported from the motherland in favor of their squaws, and vestiges of European caste-consciousness survived the Atlantic crossings of civil and military officers who were from the upper and middle classes. The *habitants,* on the other hand, were from *là-bas.* To their superiors, promiscuity could be overlooked, but their constant quarreling among themselves, the randomness of their violence, and their unrestrained use of liquor that debased the native peoples also endangered the public peace and the French-Indian alliance. The authorities were no doubt partly right in their concern for the impact of it all on the uncorrupted Amerind. But the same familiarity between Frenchman and Indian that bred contempt (and children) also bred an offsetting measure of respect, or at least interdependence.

However much the French viewed with alarm the lawless situation in the Illinois Country, the relative success of the region spoke for itself. Besides trading for furs, the inhabitants occupied their spare time with planting, and the virgin prairie brought forth wheat and corn in such plenty that it became, with no great effort on the farmers' parts, the granary for all Louisiana. Each spring a convoy with one hundred to two hundred men took the milled grains, as well as furs, hides, and lead, down the Mississippi from a seventy-mile stretch of settlements lying between the entries of the Missouri and Kaskaskia rivers: Cahokia, Prairie du Rocher, Saint Philippe, Fort de Chartres, Kaskaskia, and on the west bank of the aortal river, Sainte Geneviève.

In all, this Illinois Country (or Upper Louisiana, as it was also called) was a bountiful land praised for its climate and natural endowments by literate Frenchmen who paid it a visit. By the mid-eighteenth century it was also coveted by the approaching English and therefore given military muscle in the reconstruction of Fort de Chartres, the strategic east-bank redoubt dating from 1720. Work began in 1752 on a massive stone structure complete with two-foot-thick walls, plastered and pierced with loopholes and equipped with interior banquettes. It was muscle never to be flexed. By the time it was finished France had already lost the continent, and the victorious British, who invested it without a shot being fired, correctly pronounced Chartres the best fortification in all North America.

The Illinois Country differed from the rest of Louisiana in another curious respect: it was the one place where Catholic missionary toil bore spiritual fruit. The *voyageurs* and other free-spirited adventurers who came west and south out of Canada did not come alone. Clergymen were with them, sharing equally in the early honors of discovery and occupation, at least until they reached the Mississippi. A few priests wandered up the Missouri River in the north and the Red River in the south, but they were accorded a cold reception there, and the western banks of the

Mississippi became a figurative levee for the tide of the true faith.

One reason was that Frenchmen-become-half-Indian were not ideal traveling companions or neighbors for devout priests intent on converting savages to the word of Christ. Complaints from the Illinois clergy were not long in reaching governmental authorities, and they were not different from those already voiced in Canada. The rowdy fur traders were setting a bad example for Indian converts, particularly the women they were bedding down with. The clerics also objected to the continuing use of alcohol in the trade for furs, for it made the Indians wild and unresponsive. Those in charge of administering French colonial destinies — even Minister of Marine Pontchartrain, who was a religious man and believed that the purpose for being in the new lands was "in the first place the instruction of these savages and the knowledge to be given them of the Christian faith" — fell back on a pat answer. Yes, liquor was bad for the red man, but that was what he wanted. As was well known, English trade goods were cheaper and better than those of the French — except for spirits. Happily, French brandy best passed the taste test. So wasn't it better to live with the lamentable vice, especially when the English would only make Protestants of the Indians? The point was well made, and made often in the name of expediency.

Yet, the Church's greater problems were unrelated to the carryings-on of lusty French frontiersmen. They were internal; or when external, they were rooted in European politics, like so much else of early North American history. Pontchartrain wanted Jesuits for Louisiana. So did Bienville, who preferred them because they were "worldly" and could be counted on to learn the Indian languages. The consensus did not extend much further, however, and the Society of Jesus had more enemies in the eighteenth century than even it could handle. Rival orders wanted the chance to proselytize in Louisiana, foremost among them the Seminarian fathers from the *Séminaire des Missions Étrangères* in Paris, who had already clashed with the Jesuits in the evangelical vineyards of China on niceties of theological doctrine. Examined now, the "Chinese rites" have the same relevance as some twelfth-century monastic spat over dancing angels, disputes about what name God should be called in Chinese, and whether the homage paid Confucius should be branded idolatry or simply an example of local patriotism. No matter. The ill feelings prevailing in Paris spread to Upper and Lower Louisiana, where the Jesuits were denied the spiritual monopoly they wanted.

Jesuit setbacks began at the turn of the eighteenth century in the lower corner of the Illinois Country, known after 1765 as the American Bottom. The Seminarians were the first to get there. In 1699, Henri de Tonty led three of the fathers — François de Montigny, Antoine Davion, and Jean-François Buisson de St. Cosmé — to the Tamaroa Indians living on the east bank of the Mississippi a few miles south of where the Missouri made its muddy rush in from the far country. There they established the mission of Cahokia before moving downriver in search of new souls for saving. Then, in the following year, the Jesuit priest Marest brought a group of Kaskaskian Indians and French traders married to women of the tribe from their home on the upper Illinois River to the mouth of the Des Pères River, opposite Cahokia and near modern Saint Louis. Three years later Marest moved the settlement southeast across the Mississippi and a few miles up the Kaskaskia River, founding the village of Kaskaskia. The two orders jealously eyed each other, until the Church decreed that Cahokia was to remain a Seminarian preserve and Kaskaskia Jesuit territory.

Other missionaries from both orders spread down the river valley anticipating, as St. Cosmé said, "that so many nations having lived for so long in ignorance and infidelity will know and will love the true God and their Savior and Redeemer Jesus Christ." The infidels chose ignorance. The fathers believed they were competing with one another when all along it was an alien land of alien peoples that opposed them and frequently made martyrs of them. Montigny put up a cross among the Arkansas before opting for less demanding duty east of the Mississippi; Davion settled among the Tunicas on the lower Yazoo River without converting a single living member of the tribe; and St. Cosmé was murdered by the Chitimachas while sailing down the Mississippi in a pirogue.

The Jesuits also sent their men among the Indians of Lower Louisiana, but with little more success than the Seminarians.

While they contributed to the colony by operating a thriving plantation, by milling grain, and by such acts as assisting in the construction of a combination orphanage-hospital-convent in New Orleans for the Ursuline nuns, in 1726 they received with ill humor the news that the Capuchins were to share Lower Louisiana with them. Subsequent efforts in this colony to which they were denied apostolic exclusivity seem to have been halfhearted.

As the century wore on, the outlook became even darker for the Society of Jesus. Their foes went beyond fellow Catholic orders that envied them their material wealth and political independence. A storm was gathering in Europe. Lightning struck first in Portugal, where Minister Pombal divined a conspiracy against the monarchy and crushed the Jesuits over the objections of Rome. The long-established resentment against them shortly thundered through France. Under the pretext of a commercial lawsuit involving Jesuit speculation, a coalition of nationalists, anti-clerical philosophers, politically powerful Jansenists, and the royal concubine, Mme. de Pompadour (to whom they had refused confession), saw that the order was broken and in 1764 banished from Old France and New. Spain, the Bourbon tail, wagged in 1767. The purge of the Society and confiscation of its extensive properties removed the Jesuits as a force from North America and the West.

It can be argued that the followers of Ignatius Loyola (and rival orders as well) never really were an influence in the French West of the Plains Indians, who stayed unrepentant pagans living on the wild side of life. After 1763, neither was France. But individual Frenchmen remained—in 1763, and 1776, and a long time thereafter. Acting for themselves or as agents of Spain, England, or later, the United States, they would leave behind their culture and customs and place-names on grand expanses of the American West, which they had been the first to see.

Chapter 10

The Farthest
with the Fewest

IT WAS ALMOST AS THOUGH SOME FRENCHMEN who removed to the New World were themselves made new men; as though the place that had been denied them in Provence or Normandy or Gascony was to be found in the West of New France, where first the sun downed behind the purple shimmer of northern lakes, then beyond the waving curtain of breast-high prairie grass, and finally over the backlit shark's teeth of distant mountains that still beckoned. It amounted to a kind of tropism for those who dressed like Indians in the skins of animals and wore moccasins or snow-shoes to follow the light. It was westering, more than a century before there was an English word to describe the phenomenon of chasing the sun over the American West.

Nobody knows how many of them did it, for most left no records, not only because they did not know how to write but because they did not feel the need to tell of where they had been and what they had seen. It was sufficient to have known festive summers followed by indescribable autumns and forgettable winters and welcome springs when the year was renewed. Not that calendars mattered much; for them, time did seem to have a stop.

They chose mostly the rivers as avenues into the open-ended land they called Louisiana. The rivers of Canada had already served them or their fathers or their grandfathers well. Where the rivers took them was always a place beyond the white man's laws and customs, so that whatever they became known as—*voyageurs, coureurs de bois,* fur hounds, squaw men—they were in a real sense what many called them: outlaws. Those who lived beyond the law; those who preferred the company of *sauvages* to their own kind. Fortunately, a few who went west were men of higher station—gentlemen-born, or self-made, or gentlemen-in-the-making—who were literate and who left records, fragmentary though they be. This handful was no less brave or resourceful than their unlettered countrymen, and it was they who left upon the West larger-than-life legends with their wit, daring, and plain old *panache*.

No sooner was France precariously positioned in the Mississippi Valley than she began looking westward, the direction of rival Spain and the metallic plum that seemed not far from imperial reach. As early as 1705, Bienville had sent men exploring up the Red River, perhaps as far as the Rio Grande, and already French clothes and arms were turning up at the Taos trade fair. Then, in 1713, when Louisiana was a private enterprise under Crozat, who expected his wealth to come from trade with the Spaniards, Governor Cadillac dispatched another party up the Red in answer to a singular letter from a priest named Hidalgo. The unhappy Franciscan had been forced to abandon his mission of San Francisco and thought that by inviting the French to come west, he could prod his own neglectful Spanish sponsors to reoccupy Texas. (Hidalgo was no doubt also aware that a certain Spanish Jesuit had said it would be best "for the glory of God" if the French with their Jesuit missionaries were to take over in Texas.) Cadillac did not view the invitation as an official carte blanche to westward expansion, but he knew an opportunity when he saw one, even if it was risky. To head the twenty-four-man mission of questionable mercy, with its ten thousand *livres'* worth of trade goods, he chose a thirty-five-year-old Canadian who had been with the LeMoyne brothers from the first occupation of the delta.

Cadillac could not have chosen better. Louis Juchereau de St. Denis was the first, if not the foremost, of France's westerners. He was a flesh-and-blood fugitive from picaresque fiction, tall, handsome, educated, polite, diplomatic, witty, and above all brazen—an adventurer with an instinctive knowledge of the weaknesses of those who would stand in his way. Soon after founding Natchitoches, in the midst of the Red River Indians after whom the trading post was named, he set off with three other Frenchmen south over red hills toward the Sabine River. An Indian attack

The archetypal French westerners Radisson (standing) and Groseilliers defected to the English; most others stayed true to France.

only delayed him. When he reached the Rio Grande, the sunny Spanish settlement of San Juan Bautista had reason to rouse itself from siesta.

No one was more aroused than Don Diego Ramon by the arrival of the Frenchman who came out of the dust dressed in tailored finery, well cared for by his part-time valet, part-time press agent, Medar Jalot. What was the meaning of this? the Spanish commander must have asked himself. Did the upstart not know that foreign trade with New Spain was forbidden by royal edict? The upstart knew, all right. There was little that St. Denis did not know, including an opportunity supported by the bluff of Hidalgo's letter and a passport signed by the governor of Louisiana. He also knew a pretty girl when he saw one. While Don Ramon took St. Denis and his French companions into comfortable custody and waited for Mexico City to decide what to do, the charming cavalier, who entertained his hosts at dinner with scintillating puns in Spanish, courted the seventeen-year-old granddaughter of Señor Ramon, Doña Emanuelle, regarded as the greatest beauty in all northern Mexico. It was a confection, a cotton-candy romance — dashing young blade meets fiery Latin beauty among the soft earth colors of adobeland. St. Denis won Emanuelle's heart and Don Ramon's interest in his proposed trade before being summoned to Mexico City, where he met his stern inquisitors in June.

The gallant was as witty and winning as usual. He did not know he had broken any rules; he had only come to help the missionaries, whose religion they all shared. Then, too, he had lost his heart to a Spanish girl. It was as good as if he had become Spanish himself. Viceroy Linares bit. Would the Frenchman then personally lead a Spanish occupation force into the east Texas of Hidalgo's hope, since he had such a renowned reputation as a friend of the Indians? St. Denis would, and he did, but not before secretly informing Governor Cadillac what was afoot and giving time for Natchitoches to be fortified. He also stopped first in San Juan Bautista to marry his beloved in a frontier gala that warmed the winter of 1715. Then he shepherded a recolonizing and re-missionizing party led by members of the Ramon family into a Los Adaes settlement only a coin's throw from his own Natchitoches, where goods could be got for the right amount of silver.

St. Denis had left his pregnant wife in San Juan Bautista, and he now returned to Mobile and amassed one hundred thousand *livres'* worth of goods, which he brought back to Natchitoches, trading them with the Indians and Spaniards, and trying to smuggle some on to his new in-laws. But he was caught. Envy was as much a condition of southwest frontier life as it was in Madrid and Paris. The Governor of Coahuila and Texas, Alarcón, squealed, and once again St. Denis was packed off to a Mexico City jail for violating the trade laws. But again the brazen-tongued cavalier had his answer. No, he wasn't smuggling anything, merely bringing thirteen mules (that is all the Ramons admitted to receiving) with his own personal belongings, including some brocade for his wife, who was expecting and was, of course, Spanish. Somehow the rascal managed to escape the calaboose and head north again. The Spanish would never again have a chance to let the glib gallant slip through their fingers. This time he took his wife to New Orleans, just before the outbreak of the War of the Quadruple Alliance, which pitted Spain against France on the continent and, when word crossed the Atlantic, in North America, too.

On the Gulf Coast the French struck first, taking Pensacola; then the Spanish took it back; then France was the winner again with St. Denis and his Indian allies the decisive factor—all this within two months' time. It was a gentleman's war, victors and vanquished exchanging courtly compliments and sharing their stores of fine spirits. To the west, in the Natchitoches country that St. Denis had temporarily left, the war amounted to a comic opera. In June of 1719 a French officer took seven men and marched fifteen miles west to seize Los Adaes (which St. Denis had helped the Spanish build), capturing its "garrison" of one ragged Spanish soldier and several squawking chickens. The frightened missionaries and settlers raced south to San Antonio, the new mission and town founded in 1718 by Alarcón. Spain was out of east Texas again, and in Paris it was decided to finish the job by commissioning St. Denis to drive Spain south of the Rio Grande. Unhappily, for France, the ship carrying St. Denis' orders was captured by Spaniards.

Proud Spain had another wound to lick. Not only had she given up east Texas without firing a shot or drawing a saber, she had also suffered a stunning defeat far in the north, at a place that wasn't even on a map. For two decades Spaniards had worried about the spreading French influence among the Indians of the Great Plains, to whom the French had come with trade and guns. Concern ran deepest in Santa Fe, where, upon instructions from the viceroy, Governor Valverde decided someone had to go out and reconnoiter French activity. In 1720 he sent Don Pedro Villasur and more than a hundred Spaniards and friendly Indians north over the Sangre de Cristos and onto the unfriendly shortgrass flatlands. Villasur was not the man for the job. He went too far, angling up through eastern Colorado and then on to the banks of the northern branch of the Platte River, near the present town

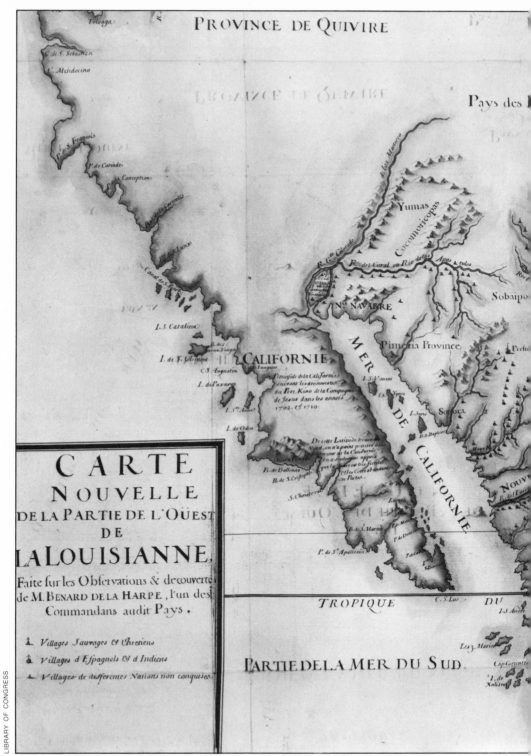

PROVINCE DE QUIVIRE

Pays des

Yumas
Cocomoricopas

N. NAVARRE

Pimeria Province

MER DE CALIFORNIE

Sobaipo

Sonora

CALIFORNIE

Presqu'isle de la Californie
suivant les decouvertes
du Pere Kino de la Compagnie
de Jesus dans les annees
1702 et 1710.

TROPIQUE

PARTIE DE LA MER DU SUD.

CARTE
NOUVELLE
DE LA PARTIE DE L'OÜEST
DE
LA LOUISIANNE,
Faite sur les Observations & decouvertes
de M. BENARD DE LA HARPE, l'un des
Commandans audit Pays.

Villages Sauvages & Chretiens
Villages d'Espagnols & d'Indiens
Villages de differentes Nations non conquises.

La Harpe's map of 1720. He had been west, but not far enough to shed much light on the shadowed lands still controlled by Spain.

of North Platte, Nebraska. Here, through indecision and stupidity, Villasur invited a massacre by French-armed Pawnee warriors that cost New Mexico more than thirty of its non-Indian defense force, a third of the province's finest troops.

The time had come to avenge such indignities. Time for a show of force in the West, which Spain thought of as her own land. But she acted with typical deliberateness, and that, as usual, cost her. By the time an army of five hundred men was assembled, provisioned, and organized to retake the lost Texas territory, its proud commander José de Azlor, the Marqués of San Miguel de Aguayo, who was determined to push France back across the Mississippi, received word that peace had been made between Spain and France, on May 16, 1721. Deflated, Aguayo marched on to reoccupy Los Adaes. There he received under a safe-conduct pass the man the Indians called "Big Leg." St. Denis asked if Aguayo meant to respect the peace agreed to by their respective countries, or whether he chose to fight. The marqués, having observed the heavily armed coalition of Indian tribes that St. Denis had put together with his customary skill, chose peace. So the status quo returned to the blurred boundary between the red-earth hill country of Spanish Texas and the reedy swamps and giant cypresses of the French Red River valley.

St. Denis, who had been made commandant of Natchitoches and was to remain in that capacity for another twenty-three years as an immovable barrier to Spanish expansion east, probably welcomed the return of his wife's nation to Los Adaes. He was as much a trader as a French hero, and his best customers were back, short as always of everything he just happened to have in stock. The fact that His Most Catholic Majesty forbade his colonial subjects to trade with the French was conveniently forgotten most of the time on the Texas-Louisiana border, where a succession of Spanish commanders and padres supplemented their incomes in a lively trade with the puzzling gentleman who wore silver-braided damask and taffeta uniforms and resided in a well-appointed wilderness mansion.

Another Frenchman opposed to the hostilities was Jean Baptiste Bénard de la Harpe, like St. Denis an officer-explorer who left records. In 1718 he departed New Orleans with the blessing of Bienville and a concession from Law's company to go up the Red River well beyond Natchitoches and initiate trade with the Spaniards, wherever they might be found. The following year La Harpe built a trading post among the Caddoan Nassonites near what is now Texarkana and sent out the word that he was prepared to pay 5 percent commissions to any Spaniards that would fence for him. Again, the impotent Spanish authorities were in a rage. Frenchmen were popping up everywhere, and their insolence knew no bounds. Neither did their wanderings. After reminding the Spaniards that Texas really belonged to France by dint of La Salle's colonization there, La Harpe traveled to the Canadian River in modern Oklahoma, befriending Indians as he went and cataloging the flora, fauna, and geological finds in commendable French detail. The War of the Quadruple Alliance and the flight of the Spaniards after the "battle" of Los Adaes dashed La Harpe's hopes for commerce, and in 1721 he was ordered to proceed by sea and take Matagorda Bay (called St. Bernard by the French and Espíritu Santo by the Spanish), where La Salle had made his fateful landfall. La Harpe missed Matagorda Bay and put in at Galveston Bay. Only the year before a Frenchman named Béranger had arrived there to carry off the fairest Indian damsels of the land and leave sickness behind. La Harpe's blandishments gained him nothing. He had no choice but to sail away, back to Louisiana, while Aguayo found the right bay and fortified it.

The resolute La Harpe might be done in Texas, but he was not through in the West. Later in 1721 he took three pirogues out of New Orleans laden with trade goods and headed north to the Arkansas River, up which, he said, he traveled three hundred miles before he lost a third of his stores in striking a reef and had to return. "I did not obtain any advantages from this discovery," he later wrote with regret, "except to have looked over a very beautiful country, prairies covered with oxen and other animals whose skins are valuable. Turtles are very good there. There are birds of all kinds there. Turkey-hens and black bears are common [as are] trees suitable for clapboards . . . and others of fruit, wild vines, and white mulberry trees." It was a river worth fortifying, La Harpe advised his countrymen in 1763, when he was an old man and France had just given that river and many others away to the nation that had once blunted his enterprise. Rising in the alpine heights of the southern Rockies, the Arkansas was truly a worthy river, an important river. But there was another that drained the West even better, one that was even more important.

FATHER MARQUETTE, when he saw the Missouri roaring in from the West in June of 1673 with its cargo of uprooted trees and mud in solution, called it the Pekitanoui. Father Charlevoix, traveling down the Mississippi on a royal inspection trip in 1720, described the Missouri's entrance as the "finest confluence in the world." "The Missouri is by far the most rapid," he wrote, "and seems to enter the Mississippi like a Conqueror, through which it carries its white waters to the opposite shore, without mixing them; afterwards it gives its colour to the Mississippi, which it never loses again, but carries it quite down to the sea."

So forceful and promising a river was irresistible to westering Frenchmen from the first, and after La Salle they began to work their way up it in ones and twos, most of them anonymous adventurers looking for mines and trading for furs. The first official expedition to penetrate the interior of the Missouri country (at least the first of record, for the French traders turned up virtually everywhere before they were permitted to and deliberately left no records) was not sent until 1719, when Governor Bienville again gave the order. The Illinois Country had only recently been added to the jurisdiction of Louisiana, and the prevailing belief was that the shortest way from there to Santa Fe was up the Big Muddy. Leading the party of trader-diplomats that set out from Kaskaskia was Charles Claude du Tisné, a man stamped in the St. Denis mold who had taken over the command of the Natchitoches post when his superior went wooing in Old Mexico. Du Tisné was a gentleman, a Parisian, clever, literate, blessed with the gift of mirth, and if some tales told of him are true, the first great prankster of the West. (Among other tricks, he is suspected of having salted the Illinois Country with silver-bearing ore from Mexico, howling when the assay reports sent the colony into a tizzy.)

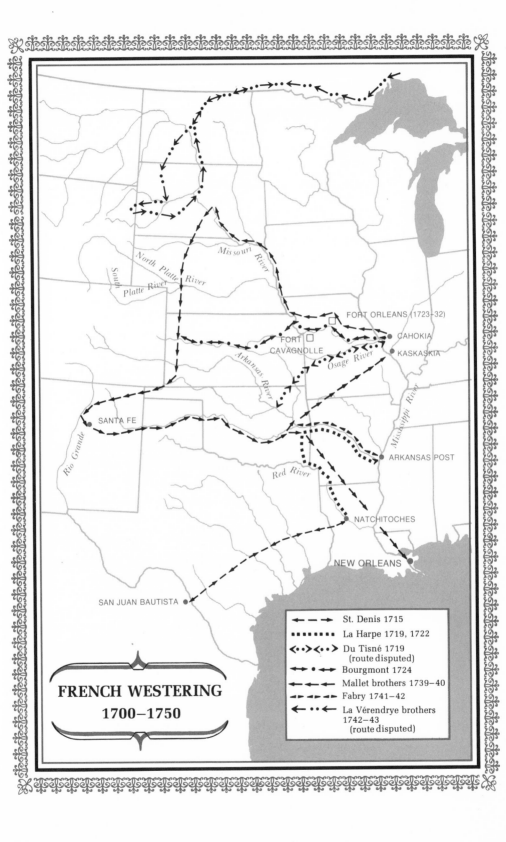

FORT ORLEANS (1723-32)

CAHOKIA

KASKASKIA

FORT
CAVAGNOLLE

Missouri River

North Platte River

South Platte River

Arkansas River

Osage River

Mississippi River

SANTA FE

Rio Grande

Red River

ARKANSAS POST

NATCHITOCHES

NEW ORLEANS

SAN JUAN BAUTISTA

	St. Denis 1715
	La Harpe 1719, 1722
	Du Tisné 1719 (route disputed)
	Bourgmont 1724
	Mallet brothers 1739–40
	Fabry 1741–42
	La Vérendrye brothers 1742–43 (route disputed)

FRENCH WESTERING
1700–1750

In 1719, du Tisné headed up the Missouri until he met the Osage Indians, with whom he traded. When they heard du Tisné's intention to go farther west and make peace with the Pawnees, the Osages objected. The Pawnees were their enemies, a people they were accustomed to enslaving and trading to the French. Eventually du Tisné managed to get past them, but only on the condition that he take no more than three guns with him. Following the Osage River southwest, du Tisné finally reached a tribe of Pawnees in Oklahoma. Here he bartered away his last three weapons and told his hosts that he was now ready to proceed west to the Comanches, to which the Pawnees gave an emphatic "nothing doing." Comanches were their most hated foes.

There is a story that the Pawnees first planned to scalp du Tisné and appropriate his goods. But the little Frenchman overheard them. Boldly he confronted them shouting, "Do you want my scalp? Pick it up if you dare." Then he yanked a wig from his cue-ball head and threw it at their feet. The astonished Indians gaped at the wonder. Then du Tisné thundered, "If you attempt to harm me I will burn your rivers and fields!" To prove his powers he took some water, poured on a little brandy (the *eau-de-vie* was still unfamiliar to the Pawnees) and set it aflame. Next he took a magnifying glass with which he set a log on fire. It was strong medicine well taken by the Pawnees, who lavished gifts on the miracle man and looked carefully after his safety. On September 27, 1719, du Tisné planted the royal white flag of France in their village, then returned to the Illinois Country with an especially nice haul of furs.

The westward thrust of France was hardly massive, but the few took it far. Discouraged by the international stalemate on the Louisiana-Texas frontier, France turned more and more to the Missouri as the way to bring New Mexico within striking, or at least trading, distance. Lacking manpower to fortify the route, she decided to unite all the Plains tribes under the fleur-de-lys in treaties of peace—a plan as likely of success as that of some Asiatic potentate, arriving in eighteenth-century Germany, to bring the many principalities together in a lasting understanding.

Yet, the French gave it their best and chose one of their best for the task. Étienne Véniard, Sieur de Bourgmont, had many qualifications and a few failings that perhaps only the French could have found forgivable. The competent officer had been commandant of Fort Detroit before running off into the wilds with a married Frenchwoman. Though he and his ladylove were captured and returned in 1707, the philanderer deserted again in 1714, this time enamored of a Missouri Indian girl. For some years he lived with her and her people, learning much of the long river and its tribes, which he had the good sense to put on paper.

The year 1719 found Bourgmont leading a group of Missouri warriors against the Spanish on the Gulf Coast before returning that fall to France in honor, having been nominated for the Cross of Saint Louis. There he is said to have married a rich widow, and in 1722 he was commissioned by the Company of the Indies to build a fort on the Missouri, pacify the river tribes, make an alliance with the Comanches, and open trade with New Mexico. It was a tall order, but the colorful Bourgmont, who had a respect from the red man that seems to have bordered on idolatry, was up to filling it. By winter of 1723 he had constructed Fort Orléans on the north bank of the Missouri (near modern Brunswick), complete with personal quarters, barracks, church, and icehouse. Then the bringer of mutual friendship and fidelity called together the Missouris and Osages and Otoes and Pawnees—tribes not always the best of friends. It was time, Bourgmont told them, to make peace with the Comanches, who happened to be the enemies of all.

In the summer of 1724, Bourgmont headed more than one hundred fifty Indians and eight Frenchmen up the river to collect some Kansas for the trip to Comanche territory. Sickness delayed the stouthearted captain, but in October he was back at it, leading a column across present-day Kansas with drums rolling and banners flying, a microscopic disturbance on the stubbled floor of the sky country.

At last smoke was seen on the afternoon horizon, which Bourgmont answered by setting the prairie afire. He had had the wit to purchase two Comanche slaves from the Kansas, free them, and send them ahead as goodwill messengers with the white colors of France. It was a glorious coming together: whooping and pistol shooting, handshaking all around, passing the peace pipe, and other signs of brotherliness. At six the next morning Bourgmont unpacked and carefully sorted out a veritable storehouse: axes, blankets, red cloth, blue cloth, mirrors, knives, shirts, scissors, combs, awls, kettles, bells, beads, brass wire, and, bad news for the Spaniards, guns, powder, and balls. Then, French flag in hand, he addressed an assembly of two hundred notables: "I bring you the word of the King, my master, who is the big chief of all nations, our allies, with whom we have acquaintance and who are the Missouris, the Osages, the Kansas, the Otoes, the Panimahas [Pawnees], whom you see with me and who are witness of this, so that hereafter you may live in alliance and . . . visit each other and trade with each other. . . ." Bourgmont also appended a warning to the Comanches that it could go hard on them if the trust was broken, or if Frenchmen coming later were stopped on their way to trade with the Spaniards. At last, handing his flag over to the chief with the command that he keep it spotless for the French that would "from now on come to see you," Bourgmont offered them the treasures and trinkets displayed, gratis, in the name of his king. The Comanches were overwhelmed. They accepted unconditionally, the chief bad-mouthing the Spanish and giving eloquent protestations of eternal friendship with France. Then lions and lambs sealed the pact with a festive buffalo banquet.

Bourgmont had done everything expected of him, except to reach New Mexico. His summer illness prevented him in that, and he probably figured the treaty he had arranged was sufficient, having no real way of knowing that the Comanches were not a single tribe but many bands unified only by a common language and ferocity. Nor did he know that the French would prove unable to maintain such a bountiful supply of goods on which the peace would depend.

Whatever, Bourgmont returned to Fort Orléans and called a great council of his new confederacy. It was time, he concluded, to introduce these newest subjects of Louis XV firsthand to the might and grandeur of his nation ("*pour leur donner une idée de la puissance des Français,*" as his sponsoring company had said). The Superior Council of New Orleans pared down his original entourage to one Missouri chief, one Osage, one

Illinois, one Oto, one Metchigami, and a young Missouri princess—the last, we may guess, at Bourgmont's insistence.

Oh, what a Paris gala when the visitors arrived in September 1725! The *peaux-rouges* were regaled in grand style and dressed in finery of blue and gold. They attended a fancy reception given by the Duke and Duchess of Bourbon and the directors of the Company of the Indies; they even had an audience with the handsome Louis himself. For the pleasure of Parisians, they performed war dances at the Opéra, and put on a demonstration of stag hunting in the Bois de Boulogne. The Missouri princess was baptized and then married off to one of Bourgmont's sergeants in the Cathedral of Notre Dame. (Madame Bourgmont must have put her foot down.) When the Indian delegation left Paris to return to their uncouth West, they did so without Bourgmont, who, rich in honors, decided to stay in France.

If victories were won on brilliant gambits, grand gestures, or *courage sans peur*, the American West might be French today. But there was more to it than that. The foundations laid by du Tisné and Bourgmont were not built upon. By the close of 1732 Fort Orléans was abandoned by missionaries and traders alike. The bonds that were to hold red men to red men, and red men to Frenchmen, came unstuck, out of neglect and the normal strains of rowdy life on the Plains.

This was not to say that individual Frenchmen gave up the idea of reaching New Mexico by the Missouri, which turned away from that direction by a quadrant. In 1739 eight Frenchmen led by the Canadian brothers Pierre and Paul Mallet actually reached the pot of sand at the end of the rainbow by that circuitous route. After following the Big Muddy, not quite as far as the Arikara Indians in South Dakota, they turned about and headed south across the Platte and through the Comanche curtain to New Mexico. The ringing of Spanish bells greeted them in Taos along with a most hospitable detention in Santa Fe when they arrived there on July 22, 1739. It was a grand detour from the Santa Fe Trail of future lore, and yet it had been done; New Mexico was reached by the first white men to have crossed the full girth of the Great Plains.

The purpose the Mallets gave for coming, opening trade,

delighted many including the clergy, who had also responded to St. Denis's overtures. The French could promise dry goods and luxuries the Spanish lacked, in exchange for horses and silver coin. The old proscriptions against trade no longer seemed reasonable since Bourbon Spain and Bourbon France had buried the hatchet in 1733, coming to the realization that England was more a threat to them both than they were to each other.

The Mallets stayed nine months in Santa Fe, noting that the garrison was small and raggle-taggle, and convincing themselves there were mines in the vicinity that the Spanish were too lazy to work. In May of 1740 all but one of the Mallet party (he'd married a local girl) departed the province. By now they had their geography straightened out somewhat, and this time they followed a new route along the Canadian and Arkansas rivers before splitting up, some returning to the Illinois, others making an uneventful journey to New Orleans, where they were received with surprise and pleasure by Bienville. The governor was so pleased with the news of how graciously the Mallets had been treated that he sent them back in the same direction the next year under the leadership of a clerk named Fabry de la Bruyère. Fabry was apparently a dolt, at least in the wilds, and the expedition bogged down on the Arkansas River, where the September waters were too low for travel by boat. Dissension scattered the party. Fabry was unable to get horses from the Comanches, so the Mallet brothers finally went their own way on foot.

The Fabry failure proved only an isolated stop to the French movement west. So many unlicensed *voyageurs* and *coureurs de bois* were operating along the Missouri and its tributaries (and more than a few of them with the kinds of methods that earned them surprise deaths) that Louisiana's Governor Vaudreuil farmed out the whole region in 1745 to a single trader, Sieur Deruisseau. Soon afterwards Fort Cavagnolle was erected on the Missouri River near modern Kansas City to control abuses in the fur trade and make safe the way toward Santa Fe. An insistent trickle of Frenchmen now headed westward via the Red River and the upper Arkansas. Some went with official approval, some were free-lance traders, and some were simply deserting the frontier army with its harsh discipline.

Distressed Spanish officialdom could agree on no consistent policy for dealing with the intruders. In Mexico City, where suspicion of French intentions remained despite the new era of peace between the two nations (why else would anybody give guns to Comanches?), authorities tended to take the hard line on enforcing royal regulations that forbade colonials to trade with outsiders. Not so in New Mexico. The monopolistic practices of licenses, duties, and ports of entry made prices exorbitant for goods that might or might not arrive on the once-a-year mule train up from Chihuahua. French wares were not only less costly and better, they were also readily available from the enterprising visitors who crossed a hostile wilderness to reach them. What the viceroy didn't know wouldn't hurt him, but it would certainly help his neglected servants scratching a living from the valley of the Rio Grande del Norte. Illegal trade in New Mexico became almost as common as Apache attacks.

Nevertheless, some northern governors, either because they were short-timers answerable to higher authorities, or because they saw a connection between trading and raiding, were zealous and meant to enforce the law to the letter. Now and again an unlucky French trading party was arrested, and its coveted goods auctioned off to pay the royal expenses of custody while authorities decided what to do with them. That was the rub. What to do with them? Spanish responses varied. One intriguing case involved three French deserters from the Arkansas post who showed up with Comanches at the Taos trade fair in 1749 and were arrested. Governor Tómas Vélez Cachupín aired his predicament in an exchange of letters with the viceroy. These Frenchmen were, of course, lawbreakers, Cachupín admitted. But they had skills. One was a carpenter, another a tailor, and the third a barber and bloodletter. The province could use men of such extraordinary talents. The viceroy acceded. They might stay in New Mexico, but under no circumstances were they to be allowed to return to Louisiana and encourage others to come.

Others did come. Some were caught and dealt with more severely, among them Messrs. Jean Chapuis and Luis Feuilli, who arrived at the Pecos pueblo in 1752 pleading ignorance of any trading prohibitions. They did time in a Mexico City jail before being shipped to Spain as prisoners. One Joseph Blanc-pain, apprehended in 1754, died in a Mexico City prison the following year, causing Governor Kerlérec of Louisiana to pro-test. Spain remained inflexible. A new royal order decreed deportation to South America for any Frenchman caught trading in its territories.

So much for appearances. In reality, contraband trade in the Southwest continued — with a gubernatorial connivance here, a *mordida* there — until 1763, when the West that was France's became Spain's and the westering trails blazed by St. Denis, La Harpe, du Tisné, Bourgmont, and the Mallets reverted to nature and the savagery that was the natural condition of life on the southern Great Plains. They would be recut and recrossed again generations later by white men who spoke neither French nor Spanish.

T HE RIVERS OF LOUISIANA were not the only ways west. An-other way was from the far north, north of the Fox Indians who for many years blocked French expansion west, from Can-ada, the broad shoulders of the continent, the prime fur country that brought many a trader from river to lake to river to lake, chasing the sun and the diminishing beaver for personal profit and the chance to live life at its freest among the hospitable Chippewas and Crees.

There was one who came west for another reason. His name was Pierre Gaultier de Varennes, Sieur de la Vérendrye, a Canadian-born soldier who had fought for France in Europe, been wounded there, and afterwards returned to his native land in his middle age to pursue what became his life's consum-ing passion: to find the elusive western sea that two centuries of French savants had believed in. Perhaps the passion ran in the Vérendrye blood, for it was shared by his four sons, Jean-Baptiste, Pierre, François, and Louis-Joseph, and by a nephew, La Jemeraye.

The family saga took two decades to unfold. In 1730, La Vérendrye presented his design for discovery to the Canadian governor, Charles de la Boische, Marquis de Beauharnois, hoping for royal funds to outfit a group of proven frontiersmen for the expedition. The minister of marine, Comte de Maurepas, said no. The best he could do was to grant La Vérendrye a fur monopoly in the unopened country and some royal presents for the Indians who would lead the party to the western sea. With his own resources meagre, the Canadian had no recourse but to go for financing to the Montreal merchants—a grasping, backbiting lot who had been the ruin of more than one good man. He was advanced equipment and stores, but on terms that stood to enrich the backers at the expense of the visionary.

The summer of 1732 found the Vérendrye clan at Lake of the Woods, where they built Fort Saint Charles; by the autumn of 1734 another fort was built on the Red River of the north, though the senior La Vérendrye had to go back to Montreal to placate the merchants, who wanted more furs for the provisions they were forwarding. Then a double tragedy befell La Vérendrye in 1736. First, his nephew La Jemeraye died; next, his oldest son Jean-Baptiste and nineteen other Frenchmen were murdered and decapitated by the Sioux at Lake of the Woods.

But there was no turning back for the man and his surviving sons. The Indians they met and befriended continued to fill their ears with stories of a range of tall and shining mountains to the west, and beyond that a sea whose waters could not be drunk. In 1738, La Vérendrye left his farthest outpost at Fort La Reine for the southwest, where, his Assiniboin friends told him, were a people who could tell more of the western sea. On a North Dakota December day, La Vérendrye and his party were welcomed in a Mandan village beside the Upper Missouri. La Vérendrye found the Mandans an impressive people. In his journal he described them as clean and industrious, shrewd traders, "the most skillful in dressing leather," and working "very deliberately in hair and feathers." The village (one of seven the Mandans had) consisted of one hundred thirty large earth-covered lodges laid out with geometric precision, the whole enclosed with defensive ramparts and a palisade. As for their physical appearance, La Vérendrye left a puzzling description, which would later be cited by Madoc boosters: "This tribe is of mixed blood, white and black. The women are rather hand-

The brothers La Vérendrye look to the "Shining Mountains" (in a latter-day painting). What range was it? The debate continues.

some, particularly the light-colored ones; they have an abundance of fair hair."

All the same, La Vérendrye was disappointed. His interpreter had run off, making communication difficult. Worse, of the western sea the Mandans apparently knew nothing. Then La Vérendrye fell ill, and on December 13, still sick, he departed, leaving two Frenchmen with the Mandans to learn their language. For the next two months he retraced his steps in agony, his health broken. "Never in my life," he wrote, "did I endure so much misery, pain and fatigue as on that journey."

The senior La Vérendrye was never to make it as far west as the Mandans again. His supplier had seized what goods the explorer had stored at Michilimackinac, and he had to return to Montreal to seek redress. Much of his time was now spent trying to keep his tenuous enterprise alive against Sioux war parties and the more corrosive hostility of the cheaters and gougers in Montreal.

Nevertheless, the family search for the western sea did not

end. In May of 1742, sons François and Louis-Joseph, known as the Chevalier, returned to the Mandan village; and that long-ago summer they wandered west among tribes the Chevalier came to know as the Beaux Hommes, the Petits Reynards, the Gens des Chevaux, the Gens de la Belle Rivière, and the Gens de l'Arc, a brave people that at the time were assembling an army to fight the most dreaded enemies of all, the Gens du Serpent, who lived at the base of the tall and shining mountains over which there was a sea where white men lived. What did the Gens de l'Arc know of these white men? the Chevalier inquired. He was told that those on the coast were numerous and lived in separate apartments, having many slaves and horses and animals used in tilling the land. They also had "many chiefs," some for their soldiers and "some also for prayer."

Spaniards, the Chevalier concluded with a heavy heart. The western sea was the South Sea and in no need of discovery. The brothers accompanied the Indian army anyway, until on January 1, 1743, they saw on the western horizon their shining mountains. Unfortunately, the Indians soon gave up their chase and retired in disorderly fashion, leaving the brothers La Vérendrye no choice but to follow.

Pinning down the various "gens" the Chevalier met has been the center of continuing controversy, as has determining the range of mountains he saw capped with snow. Some have said they were the Bighorn Mountains of Wyoming, some the Wind River range. The most conservative suspect they were the Black Hills of South Dakota. The Chevalier's report is sketchy enough to raise doubt as to whether the whole thing wasn't a dream, were it not for the probity of the man himself and a March entry made on the way back that reads in part, "I deposited on an eminence . . . a tablet of lead with the arms and inscription of the King." In 1913 a schoolgirl playing on a hill near Pierre, South Dakota, found the long-buried plate, which bore the names of Louis XV, Governor Beauharnois, and Pierre Gaultier de la Vérendrye.

Meanwhile, the elder La Vérendrye's situation worsened. It wasn't enough that he had a wilderness and the fur barons of Montreal against him. Poison pen letters carried libels back to

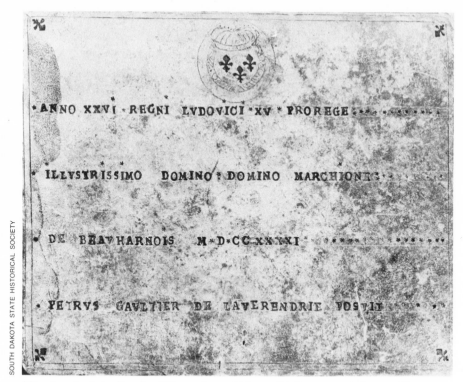

The lead plate the La Vérendryes "deposited on an eminence" was found by a schoolgirl on a hill near Pierre, South Dakota, in 1913.

France, where Minister Maurepas issued a barrage of carping letters that crossed the North Atlantic to Governor Beauharnois. The minister expressed the hope that La Vérendrye would "succeed in removing the suspicions for which, up to the present, he has given cause." He was charged with favoring his own sons over others better qualified and "for several years [being] solely occupied with his own affairs, [having] done nothing for the service." What is more, La Vérendrye was said to be "content with the profits accruing from this trade [and] very slack in pursuing the discovery which ought to have been the principal object of his efforts." By Maurepas's choplogic La Vérendrye was guilty of trying to pay his bills instead of finding the western sea, a project for which the Crown in its wondrous parsimony had extended very little. But at least Maurepas was consistent. After looking at maps drawn by charlatans who, like himself, had never seen the other side of the Atlantic, he also found reason to fault the directions the La Vérendryes were traveling, being far from "the one that would lead to what they were commissioned to discover."

Governor Beauharnois bravely stood up for the "mild and firm" man who had such a knack for winning over savages and who, contrary to what was being said in France, was becoming poorer, not richer, in his quest for the western sea. It was no use. The harassments continued until, in 1744, Beauharnois had to ask for La Vérendrye's resignation. The journeyman officer sent to replace him left the enterprise a shambles before asking to be relieved. That left a vacancy. There was only one man in New France qualified to fill it: Pierre Gaultier de Varennes, Sieur de la Vérendrye. Having received his long-delayed promotion to captain, the old man now in his sixty-fourth year was overjoyed at another chance and began making plans. "I shall be only too happy," he wrote the minister of marine in September 1749, "if after all the trouble, fatigue and danger I am about to encounter in this long exploration I could succeed in proving to you the . . . zeal of myself and my sons for the glory of the king and the welfare of the colony."

The nonexistent western sea could not be found by Père Vérendrye. A few months later the man who had given France thirty-nine years of service, taken nine wounds on her battlefields, sacrificed a son and a nephew to a patriotic dream, and carried the flickering light of his nation into a thousand miles of geographical darkness, died. No Frenchman acting officially for France would ever again go so far.

La Salle, had he come back from his Texas grave, would have been sadly amused. Nothing had changed. A man who had been West and had dreams didn't stand a chance with the pound-of-flesh merchants of Montreal and the myopic ministers back in what was sometimes thought of as home.

Chapter 11

Loose Chip in the Imperial Game

IN THE INFLATIONARY SUMMER OF 1763, Pierre de Laclède Liguest went upriver from New Orleans to find a place to store his bulky cargo. The firm of Maxent, Laclède, and Dee had just received a monopoly to trade with the tribes of the Missouri for six years, granted by Governor Jean Jacques Blaise d'Abbadie, who feared that the financial dislocations brought on by the Seven Years' War were going to be the ruin of Louisiana's entrepreneurs. Acting with the blessing of Maxent, his senior partner, Laclède sought a post that was convenient to the red men as well as to the arterial rivers, the Missouri and the Mississippi. He found his place, and in mid-February of 1764 construction began a few miles southwest of where the rivers met. From the first the settlement showed signs of health, attracting families from Cahokia and other French villages on the east side of the Mississippi. Later it was to be known in slogan and in function as the Gateway to the West. Laclède called it Saint Louis, in honor of Louis XV. What Laclède did not know was that his king no longer had title to the property, that he had palmed it off on Spain as he might an old and tattered beaver hat. What the trader had not yet heard was that he and his fellow Louisianans had been sold down the river, down both rivers.

Who was responsible? While the Duc de Choiseul was present at the dismemberment of France's colonial empire, so painstakingly put together first by Cardinal Richelieu and then by Louis XIV's minister, Colbert, he arrived on the scene too late for blame. The finger of suspicion shifts elsewhere, to the man Louisiana historian Charles Gayarré said "never had either the

A portrait of Pierre de Laclède Liguest, who in 1763 selected a site on which to build a trading post. He named it St. Louis.

tenderness of a woman's heart, the pride of a king, or the courage of a man."

Apologists for Louis XV point out that he was not an unintelligent fellow and that his illustrious father, the Sun King, had left him a treasury emptied by the costs of his never-ending wars. True, but that did not explain away the royal flaws in the royal character, which included timidity, duplicity, indecision, sloth, and sensual appetites that a succession of mistresses and a private brothel could not satisfy. He was no Sun King, more a Moon King, whose very longevity led France into five decades of steady eclipse, and who toward the end of his reign attended more to scotching rumors of his scabrous reputation as Europe's premier lecher than he did to vital matters of state.

The army of Louis XIV had been the envy of Europe. Under Louis XV it became a flabby refuge for bureaucratic *plume-pushers*, overloaded with officers who purchased their commissions and congregated in high society's watering spots, far

The beginnings of St. Louis. Land was cleared and buildings raised in 1764. The settlement drew Frenchmen from across the river in what was now the English Illinois Country.

BY OSCAR E. BERNINGHAUS; COLLECTION OF AUGUST A. BUSCH, JR.

from the troops they seldom if ever saw. As for the navy, the perennially weaker link that had been humiliated by England in the Seven Years' debacle, and which his foreign minister now worked feverishly to rebuild, Louis delivered himself of this opinion: "My dear Choiseul, you are as mad as your predecessors. . . . There will never be any other navies in France than those [painted by] Vernet, the artist."

Louis Quinze was by no means an absolute monarch. Under his diffident rule the traditional institutions with whom the king shared power began to break down. The center did not hold. Division had become endemic. The judicial authority of the *parlements* was challenged by administrators who claimed to

be acting in the name of the Crown, and the *parlements* in turn invaded areas of royal rule. The rise to influence of the bourgeoisie pitted them against the noble caste for political influence and offices. The Church found itself set upon by both patriotic nationalists and skeptical *philosophes*, who showered bouquets on the "enlightened" Prussian enemy Frederick at the very height of the Seven Years' War. The intellectual climate (always more meaningful in France than in other nations) was changing. It was the time of Rousseau and Voltaire, Diderot and D'Alembert. There was talk about natural law and talk critical of despotic kings and laudatory of the rights of man. That talk wasn't contained in France either; it spilled across the ocean to colonials who

Louis Quinze in all his finery. The ineffectual Bourbon played no small part in France's colossal failure in North America.

spoke English but could think in French. It even seeped farther west to a disowned people who actually spoke French. They now lived in Spanish Louisiana.

Choiseul clearly identified England as the one and only enemy of France; he considered the settlement of the Seven Years' War no more than a bad hand in an unfinished game that would be resumed later, after he had rebuilt the army and navy of France to supremacy. What part Louisiana might play in the cagey foreign minister's vision of a French-dominated future is less clear. Louisianans did not learn of their subjection to the Spanish crown until September 1764, and the news was not well received. But when a full year passed and then another without the Spanish arriving to implement the take-over, the colonials took heart. Perhaps it had been merely a rumor. Or maybe France had seen the absurdity of it all and had revoked the cession. Then hope dissolved in the spring of 1766 when a small Spanish contingent, which included the new governor, belatedly arrived in New Orleans to raise the flag of Spain.

Antonio de Ulloa was a widely respected scientist and engineer, but a poor choice to govern a colony of seething Frenchmen. First of all, he came with only ninety slovenly soldiers, an insultingly small number even if they had looked able to defend a quarter of a continent. An arrogant yet retiring man, Ulloa chose to rule through the resident French governor, Philip Aubry, ignoring the New Orleans Superior Council. The widespread grumbling became cries of outrage when Ulloa gave signs of enforcing the Spanish mercantile dogma that no trading ships were to be allowed in the colony which were not Spanish-crewed and from Spanish ports. No such vessel had ever put into Louisiana, and what items might be shipped out of New Orleans Spain could get cheaper from her own colonies. Since trade with traditional French markets would be stopped and smuggling cracked down on, the colony was left to its own devices, which weren't enough without either French or Spanish laws or subsidies. The effect was to make prisoners of the French in a commercial leper colony.

The predictable revolt came in late October of 1768, when a mob of several hundred took to the streets and the Superior

The Duc de Choiseul had to deal away Canada and Louisiana in the settlement of the Seven Years' War.

Council labeled Ulloa a usurper. The frightened Spaniard and his family boarded an anchored frigate, whose moorings were then sheared by the governed. He drifted down river through the cool bayou country and out into the warm Gulf of Mexico, no doubt dismayed by his ungrateful send-off.

Some Louisianans were jubilant after their bloodless revolt. They sent petitions and ambassadors to Versailles, begging the Crown to make them French again, since the Spaniards were obviously not concerned with their welfare and through weakness would only invite England to become their colonial masters. In the supporting pamphlets written by a few of the insurrection's more radical instigators, there was a heavy seasoning of republican thought, even the suggestion of creating an independent republic of free men governing themselves.

Choiseul wavered. England was flush against the Mississippi River and greedily looking to the west bank. And if Spain wasn't strong enough to hold it . . . .

Choiseul got advice on how to exploit the touchy situation from

*Antonio de Ulloa,
the unpopular first
governor of Spanish
Louisiana, was run
off the continent by
rebellious Frenchmen.*

the Comte d'Estaing, a heroic soldier who would later distinguish himself in the Revolutionary War on the side of the Americans. He suggested making Louisiana a quasi-republic whose integrity would be guaranteed jointly by France and Spain. This way Spain would have her precious buffer and France would see the British halted in their imperial tracks — ends achieved without further depleting the treasuries of the two hard-pressed nations. The plan was as devious as it was ingenious. While France and Spain would direct the new republic's foreign affairs, it would be allowed a domestic independence that would be a living model of the enlightened new theories of self-government, according to d'Estaing. "To give willingly what the English Parliament refuses; to copy the form of Louisiana's government from that of the freest English colony, New York, for instance, to take from the regime of each what [it] holds dearest, what is wisest, to go beyond that and make it free; to then maintain its privileges, so worthy of the envy of these new men of England and America, and so capable of making them drunk with enthusiasm." What better way could there be to hurt England than to set her colonists against her?

Choiseul listened—to the Comte de Châtelet, the French ambassador to England, who agreed with d'Estaing, and to others, who variously suggested that France train and arm the Louisianans for an attack on England's backside or that France retake Louisiana and then trade it back to Spain for her half of the island of Hispañola. But the foreign minister did not act. He could sympathize with the colonists and regret that French ships were not able to put in and trade with them. At the same time he did not dare alienate Spain by meddling in what was now her own internal affair. At all costs, the Family Compact had to be preserved for the next showdown with England, whenever it might come.

Spain, which could tolerate no incendiary examples for its extensive overseas colonies, finally took the delicate matter out of Choiseul's hands in August of 1769, when Don Alejandro O'Reilly arrived in New Orleans with more than two thousand crack Spanish troops and much ceremonial cannon fire. French opposition, never unanimous, disintegrated under this soldierly show of firmness. Governor O'Reilly (one of several talented Catholic Celts in the service of Catholic Spain) quickly arrested a dozen of the revolt's ringleaders. He sent six to prison and five to a firing squad, thus earning himself the nickname "Bloody O'Reilly." There would be no Creole republic, only the subsiding ripples of revolt-that-never-became-revolution, and adumbrations for the near future.

Choiseul went back to building the French navy and laying away arms for the next war with England. Then, in 1770, Louis XV sacked him. It was a risk every public servant, regardless of his abilities or accomplishments, took under Louis the Effete, when shadowy cliques of courtesans, bankers, and opportunists controlled the changeable destinies of France. His successor, Charles Gravier, Comte de Vergennes, was a man less inclined to war than Choiseul but one who shared his anglophobia. France would never prosper as long as England thrived. So he continued in Choiseul's tactics of sending agents into English colonies to stir up trouble while at the same time isolating England from Europe through a series of carefully crafted alliances. Ver-

No man for his revolutionary time, Louis XVI reluctantly agreed to aid the American rebels against mutual enemy England.

gennes was also of a mind with Choiseul that England, by having accepted Canada and lands east of the Mississipppi in the settlement of the Seven Years' War, had walked into a trap. Let them dilute their strength administering their new lands while their own subjects were aided in their treasonous activities.

Louis XV departed his earthly playground in 1774, and France and Vergennes inherited Louis XVI, Louis the Pathetic, rumored to be impotent in body, suspected of being the same in mind, whose unkingly virtue was to believe that war was ipso facto wrong. Vergennes himself was no hawk, but his hatred of England was too deep to let him pass up the chance to wound the enemy across the English Channel. Through Caron de Beaumarchais and his company of *Roderique Hortalez et Cie,* he began in 1776 to send arms and materiel to the transatlantic insurrectionists under a transparent cloak of neutrality. Louis XVI had balked at first. He did not think any king should be encouraging the rabble of a fellow monarch against its God-anointed master. He wasn't so dull that he didn't feel the revolutionary tremors on his own home turf. But when England started interfering with French-American shipping, even the last Louis gave in.

France initially feared that its export of arms and "volunteer officers" would come to naught, for the first year of war became a chronicle of American defeats. Then, in October of 1777, Gen. John Burgoyne, on a campaign down from Canada, surrendered his army of seven thousand to the Americans at Saratoga. It was recognized in France as a turning point, a time for the fleur-de-lys to make its real feelings known to the world, if any nation could possibly still be in the dark. Two treaties with the Americans, the Treaty of Alliance and the Treaty of Amity and Commerce, were signed by Louis XVI on February 6, 1778. Article VI of the Alliance said France would assert no claim on any of her former territories east of the Mississippi conquered by the Americans in the course of the war.

It was a curious concession for a world power to grant an infant republic whose prospects for making it out of the cradle were no better than even. Of course, signing a treaty and abiding by it are two quite different things. Yet even as a paper agreement, it says much about French thinking at the time. As revealing was the collapse of an American plan in 1778 for a joint invasion of Canada. The Americans must have had reservations about inviting erstwhile enemy France back onto the North American continent. But the French were more than content to let Canada remain English; that way, if the Americans were successful in winning their independence, there would be two mutually unfriendly English-speaking nations tied to the soil of North America. Armies would have to be stationed there, armies that could not be deployed elsewhere, say, in Europe. As for Louisiana, the former French West, there is no indication that Vergennes ever scratched his wig over it. That was a wager lost in the last game, done with, or almost. A quarter of a century off, France would recoup the amorphous territory and hold it for a brief two years, only to hazard it as a chip in another imperial game, whose players included Thomas Jefferson and Napoleon Bonaparte.

I N THE HISTORY OF THE AMERICAN WEST no people did so much for so little return as the French. They were never many, but through their daring and sometime vision they managed to make the failure of France one of heroic dimension; through them the promise had been of everything, yet the addition came up next to nothing.

Why? The problem was made epigram by John Quincy Adams when he said that France "may well conquer colonies but how can she possibly keep them?" The resolution is perhaps to be found in the French character. There was a romantic, almost messianic flavor to French colonization world-wide. While the nation of light did not really try to bring that light to North America's *peaux-rouges* (as was the case with most of her other colonial wards), she nevertheless embraced them fraternally. Humanism tempered many an official decision.

There was also a strong element of intellectual curiosity in the French New World experience. The hunger to know for knowledge's sake alone shows through the journals and letters of individual Frenchman who had come and gone back home. The idea of the western sea brought the scholarly Charlevoix to the Mississippi Valley on a fact-finding mission in 1720. Other learned gentlemen came to catalog the flora and fauna of the new lands, even to find there, they hoped, a medicinal cure for syphilis. (It was believed then, as it still is by some, that the unspeakable pox was a disease of New World origin; therefore, God in his rational wisdom would grow its cure there, too.) Exotic seeds and cuttings were collected and taken back to French gardens, with *magnolia grandiflora* a popular ornamental.

This was all very well and praiseworthy, but in the more down-to-earth determinants of colonial success, France was deficient. Her mercantile men gave up on Canada as a paying proposition too soon, and Louisiana never got the investment monies even some Frenchmen thought it deserved. Whereas British capital was daring, to be risked on an overseas venture that might bring handsome returns, French money stayed home, in the hands of conservative men looking for sure things at the Paris Bourse. Where money goes, so do people. There is a saying that Frenchmen do not emigrate, at least in any numbers, because most already believe they are living in the best of all possible worlds.

England had populated her colonies with religious dissenters seeking to start new lives and with ambitious younger sons driven from home by the laws of primogeniture. France had consciously excluded her Huguenot minority from settling in North America, and many Frenchmen who did arrive saw their surroundings as temporary—a place to make a pile (notably in the ephemeral fur trade) before heading back home to live out their years in the center of the civilized world.

In 1760 there were twice as many English subjects in the colony of New York as there were French subjects in Canada and Louisiana combined. The one-sided outcome of the Seven Years' War in North America did not violate the laws of probability. But the seeming casualness with which France forfeited her vast claims there at the Paris treaty table begs further explanation. Where insular England looked out on the world at the end of her sea lanes, continental France always looked first to her terrestrial backside, to Europe, where her future and her fortunes always converged. Forever enmeshed in its Byzantine politics, the least imperial of the three imperial rivals worried most about what was happening in Germany or Austria or Russia or Italy. When the chips were down, her own continent came first.

In the trans-Mississippi West there were no more than a few thousand Frenchmen who found themselves disowned during the reign of Louis XV. Some felt betrayed and some had voiced their bitterness and longed for a return of what were not exactly the good old days. Still others must have taken their abandonment lightly, if it troubled them at all. Among them were men six generations removed from the France of their forefathers.

They were the cutting edge of Frenchmen moving West: those who had "gone native"; those who had taken squaws; those who painted their bodies like the savages with whom they drank and danced and laughed around evening campfires in the wilderness that owned them; those who had adopted the Indians' attitudes and blustered and bellowed and whooped when they went raiding. Genealogically they were Frenchmen, but they were not of France, the France of the salons where brittle wits crafted *mots justes* that would live a year in literary circles, the France of young schemers and fops absorbed in boudoir gallantries and fortune-hunting, the France-centered France where cynical practitioners of the expedient vied with one another for social or political survival. They were no longer emissaries from France, the torchbearer of enlightened Europe. They had found their home in the trans-Mississippi shadowlands and had become the first westerners, sleeping under stars whose light could not have seemed more distant or irrelevant than the glitter of Versailles.

Unknown Lands

Explored Lands

Known Lands

The Spanish Presence – 1776

PART IV

RESURGENT SPAIN

September 17, 1776. Ceremony was the order of that late-summer day as nearly a hundred happy souls assembled near the peninsula's white cliff, hard by the bay and its guardian presidio, which were to be formally possessed, blessed, and named with all possible Spanish punctilio after San Francisco de Asís, founder of the order of the four attendant priests. The day was not randomly chosen. It had been selected, as the senior padre Fray Francisco Palóu later wrote, because it was the day "our Mother Church celebrates the impression of the stigmata of our Seraphic Father San Francisco." Nor was new ground this minute being broken. In the usual deliberate Spanish fashion, the hilly land was familiar before the formalities were arranged. For seven years Spain had known by exploration (six separate times by land and once by water) of this remarkable inlet in the north Pacific. For more than two months soldiers and settlers and priests had been living permanently on the muscular, windswept arm of earth that nearly closed the continent to the insistent Pacific chop.

In June, Lt. Don José Joaquín Moraga had led the men, women, and children out of Monterey: one sergeant, two corporals, and ten soldiers, all with their wives, plus seven families of Sonoran settlers and a handful of servants and neophytes, who herded more than two hundred head of cattle and horses that would sustain the residents and the two missionaries, Fathers Palóu and Pedro Benito Cambón. It had been a slow march north—ten days, in consideration of the children and the women carrying children unborn. At last, on June 27, they stopped near a lagoon named for Nuestra Señora de los Dolores, where they immediately built a brush shelter in which to say Mass. Hesitant, inoffensive Indians approached them with gifts of seeds and mussels, accepting in exchange beads and food but refusing milk. With growing impatience the newcomers waited for the support vessel that Moraga had watched put out from Monterey. Three pack trains had to be sent back to California's capital for food and warm clothes to protect them from the chill weather and annoying winds. To ease their worry, the officers busied themselves exploring while the settlers and soldiers set to work building huts and cutting small trees for more permanent dwellings.

On August 18 their ship had at last come in, nearly two months delayed by strong winds that had driven it south to the latitude of San Diego before it found the north in its sheets again. When the packet *San Carlos* finally dropped anchor off the white cliff, its officers and crewmen came ashore to help lay out and construct the royal buildings, the settlers' houses, and the church of the padres.

And now one month later, all was in readiness for the dedication—the presidio this day, the mission later. After Mass, bells rang and voices sang the "Te Deum." Cannons and muskets roared, and the swivel guns of the *San Carlos* bobbing in the bay echoed the salute. The noise, doubtlessly cheering to the Spaniards' ears, was terrifying to the Indians who had come to watch. They scattered like the seabirds of the nearby marshes and would not be seen in San Francisco again for many days.

The outpost at the Golden Gate was now Spanish, with Spanish cannon guarding the entrance to what Father Pedro Font had earlier described as a "marvel of nature [that] might well be called the harbor of harbors." "Indeed," Font added, reading the future, "although in my travels I saw very good sites and beautiful country, I saw none which pleased me so much as this. And I think that if it could be settled like Europe there would not be anything more beautiful in all the world, for it has the best advantages for founding in it a most beautiful city."

While westward-bound colonists not yet become Americans were spilling down the Ohio River, through the inland valleys, and around Florida by sea, bound for the Mississippi, Spain was on the move again, covering even greater ground in the trans-Mississippi West that was now hers and hers alone. Why now, after nearly two centuries of virtual stasis, had the New World's largest colonial landholder chosen to expand its already unmanageable borders? Certainly the time was right. All Europe, and some of its colonies, knew a quickening of life, felt the prod of new ideas, smelled change in the wind. Spain was a part of Europe—now more so than she had been since the sixteenth-century reign of Philip II, when she was the first of nations.

After Philip, through a succession of lackluster Hapsburg rulers, the Iberian defender of conservative Catholicism had rested on its laurels, shielding itself from the heresies and realities beyond the Pyrenees. The price of this privacy was paralysis, and no aspect of life escaped the general atrophy. Ideas were shut out by the Spanish Church lest they corrupt a people who already had their world in scholastic order. The far-from-absolute monarchs shared administrative power with a seemingly endless number of overlapping councils and commissions, which scorned dissent and made inertia a national virtue. The economy grew sick and stagnant through a system that was medieval, agrarian, pre-capitalist; for all its wealthy colonies, most of the bullion flowing into Madrid flowed right out again to buy what Spain had not bothered to learn how to make at home. The sprawling empire won by bold *conquistadores* might still be intact, but behind the facade of gilt and grandeur Spain had become an ailing second-class power.

Spain awoke slowly from its century-plus of Hapsburg sleep when a Bourbon line took the throne in 1700, and through the reigns of Philip V and Ferdinand VI, French influence began to erode the legacies of ignorance, lethargy, and poverty. Political *regalistas* were successful in breaking the stranglehold the Spanish Church had on the Spanish Crown. A governmental reorganization that introduced the French system of departmental ministers and intendants was somewhat less successful in bucking the reactionary boards and juntas whose greatest lack was initiative. There were crackdowns on the corrupt tax collectors, and lands were distributed to some peasants among the many who remained in thrall to feudal landlords.

Reform found its greatest Bourbon champion in Carlos III, who came to the Spanish throne in 1759 after an instructive term as the King of Naples and Sicily. Carlos was an energetic, resourceful, and progressive man who meant to put Spain on the maps again—the New World's as well as Europe's—by dragging his kicking and scratching charge right into the eighteenth century. He wanted social welfare at home and respect abroad, and to get them, he further stripped the Church and the councils and the landowners of privileges and powers. Under his enlightened rule, individualism and speculative thought reappeared after a long absence in Spanish life. There also appeared a small middle class and the beginnings of industrialization. Of all the gifts of the gangly, homely Bourbon monarch, none was greater than that of drawing talented and able men into his service. At the same time America had men like Franklin, Jefferson, Washington, and Hamilton, Spain had Pedro de Bolea, Count Aranda; Count Pedro Campomanes; Joseph Moniño, the Count Floridablanca; and an Italian advisor to the king and minister of foreign affairs, the Marqués de Grimaldi. They, too, were men of stature and action. But as their American contemporaries became radicals opposed to their king, the Spaniards remained conservatives who borrowed some liberal French ideas to reform existing institutions at the behest of their king. It was Carlos III and his enlightened traditionalists who directed the resurgence of Spain, a resurgence that crossed the Atlantic and was yet to leave its high-water mark on the American West.

Chapter 12

The Pacific Defense

OCCUPYING ALTA CALIFORNIA was not unheard of before 1769. The notion had been entertained off and on for more than two hundred years before Father Junípero Serra said his first Mass in San Diego. But the desire to absorb the upper lands never exceeded the trouble of battling frustrating winds and currents that made the northwestern coast difficult to reach by sea, or of subduing the Indian-menaced arid expanse of Sonora that stood as an obstacle to supplying it by land. Under Carlos III, desire overcame the elements. Spain's poor undermanned northern territories, already more than doubled in size by receipt of the French West in 1763, were shortly to be enlarged even more.

The expansion was not as blindly foolish as it may appear. Neither was it a glorious outburst of exploratory fervor to equal the conquests and *entradas* of the sixteenth century. Rather, it was conservatively motivated, true to the same obsession with defense that had caused Spain to stay in New Mexico, to occupy and reoccupy Texas, even to accept Louisiana. What had to be defended were the mines of Mexico, and in the Spanish way of thinking, the more advanced your buffers, barriers, bastions, and bulwarks, the better.

Along with the national reawakening came another seizure of the national paranoia. The latest persecutor was divined to be Russia, with whom Carlos III had renewed diplomatic relations in 1760 after a twenty-year breach. Almost immediately intelligence reports started arriving in Madrid of stepped-up Russian activity in the north Pacific. After 1762 and the accession of Empress Catherine II, the Bear was even more restless

The San Carlos *sails from La Paz in 1769. Few aboard would survive the ravages of scurvy and stagger ashore in San Diego.*

and determined to send mariners to that mysterious western coast of North America where Spain had claims by right of previous discovery and by the Treaty of Tordesillas. It was all very unsettling, as was the fear that dynamic England—now poised a river's breadth away on the east bank of the Mississippi, doing God-knew-what up Hudson Bay way, and suspiciously active in Pacific waters—was about to grab again.

Alarmists seldom had their way in the inner councils of Spanish strategy. Granted, the intentions of other nations were invariably avaricious and irreverent, yet any response should begin with scrupulous investigation and never be rash. But in the case of Alta California, it *was* rash. Moreover, and the more amazing, the decision to occupy rather than reconnoiter seems to have been the whim (or call it vision) of one man, without the prior approval of any council or board.

Just as old Spain under Carlos had its new blood, so did New Spain, and much that was new was embodied in the man Carlos sent to Mexico in 1765 as his visitador-general. José de Gálvez was an Andalusian of modest lineage who by dint of his mind, industry, and a wise marriage rose from shepherd to bureaucrat and the high esteem of his king. He was sent to Mexico with extraordinary powers, above those of the viceroy, his major responsibility being to bring fiscal reform to a colony rife with pocket-liners and thereby increase the royal revenue. In this he succeeded very well, by establishing a tobacco monopoly, revising tax procedures, and cracking down on customs-house crooks. An arrogant, volatile, yet effective man, he didn't operate by calling together juntas to debate his plans; members rubber-stamped them or they stood in danger of losing their lives. (There were ample gory examples among rebellious Indians who had opposed Gálvez; he was wont to go to church to pray to the Virgin for guidance on what to do with the miscreants and then come out and order them to be hanged.)

Gálvez was not content merely to show a quick profit on the royal books, however. He had a fascination with the empty and

Brilliant, ruthless, and for a time quite mad, José de Gálvez was architect of the Spanish occupation of Alta California.

threatened northwest called California, which, he believed, ought to be made safe for his country and liege, and mined of the precious metals that rumor and legend said were the match of Mexico's. His authority never extended to ordering its occupation, but where Gálvez's prescribed powers ended, his willfulness began, and few in New Spain had the temerity to cross the king's man. One who lacked backbone was the new viceroy, Carlos Francisco, the Marqués de Croix, who arrived in Mexico City in 1766 and was soon in the visitador's pocket.

In 1768 word reached Gálvez out of Saint Petersburg by way of Madrid and Mexico City that the Muscovites were heading south along the North American mainland. In the communication, Minister of State Grimaldi asked that precautions be taken to protect Spanish interests against Russian encroachment. But Gálvez and Croix were ahead of the home office. In January of that year Gálvez had muscled a local junta (including the viceroy, the archbishop, and the judges of the *Audencia* of Guadalajara) into entrusting him with meeting the Russian threat. When the minister's letter was forwarded to Gálvez in the spring, he was already on his way to Mexico's west coast to construct a port and shipyard at San Blas that would supply Sonora, where he had ordered Col. Domingo Elizondo to conduct a massive campaign against rebellious Seri and Pima Indians in the vicinity of Cerro Prieto. San Blas would also serve the logistical needs of Baja California, occupied for more than seventy years, and Alta California, a void he intended to fill with leather-jacketed Spanish soldiers and leather-sandaled Spanish padres. In acknowledging receipt of the letter, Gálvez wrote to Croix, mentioning that the two of them had already had "many conversations and reflections . . . concerning the supreme importance and utility of taking possession of the port of Monterey." And, bending the words of Grimaldi and Croix to suit himself, Gálvez said he would "take such measures as I deem fitting for reaching that place by land or sea."

Not since the days of Cortés had New Spain known a more energetic and decisive administrator. Gálvez catapulted himself into action. He first personally supervised the work in the steamy coastal swamps of San Blas and then, in midsummer of 1768, proceeded to Lower California to reform local government and mining and mission operations, and to organize the expeditions that were to seize Alta California. In January of 1769, Gálvez watched as the two-hundred-ton *San Carlos,* originally earmarked for Sonoran service but careened for Pacific waters, sailed out of La Paz for San Diego. On February 15 a repaired *San Antonio* departed in the wake of the *San Carlos,* followed in June by the *San José,* which never made it to Cabrillo's port but was swallowed up by the vast blue ocean called peaceful.

Meanwhile, two separate land parties started north up the arid leg of Baja California, taking from the poor former Jesuit missions all the supplies they needed to get them safely beyond what diarist Fray Juan Crespí called "the borders of heathendom." Gálvez was not present to see them off and wish them well. He had made clear what was expected of them: California was to be taken, especially Monterey, that spacious "fine harbor" so glowingly described by Sebastián Vizcaíno after his voyage of 1602–03. For his part, Gálvez the visitador had pressing business elsewhere—in Sonora, so necessary to his more grandiose plan for a separate northern command, where the campaign he had ordered against the Indians was foundering.

Tireless and forcible as he was, Gálvez had strayed beyond his compass. The hit-and-run attacks of Apaches and Seris that had kept Sonora bleeding for decades were not to be countered with conventional military tactics, as the ever-confident Gálvez discovered after assuming personal command in May. His ordeal of failures and frustrations snapped a taut mind, and by October of 1769 he had become megalomaniacal to a degree embarrassing to his aides. At various times he imagined himself the king of Prussia, Charles XII of Sweden, Montezuma, Saint Joseph . . . even God Almighty. Authoritarian even in his madness, he ordered the treasury opened to the common soldiers so they could have what they wanted. He also had a solution to his Indian problem: six hundred Guatemalan apes were to be imported, dressed in uniforms, and made to run around the Cerro Prieto, flushing the terrified redskins into the open. There were other wonders to be worked at his bidding, including the construction of a canal from Mexico City to Guaymas—no mean feat, given the gradient. Gálvez's nonplussed subordinates covered for him until he regained his senses in the spring of 1770.

It is tempting to argue that even a stark-raving-mad Gálvez was an improvement over most of the officials New Spain had known. But more germane is the fact that Gálvez was not the only energetic or ambitious man in New Spain at the time, and a goodly number of them were among those he had sent out on the California expeditions. Their names pepper Alta California's honor roll. On board the lead ship *San Carlos* was Pedro Fages, a fiery Catalonian army lieutenant who would come to love California, explore it far and wide, and serve as its civil authority for two separate terms. Commanding the second-out *San Antonio* was Juan José Pérez, the most experienced mariner Spain had available on the west coast of North America. Included in the first of the land divisions was Fray Juan Crespí, a former student of Serra who faithfully served in the California missions and acted as diarist on more than one expedition. In the second overland party were Gaspar de Portolá, the duty-driven governor of the Californias; the sturdy Sergeant Ortega, who was to make lieutenant in the new land; and foremost, the limping Fray Junípero Serra, chosen by Gálvez to be the first father-president of the new missions of California.

Counting the total loss of the *San José*, the deaths by scurvy at sea, and the desertions of numerous Indian neophytes, fewer than half of the nearly three hundred men Gálvez had sent out made the rendezvous in San Diego. Many of these were not far from death's door, sick with the disease that caused swellings, hemorrhaging of the mucous membranes, and loss of teeth. Nevertheless, their instructions were to find and fortify Monterey, and Portolá was determined to do it. It was agreed that Pérez should take the *San Antonio* back to San Blas for provisions, leaving the crewless *San Carlos* tethered in San Diego Bay. Father Serra and a couple of others would stay in San Diego to tend the many sick, while Portolá would take the rest of "that small company of persons, or rather say skeletons," north to Monterey.

On July 14, 1769, Portolá, Fages, Captain Fernando de Rivera y Moncada, Ortega, diarists Crespí and Miguel Costansó, and fifty-seven others began a six-month journey attended by what

The party of duty-driven Gaspar de Portolá discovers San Francisco Bay late in 1769. (Painting by Arthur F. Mathews, 1896.)

the commander later described as the "greatest hardships and difficulties" in that "ungracious country." Monterey proved an enormous disappointment and a cruel deception. Although some of the landforms roughly conformed to Vizcaíno's description, Portolá could discern no wonderful harbor. So he marched his tired men farther north until they were finally halted by the uncrossable bay of San Francisco (which they mistakenly thought to be an estuary of Drake's Bay). The grim scurvy had reappeared among the starving explorers, and on the return to San Diego they had to slaughter one gaunt mule a day, to which, Portolá allowed, "we shut our eyes and fell [upon] like hungry lions."

The commander had hoped to see Pérez and the *San Antonio* when he brought his mule-eaters back to San Diego on January 24, 1770. Instead he found Serra burying more dead, and a few scarecrow invalids stripped to near-nakedness by the thieving Indians. Portolá and Serra had good reason to give up on the gamble, but they stuck it out, eating fish and fowl and what meager supplements the Indians would trade them for the clothes they wore, until, on the evening of March 22, the sails of the *San Antonio* appeared on the western horizon with its priceless cargo of corn, flour, and rice. The dutiful Portolá then ordered Pérez on to Monterey, where he was to be joined by a second land expedition to formally reclaim Vizcaíno's discovery for Spain.

Only sixteen men accompanied the governor on the second fatiguing hike to the unprotected bay, which was ruefully acknowledged to be Monterey. There, on June 3, 1770, the party did not fail "to erect a fort and defend the port from the atrocities of the Russians who were about to invade us, as was to be inferred from the terms of the instructions." His mission accomplished, Portolá turned over command to Pedro Fages and sailed back to Mexico for a military promotion and, eventually, the governorship of Puebla. A few years later he expressed his condolences for those "unhappy Spaniards" he had left behind — the twenty-odd men who manned the cannons of the presidio and the mission at Monterey, and the slab-sided diehards at San Diego. Their miseries were as numerous as the fleas of the countryside, but they did not include any "Russian atrocities."

The news that the establishments had not gone under was

Carlos III was a most capable king, though he may not look it in this candid portrait by Goya.

celebrated in Mexico City with a special Mass, bell-ringing, and flag-waving. José de Gálvez and Viceroy Croix could toast a job, if not complete, at least begun, though neither would long direct the destinies of their creation. In September of 1771, Croix left his post and was replaced by Antonio María Bucareli y Ursua, the most widely respected viceroy New Spain was to have. Gálvez, his mind back on track, stayed a while longer to counsel the new viceroy before returning to Spain in February 1772, there to become a member of the Council of Indies and, in 1776, its chief minister, the first officer of Spain's New World.

Bucareli did not have the flair of some of the new breed of Bourbon appointees, but he was a most capable administrator — intelligent, modest, rational — and what he lacked in originality he made up for in thoroughness. After assuming office, he heard new rumors of Russian and English threats to the Crown's claims, and he knew the key to the Pacific defense was Alta California, Gálvez's little foundling which the new viceroy would adopt as if his own. From 1772 through 1776, he never flagged in attending to the needs of California.

The year of decision was 1773. In the previous fall Bucareli had received Father Serra in Mexico City and listened to his requests for supplies and craftsmen and settlers. He also heard Serra's grievances against Governor Fages and his rough troops. More than personality differences divided the two. There was the ever-present friction of church interest and state interest, and a division in authority between missionary and military man that had both the father-president and the governor reporting to the viceroy. Among Serra's complaints was an uprising at the newly-founded Mission San Gabriel precipitated by a soldier who lassoed the local chief's wife as a prelude to gaining her affections, then killed the chief when he opposed him. Bucareli sided with Serra and in 1773 ordered Fages to be replaced by Rivera as the civil authority in Alta California — not a good choice, the future should show.

In April mere rumors turned to royal orders when Minister of the Indies, the Count of Arriaga, instructed Bucareli to strengthen the California posts. The viceroy already knew the extent of California's weaknesses. No more than about sixty soldiers and eleven priests were in the far province. Given their callings, they were ignorant of how to sow the earth to their benefit, and the previous year they had just escaped starvation on a diet of bear meat. If Russian or English ambition should bring either nation to the Pacific shores, that suffering handful of Spaniards could hardly offer resistance.

The answer to Bucareli's dilemma was to be found in the Old Testament's injunction to increase. That was impossible with the "perpetual and involuntary celibacy" of Spain's soldiers and the voluntary celibacy of her priests. What was clearly needed were families — settlers, not occupiers — women as well as men who would see to their own regeneration and, perforce, know a little something about farming. Such settlers could not be entrusted to the sea, as experience had made plain. Nor could they easily be recruited from Baja California. Gálvez's initial colonization had already laid a "heavy hand" on the peninsula, to borrow Serra's words. There weren't even very many mules left there for pack trips north, and as experience had again shown, there wasn't enough water or forage along the way to see them through. The only other way was across the bloodied earth of Sonora, where, in fact, the situation had improved. Whereas Gálvez's original policy of massive and quarterless war had failed, the wholesale granting of amnesties and bribes got better results. Then, too, chance and lust had come to the rescue. On one punitive expedition in 1771, a squad of Spaniards found no enemies but did discover a rich show of placer gold at Cieneguilla, not far from Altar. A rush followed. There was nothing like gold to make a man hold his ground against Indian attacks.

Bucareli came to another crucial decision in 1773. The year before he had read with interest an artless letter from an unknown officer on the northern frontier. The young man, a captain at Tubac, believed he could get to Alta California from Sonora and was requesting the authority of the viceroy and the assistance of a priest of mutual acquaintance, one Fray Francisco Garcés. The petitioner was even willing to assume the expense of the expedition himself. Bucareli submitted the proposal to a junta for evaluation. Not bad but not now, was the collective opinion. Then the

Spain's answer to France's frontier heroes was the remarkable Anza. (Conjectural, artist unknown.)

plight of the Alta Californians worsened, and after Serra and others enthusiastically endorsed the officer's plan, Bucareli convened another junta to consider it. This time, on September 9, 1773, it gave its blessing.

The captain in question was Juan Bautista de Anza, Spain's stolid, methodical answer to the flamboyant French heroes of western pioneering. Anza's father and grandfather had both been respected officers in Sonora before him, and now, in his thirty-eighth year, the veteran fighter of Apaches and Seris stood to advance his career and see something of the world unseen. A reading of Anza's reports reveals a hyper-competent, no-nonsense officer of quiet dignity whose qualities went beyond those that make a superior soldier. Indeed, he passed that litmus test that often separates the efficient military man from the true leader of men: he was respected and beloved by the lowliest who served under him.

Anza left Tubac on January 9, 1774, with thirty-three men, including the intrepid Father Garcés, bearing orders to discover a new way to Monterey without alienating any of the native peoples whose lands he crossed. Marauding Apaches ran off his horses before he was far out and forced him to round up some "stacks of bones" as replacements, but this misfortune was soon offset by encountering an Indian named Sebastian Tarabal, a runaway from Mission San Gabriel who had just made the very desert crossing Anza was about to embark on and agreed to help show him the way.

Nothing untoward happened to the party before reaching the Yuma Indians at the junction of the Gila and Colorado rivers, and there — contrary to what he'd been led to expect — Anza was hospitably received by Chief Salvador Palma, whose people helped the Spaniards ford the Red River of the West. Anza was bogged down in the dune country west of modern Yuma, the shifting sands sucking strength from his stock, which began dying off in what soon became a trackless maze even for Tarabal. So Anza wisely returned to the Yumas, then detoured south around the soft sands and set a course for the northwest that took him over the mountains and down to the delighted priests of San Gabriel. He went on to Monterey and was back in Tubac on May 26. Not only could it be done, this crossing of the desert, but it had been done with ease. The man who did it was immediately promoted to lieutenant colonel.

Bucareli was even more delighted than the lonely Franciscan friars who had welcomed Anza in the not-yet-promising land. Though Rivera had in the meanwhile escorted a small party of settlers to Alta California from its nether peninsula, the Anza route was clearly shorter and better. After meeting him in Mexico City in the latter part of 1774, Bucareli knew he had his man in Anza. Now let him really prove himself. Let him usher a group of impoverished families from Sinaloa to help populate the great void to the north.

Anza was for it. He wisely suggested paying the colonists in goods rather than specie that could be gambled away. The viceroy agreed, providing farm implements, seeds, clothing, and all that the settlers would need. On October 23, 1775, Anza led the large party out of Tubac with nearly a thousand hooved animals in herd. When he brought his charges to the Yumas, he also brought

Anza's second California expedition convoyed much-needed settlers from Sonora to Monterey in 1775–76. (Painting by Cal Peters.)

the most civil greetings from King Carlos III and personal raiment for Salvador Palma. The grateful chief assisted the Spaniards through an arduous crossing of the swollen Colorado, the non-swimmer Garcés being borne on the shoulders of three Yuma men. After a few days of recuperation on the California side, they were off again to traverse a December desert, which was abnormally cold. They stopped at a waterless camp in creosote-dotted Borrego Valley, made a sleet-numbing climb over the San Jacinto Mountains, then descended the mild coastal slope into San Gabriel, arriving on January 4, 1776.

The journey had been little short of miraculous. Anza started the expedition with 240 souls, 115 of them children, and finished with 244. To compensate for the single death on the way, a woman lost in childbirth the first stop out, he had personally played midwife to the arrival of a number of squalling infants. The only one to fault the soldier's conduct was his companion, Father Font, who was scandalized by Anza's periodic distribution of aguardiente, which resulted in drunkenness and hangovers to be worked out on the next morning's trail. Perhaps Anza knew his flock better than the fastidious Font. This was no coterie of elegant Castilians, but mostly unlettered half-breeds, hardy frontier men and women who probably wouldn't have lasted the rigors of a long, dry trail if they had been other than what they were.

Anza found no rest in San Gabriel. Upon his coming, word arrived of an Indian uprising in San Diego in which Spanish lives had been lost. With seventeen of his soldiers, Anza joined the sullen Rivera in a march south to relieve the beleaguered station. The rebellious Indians were quickly cowed by the show of force—force excessively applied by Rivera who, among other atrocities, killed a neophyte in the sanctuary of the mission church, for which Serra saw that he was excommunicated. Anza retraced his way to San Gabriel and immediately turned to the business that brought him, leading half of the hungry settlers on a month's trek to Monterey.

Rivera resented this outsider. He was not only a challenge to the acting governor's authority, but he was intent on carrying out Bucareli's instructions to establish a presidio at San Francisco, instructions Rivera disagreed with and did his best to ob-

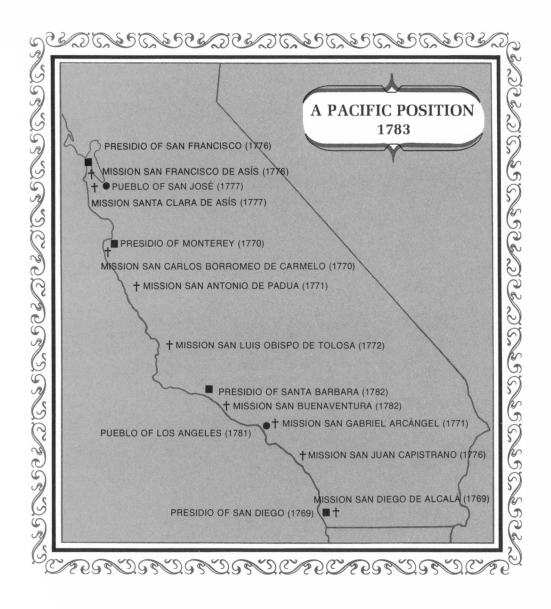

A PACIFIC POSITION
1783

PRESIDIO OF SAN FRANCISCO (1776)

MISSION SAN FRANCISCO DE ASÍS (1776)

PUEBLO OF SAN JOSÉ (1777)

MISSION SANTA CLARA DE ASÍS (1777)

PRESIDIO OF MONTEREY (1770)

MISSION SAN CARLOS BORROMEO DE CARMELO (1770)

MISSION SAN ANTONIO DE PADUA (1771)

MISSION SAN LUIS OBISPO DE TOLOSA (1772)

PRESIDIO OF SANTA BARBARA (1782)

MISSION SAN BUENAVENTURA (1782)

MISSION SAN GABRIEL ARCÁNGEL (1771)

PUEBLO OF LOS ANGELES (1781)

MISSION SAN JUAN CAPISTRANO (1776)

MISSION SAN DIEGO DE ALCALÁ (1769)

PRESIDIO OF SAN DIEGO (1769)

struct. He had already explored the peninsula himself and spoken disparagingly of its climate and cited an overextension of forces for not settling it per orders.

Anza left a sickbed in Monterey to examine the future site of San Francisco for himself, and what he saw in March pleased him as it had not Rivera. He thoroughly explored the area, designating where both the presidio and the mission were to be built, before turning south again in April. Rivera slighted Anza by not keeping a meeting in San Luis Obispo that the former had arranged; in San Gabriel the pair communicated only by letter. Then the man from Sonora, his task completed, left for home over the trail he had opened.

No doubt feeling heat from the viceroy, and glad to be rid of a rival, Rivera did a turnabout and ordered Lieutenant Moraga to effect the long overdue occupation of San Francisco. Rivera could not get along with Anza (or anyone else for that matter) and Serra could not get along with Fages or Rivera or the later-to-come Governor Felipe de Neve, who in turn had a hatred of Anza. If New Spain had long suffered from too many minnows in a lake, now resurgent, she suffered from too many big fish in a common pond, and the waters got muddied with their thrashing.

The year 1776 was no exception. While delegates from the thirteen English colonies were organizing departments of a new Continental Congress, a drastic organizational change was ordered in the administration of northern New Spain that would have far-reaching consequences. What had been suggested in 1768 by Visitador-General Gálvez and Viceroy de Croix became policy under Gálvez the Minister of the Indies: New Mexico, Texas, Coahuila, Nueva Vizcaya, Sonora-Sinaloa, and the two Californias were removed from viceregal control as the *Provincias Internas* and placed under a commandant-general in whom civil and military authority were vested. The man appointed to the new post in August of the decisive year was Teodoro de Croix, nephew of the Marqués de Croix. Teodoro was effective where he knew his ground, and the ground he knew was Texas, New Mexico, and Coahuila, where he spent most of his years on the northern frontier fighting Indians. He had never been to California and never would go, and California was to know his far-from-benign neglect.

Bucareli could not have been pleased with the arrangement. Even before the reorganization he had asked to be allowed to resign and live out his last years in Spain. But he was too valuable where he was, so the ever-obedient civil servant continued on as viceroy, divested of authority over California but still responsible for supplying it out of San Blas. This he did faithfully. But supplies were not enough for those few on the oak-dotted hills of the Pacific slope—not enough to make healthy what was now the younger Croix's stepchild.

If the occupation of California was a strategic success, in most other respects it had been a failure. Far from being a producer of revenue as Gálvez had intended, Alta California had drained Spain of half a million pesos by the end of 1773. The Spaniards holding it were still pitifully few and malnourished, and Serra and his zealous Franciscans had baptized fewer than a thousand children and aged into their religion. Had it been worth it? The question was probably not even asked by the on-site padres and soldiers. They were not reflective thinkers but day-by-day problem solvers. Certainly Serra did not look back. On November 1, 1776, he refounded the swallow-favored Mission San Juan Capistrano, and on January 12 of the following year Mission Santa Clara.

Felipe de Neve, who replaced Rivera as the civil authority and received his instructions on Christmas Eve of 1776, was likewise a doer. He immediately asked Bucareli for at least three more missions between San Gabriel and San Luis Obispo, and three pueblos as well. For this, and to strengthen existing posts, he needed reinforcements and soldiers and settlers and supplies. Bucareli forwarded the requests to Croix for action, along with advice for establishing civilizing missions among the Yumas, who controlled California's lifeline. The commandant-general tried to toss the hot potato back to the viceroy, then juggled it for a time, then more or less let it drop.

Alta California was virtually on its own, run by the industrious Neve, who as the secular authority pushed secular expansion. In November of 1777 he took some residents of Monterey and San Francisco to start a pueblo on the banks of the Guadalupe River; it was called San José. In September of 1781, Neve ordered forty-four men, women, and children, newly arrived from Sonora, to found El Pueblo de la Reyna de los Angeles near the banks of the Los Angeles River about seven miles seaward of Mission San Gabriel. There might have been many more pueblos were it not for the bloody uprising of the Yuma Indians on July 17, 1781. Among the on-the-spot casualties was the expendable Rivera, who had brought the last contingent of settlers, and the innocent

Mission San Carlos Borromeo de Carmelo, based on a 1792 drawing by one of English explorer George Vancouver's crew.

Garcés. The much greater, never-to-be-recovered loss was Anza's overland trail. California was orphaned, its growth stunted. Yet it did not perish, thanks to the able men already there. When Neve left to succeed Croix as commandant-general of the Interior Provinces in 1782, Pedro Fages returned for another stint as governor. After Father Serra's death at Mission San Borromeo de Carmelo in 1784, his Franciscan friend and colleague, Father Fermín Lasuén, took over and in his steady, workmanlike way added nine missions to the nine founded by Serra.

At the close of the American Revolution, Spain's California was not yet the storied one of swollen cattle herds, of ranches and romances and fandangos and bull-bear matches. Fewer than one thousand non-Indians were scattered along the Pacific littoral, from San Francisco south, growing crops, raising stock, and showing neophytes how to do the same for the greater glory of God and the redemption of their souls. Their number was just enough to hold their own against Indian opposition, enough to assure California of a Spanish future.

HE SPINE OF BAJA CALIFORNIA tapers to barren humps at
Cabo San Lucas, ending in a row of sinking sharktoothed
islets awash with sea foam. These days cruise ships pass close to
the cape returning from California-to-Mexico pleasure runs, part-
ing schools of cavorting dolphins and sending flying fish skimming
the blue, as the captain gives his passengers a look at the land-
mark. The passage is now a breeze, a piece of cake. In the 1770s
it was a horror for the most experienced master of sail. It meant a
long reach west before wind and water even permitted a climb
through the northern latitudes and a doubling back to find the
landmass of North America. Spanish sailors had learned that
lesson as early as the sixteenth century, but it had to be relearned
in the eighteenth century when worried Spain launched its northwestern defense. Bases in Alta California were not enough; the
Russians had to be found and their mischief monitored. Since the
Tsarina's men had not reached Monterey (had not even come
within a thousand sea miles of it, really), that meant going beyond Alta California to find them.

That distrust of Russian intentions overlapped a similar distrust of England, about to chase again that long-lived phantom,
the Northwest Passage. Historically, Spain's attitude toward the
Strait of Anian had wavered from doubt that it was there to fear
that it might actually be found. More than once her mariners had
been discouraged from seeking it; if it were found, the word was
bound to leak out and the world (or all nations with navies) would
be intruding into an ocean that was thought to be rightly Spain's.
But now the time had come to move — move by sea above California and perhaps settle, if not the land itself, then at least the
question of who was there and what they were doing.

So it was that in 1774 the frigate *Santiago* left San Blas carrying secret orders from Viceroy Bucareli, which were not to be
opened until after the vessel had reached and departed Monterey. The skipper of the eighty-two-foot craft was Juan José
Pérez, the man who did so much to supply the California colony.
Bucareli's sealed instructions were opened at the appointed time
and Pérez found his mission described in great detail. The *Santiago* was to proceed to at least sixty degrees and then hug the
coast on its southerly return, Pérez to go ashore, claim sites

worthy of settlement, and plant there a cross and cairn. If other Europeans were encountered, they should be observed from a distance and not provoked by hostile action. The Indians met on land were to be treated most kindly, queried about other visitors, and won over with presents. In that way would the king's purpose be served, Bucareli stated, not only in "conserving these vast domains, but also in trying to augment them insofar as possible, by means of new discoveries in unknown areas, so that numerous Indian inhabitants drawn into the sweet, soft desirable vassalage of His Majesty may be bathed in the light of the Gospel by means of spiritual conquest."

Pérez finally got the wind he wanted on June 14, and with eighty-five aboard, among them Fathers Crespí and Tomás de la Peña, the *Santiago* tried the untried, with fear and scurvy to be their constant companions. Land was seen in mid-July near the present boundary between Alaska and Canada. Pérez was a cautious man—perhaps too cautious, his detractors have suggested. He met Indians off the Queen Charlotte Islands and, while becalmed, carried on a frigate-to-canoe trade without accepting the outwardly friendly tribe's invitation to come ashore. He had his suspicions, and neither his need for fresh water nor his instructions to erect his nation's markers was enough for him to send a landing party ashore.

The *Santiago* drifted slowly south around shoals and through fog blankets off the uncharted shore, finally anchoring off the west coast of Vancouver Island on August 8 at the mouth of an inlet. Indians appeared in dugout canoes, singing and scattering feathers on the water in welcome. The following day they bartered sea-otter skins for abalone shells and metal of any kind. The inlet was Nootka Sound, the first sighting of the place where history would rendezvous within a sailor's lifetime, when Spain and England would go just to the brink of war for control of it.

Pérez tried once to send a party ashore, but as soon as a launch had been put over the side, the wind kicked up and both craft were imperiled. The anchor chain on the *Santiago* had to be cut to keep her from going aground and the launch was quickly retrieved. There was no further attempt to put men on land for the duration of the cold, damp voyage, which had Pérez and his ship staying well out from shore. The giant white shape of Mount Olympus was observed and named the Sierra Nevada de Santa Rosalía, but otherwise knowledge of landmarks and coastal conformation remained slight.

Bucareli commended Pérez after his return to San Blas, but the viceroy was in fact deeply disappointed that so little had been accomplished and that no Spaniard had touched land and formally claimed it in the name of his king. Immediately he ordered another voyage and Pérez to accompany it, though as second-in-command to Bruno de Heceta aboard the same *Santiago*. Heceta was only twenty-four years old, one of six young naval officers just transferred to San Blas. The *Santiago* was to have an escort ship this time, the *Sonora,* a pitifully small schooner not much over thirty feet long that was not designed for ocean-crossing. Its command was given to another of the young officers, Juan de Ayala. A third, Miguel Manrique, was put in charge of the *San Carlos*, a supply ship that would accompany the explorers as far as Monterey. Finally, there was Juan Francisco de la Bodega y Quadra, a thirty-two-year-old Peruvian Creole who had been slighted when the assignments were passed out but, when faced with at least a year of boring shore duty, volunteered to serve as second officer aboard the tiny *Sonora*. Spain was fortunate that he did.

Bucareli's plan for a second expedition to the Northwest coast was approved in Madrid, where worries about the Russians were greater than before. In fact, the Ministry of the Indies sent instructions back to the viceroy that carried a new militancy: if the explorers discovered intruders on Spain's coast, they were to order them out, even if that required force. By the time Bucareli received the communication, however, the three ships had sailed away.

The start was not auspicious. A few days out, Captain Manrique went mad. This called for a shift of personnel, with Ayala transferred to the *San Carlos* and Bodega y Quadra, the bold young man with the sea fever, succeeding to the command of the *Sonora*. The next three months were slow going in buffeting seas, the explorers proceeding north of Monterey and landing at Trinidad in California's redwood country to take formal possession. Then, in mid-July, the *Santiago* and the *Sonora* crowded the coast of Washington south of the Quinault River, where they planted a wooden cross on shore and engaged in trade with Indians who seemed amiable. But when Quadra sent a party to shore in a small boat for wood and water, the six-man crew was ambushed and hacked to pieces, their boat reduced to kindling by the natives, who stripped it of every iron nail. War canoes soon surrounded the *Sonora*, retreating only when Quadra's swivel guns opened fire and killed six of his besiegers.

Quadra was hot for revenge, but Heceta and other officers aboard the *Santiago* overruled him. Their present anchorage was unsafe, neither vessel was deemed very seaworthy, and too many men were down with the scurvy. What ought to be seriously considered, went the gist of continuing parleys, was an early return to San Blas, even though the viceroy's instructions to reach sixty-five degrees had not been carried out. Quadra and his twenty-one-year-old pilot, Francisco Antonio Mourelle de la Rúa, bowed to the general will—or seemed to. On the night of July 29, at sea, Quadra and Mourelle conveniently got their cramped little schooner lost from the *Santiago*.

Heceta feared for those aboard the *Sonora*, and after sailing briefly north beyond the Strait of Juan de Fuca (which he did not see), he also feared for his own crew, who begged him to turn back. This he did on August 11. On his downcoast run he spied a great inlet between two headlands, which he tried vainly to enter against a strong adverse current. He called it Bahía de la Asunción de Nuestra Señora and supposed it to be the fabled Strait of Juan de Fuca, not rediscovered because its latitude had been erroneously calculated. In fact, it was the Columbia River. After charting the mouth as best he could from outside its protective sandbar, he hurried south to Monterey with his invalids.

Meanwhile Quadra and Mourelle were hard at their heroics. Short of water, short of food, short of space, short of able-bodied hands—short, in short, of everything save young men's courage—they pitched on through the North Pacific. On August 15 they made landfall in Alaska at fifty-seven degrees, not far from present-day Sitka. The king no longer lacked for standard-planters. Quadra and Mourelle took possession near Salisbury

Spain began exploring the Northwest Coast in 1774 and continued doing so into the 1790s. (Drawing ascribed to José Cardero, 1792.)

Sound and again on Prince of Wales Island at the sound they named Bucareli. Though scurvy did its worst, Quadra did not hurry home, but explored the maze of islands and passages as thoroughly as the debilitated state of his crew allowed, fighting dangerous winds and storms that forced him and Mourelle alternately to man the bilge pump to keep their ship afloat. By October 7, when the *Sonora* finally reached Monterey Bay, Quadra and Mourelle were so sick with scurvy they had to be carried ashore. Few stories in the annals of man versus sea match Quadra's for drama and determination. But in keeping with the Spanish penchant for secrecy, it was drama and determination kept under wraps. Well, almost.

Bucareli was pleased and reassured that Russians were not breathing down Spanish necks, and 1775 (thanks mainly to Quadra) had been a very good year on the Pacific coast. Every year, however, will turn and bring another. The following one, 1776, was a supra-national year of decision—particularly for those nations with a stake in the New World. Eternal vigilance, internationally applied, was the price of imperialism, no less for Spain than for England or France. The year that found England at war with her American offspring also saw Spain distracted by colonial upheaval in North Africa and armed confrontation with Portugal in South America over the Río de la Plata.

Bucareli must be excused his lack of interest in the north-of-California coast where no dragons had been found. Carlos' own attention was diverted elsewhere to flash points all over the world. But not so for the newly named minister of the Indies, José de Gálvez, he of the once-warped mind, he of the first Pacific gamble, he of the great obsession with California and a new empire north of Mexico. Gálvez was frantic over reports from England that Capt. James Cook, renowned for his two previous voyages that had revealed to the world secrets of the Southern Hemisphere, was about to sail again, this time for the north Pacific coast, where among other duties he would seek the Northwest Passage. Cook wasn't exactly sailing into the great unknown, either. In spite of Spanish secrecy, summaries of the explorations of 1774 and 1775 had been published in London in 1776; Cook even had access to a copy of Mourelle's journal.

Early in 1776, Gálvez drafted new orders for Bucareli: commanders of Pacific outposts were to be alerted of Cook's intentions. There would be no comfort shown the Englishman; every obstacle short of military force was to be put in his way. In May, after reading Heceta's report of sighting that large waterway between forty-six and forty-seven degrees—the Northwest Passage?—he sent instructions that a third voyage was to be immediately readied to intercept Cook and arrest him as a trespasser.

Bucareli was uncooperative. In March he had been told by the foreign office to give his undivided attention to the Caribbean, where for more than a century England had been nibbling away at Spanish possessions. Now that England was sending more men and ships to her rebellious colonies, more trouble could be expected in a sea that had long been congenial to pirates. A bottom-line man, Bucareli could show that the first two expeditions had cost the Crown more than fifty thousand pesos. Besides, no Russians had been found close to California, which should be the first line of defense anyway. As for intercepting Cook in the north Pacific, that was about as likely of success as finding a single sardine in the sea.

Throughout the summer of 1776, while Cook headed toward the Cape of Good Hope, Gálvez and Bucareli wrangled by trans-oceanic communiqué. The angry Gálvez insisted on another voyage. Bucareli pledged obedience but pointed out that such a project was really no longer in his jurisdiction, belonging now to Teodoro de Croix, the commandant-general of the brand-new *Provincias Internas*, of which the minister himself had been architect. Gálvez was not one to appreciate being hoisted by his own petard. Even more annoying was the general agreement of his sovereign, Carlos III, with the opinion of Bucareli.

In the end Gálvez got his way. In February of 1779, six months after Cook had finished charting the Northwest coast, two frigates built in Peru specifically for the purpose sailed out of San Blas. The flagship *Princesa* was commanded by Lt. Ignacio de Arteaga and the *Favorita* was captained by Bodega y Quadra, the man whose daring had not gone unremembered. The month of May saw them to Bucareli Sound, where they explored the convoluted waterways of the archipelago and had their numbers thinned by a sudden outbreak of an unknown disease. In summer Arteaga took the claim of Spain far north into Prince William Sound and onto the Kenai Peninsula just below modern Anchorage. Storms and scurvy made grim visitations before the two vessels turned about for home.

Even without their having met the celebrated Captain Cook, it was a creditable feat, but one that events made strangely anticlimactic. While Arteaga plowed icy waters among misted forested islands, Spain had gone to war with England, reluctantly on the side of the American insurgents but as an ally only of France, where her Bourbon sister and *realpolitik* had led her. Now she had to face matters more urgent than how two of her mariners had done on so remote a coast, such as defending herself against possible aggression in the Gulf of Mexico, the Philippines, South America, and the Mississippi Valley, and prosecuting an old war against a different enemy in, of all places, New Mexico.

Chapter 13

A State of
Less Than Enchantment

SPAIN KNEW NEW MEXICO a quarter-millennium before fraternal blood was spilled on Concord Bridge. Coronado passed through in 1540, before there was a Saint Augustine in Florida, and in 1598 Oñate brought countrymen bent on staying in its valleys, before there was a Jamestown in Virginia. Physically, it looked like a place for Spaniards — horse country with bare earth colors and a bowl of blue sky, not unlike Estremadura, the birthplace of so many of the first *conquistadores*. But by the middle of the eighteenth century, the Spanish salient that protruded upstream along the Rio Grande del Norte was tired, as creaky as a *carreta* wheel, old without ever really having been young. In truth, the quality of life on the river was never much from the first, and the quality of those living beside it had become progressively worse with the passing of years.

In the beginning, when the province was given its name grand with promise, it was thought that New Mexico would prosper from mining. But nature decreed otherwise. No gold or silver meant no influx of the industrious greedy, who, with all the woes they can bring, at least give life and vitality to a place. Manufacturing did not develop either, because there was little to manufacture from, no one with the skills to manufacture well, and too few with money to buy finished goods anyway. Rather, the mainstays of the far-northern colony became subsistence agriculture, the raising of cattle and sheep, and trade with the nomadic Indians. No wonder those in New Spain with talents chose to apply them elsewhere.

What collected in the eddy that was New Mexico was mostly

Coronado didn't find the riches he was after in New Mexico in 1540.
Neither did other Spaniards in the next 282 years.

human sediment. Caste-conscious Spaniards, who had names for every class, could not count among the permanent settlers many *peninsulares,* the elite born in Spain. There were not even very many Creoles, full Spaniards in blood but, to their misfortune, born on the wrong side of the Atlantic. Instead, the bulk of the "Spanish" population was made up of *géntes de razón,* mixed bloods redeemed by some Iberian genetic heritage and a patina of civilization, and *genízaros,* domesticated non-Pueblo Indians, who often as not ended up serving in their masters' fields and ranchos without pay. In 1754, Governor Pedro Fermín de Mendinueta described the inhabitants of New Mexico as "perverse, poor and lazy," and forty years later Governor Fernando de la Concha saw concealed behind their "simulated appearance of ignorance and rusticity . . . the most refined malice." On the other hand, the governed did not have much to say in praise of their corrupt officials, as countless court records show, nor for the outposts where life had dropped them and where they passed the time of day in idling, gambling, quarreling, cheating the Indians and one another.

Poverty was the central fact of life in New Mexico in 1776, as it always had been. The cultivation of corn and beans and squash depended upon natural rainfall, which the seasons sometimes brought and sometimes did not. Herds of livestock grazing over the open countryside were subject to unpredictable and indefensible Indian theft. No wonder that in the eighteenth century the Indians of the pueblos were excused from paying tribute to the Crown, required elsewhere throughout New Spain, and sales taxes, which ran as high as 14 percent in Mexico, were apparently dispensed with in the province for the very sound reason that nothing could be taken from nothing. New Mexicans were constantly in debt to the far sharper traders of Chihuahua, and when coin moved from south to north, it was in open subsidy paid to soldiers and priests and governors by the king. Antonio de Bonilla, adjutant-inspector of presidios, reported in 1776 that from the time of the conquest "the conservation of New Mexico has cost, and continues to cost, the king many hundreds of thousands of pesos." (The figure ran to about fifty thousand per year.) But Bonilla was one of those men who strain to see silver linings.

"Although this province has not contributed so much as the rest of the Interior Provinces in fattening the royal treasury," he continued in gross understatement, "the glories of seeing reduced a part of the numerous heathen which live in these territories are worthy of attention." The Church might have wished that "part" was larger than it was.

Spaniards on both sides of the Atlantic took their religion and its evangelical obligations deeply and personally. Whereas Frenchmen on the whole had a greater tolerance for the varieties of religious experience, and Englishmen could seldom accommodate red men in their protestant denominations and sects, the Spanish church was in every way catholic, open to all. A baptized soul thereby saved from hell or limbo and sent on to the company of God was something every good Spaniard could rejoice in. Missionaries were not sent out into heathendom purely as a cover for imperial gain. Indeed, when the whole New Mexico experience began to sour, when it became clear in the early seventeenth century that the distant province would never pay its way, the Spanish monarchy assumed it as a perpetual financial liability primarily in order to minister to those Indians who had already been converted and to gather yet others into the fold.

It didn't turn out quite that way. The Faith in this instance did not go forward toward more and better, but did the reverse, in the direction of disillusionment and less. After the reconquest the authority of the priests was curbed, while that of civil officials was enhanced, until the Indians began going to the clergy with their complaints against venal authorities and settlers, though not for spiritual aid. The missionaries found themselves guardians of Indian rights and property, but not of their souls, which belonged to other gods, false gods. Despair and corruption appeared more and more among those anointed with the holy oil.

When Bishop Pedro Tamarón y Romeral made the long journey from Durango to New Mexico on an inspection tour in 1760, he was greatly saddened. Only a few of the twenty-eight resident Franciscan friars had learned the languages of the Indians they were ministering to, though some had been there for over twenty years, and the Spanish understood by the Indians was the wrong Spanish. "In trade and temporal business where profit is involved, the Indians and Spaniards understand each other completely," the Bishop wrote. "This does not extend to the spiritual realm with regard to which they display tepidity and indifference." Tamarón was reluctant to bestow the sacrament of confirmation on insincere Indians who confessed their sins only on their death-beds and then through an interpreter—if one happened to be at hand. A gentle and politic man far advanced in years, Tamarón nevertheless left the priests firm orders to learn the local languages and so better perform the religious offices for which their king was paying them three hundred pesos a year.

Sixteen years later, in the spring of 1776, Father Francisco Atanasio Domínguez arrived in New Mexico as commissary-visitor with instructions to make his own exhaustive evaluation of the spiritual and economic situation. A younger man than Tamarón (he was then in his mid-thirties) and accustomed to the civilized life and amenities of his native Mexico City, Domínguez was appalled by virtually everything he saw except the land-scape. Of Santa Fe he said, "Its appearance, design, arrangement, and plan do not correspond to its status as a villa nor to the very beautiful plain on which it lies, for it is like a rough stone set in fine metal." To him the capital looked "mournful" because the houses were all made of earth and "not adorned by any artifice of brush or construction." In sum, he said, "it lacks everything." He found the Indians mostly destitute and pitiful (those in Galisteo had neither horse nor cow and were reduced to toasting old shoes for food), and nearly everywhere the natives showed a "repugnance and resistance to the most Christian acts," which they performed only "under compulsion." The state of religion was most distressing in the pueblos of Taos and Picuris, where the Indians were so "notably opposed to Christianity that they cannot even look at Christian things." The visitor unhappily concluded that the Indians were as much neophytes as they had been at the time of the conquest.

Domínguez' appraisal of the settlers was no higher. Some had sunk so low as to become hired servants for the Indians. He singled out Albuquerque for special censure, charging its citizens "to abandon the lethargy and laziness in which they have lived up to now, to the loss of many graces and indulgences." As for the twenty priests responsible for the more than eighteen thousand nominally Christian souls in the territory, he found some good and loving men laboring under almost impossible conditions. But he also found some bad apples, "insolent and haughty of spirit," who were more interested in advancing their temporal fortunes in illicit trade and consorting with "notorious women of evil." In the five missions of El Paso, particularly, he discovered a veritable orchard of drunkards living in sin and swindling the Indians.

Domínguez' detailed report could not have surprised Spanish churchmen or civil authorities. The deteriorating situation in the north was already well known. As bad as things had been, they were made worse in the quarter-century after 1750 by an Indian problem unparalleled in two hundred years of Spanish experience. The Comanches had driven the Apaches off the southern plains, driven them south into the arid lands east and west of the Rio Grande, where the hunted became hunters, with stolen Spanish horses and stolen Spanish weapons hunting more of the same. To the east, in Texas, the Comanches drove the Lipan Apaches temporarily into the arms of the Spanish, to whom they appealed for help at midcentury. Coming as it did at a time when Spain was in an expansive mood in the provinces that make up modern-day Texas, and coupled with new reports of silver deposits in Apache territory, the Spanish responded by establishing a new mission and fort on the San Sabá River in 1757. The mission never drew a single permanent Apache resident within its walls, but it did arouse the anger of the Comanches, who struck it, first in 1758 and again in early 1759, burning the fort and massacring some thirty souls. A punitive army led by Col. Diego Ortiz Parrilla sought the enemy as far north as the Red River, where on October 7, 1759, an entrenched and French-armed force of Wichitas roundly defeated and routed the Spanish troops.

The Comanches themselves came raiding farther south and west when they had a mind to, and after 1763, when English traders replaced the French as suppliers of firearms, they came with awful regularity. The depredations in New Mexico didn't stop there. Amerindian hunters had instincts that drew them to the stricken, and in 1775 restive Navajos to the west joined in the raiding.

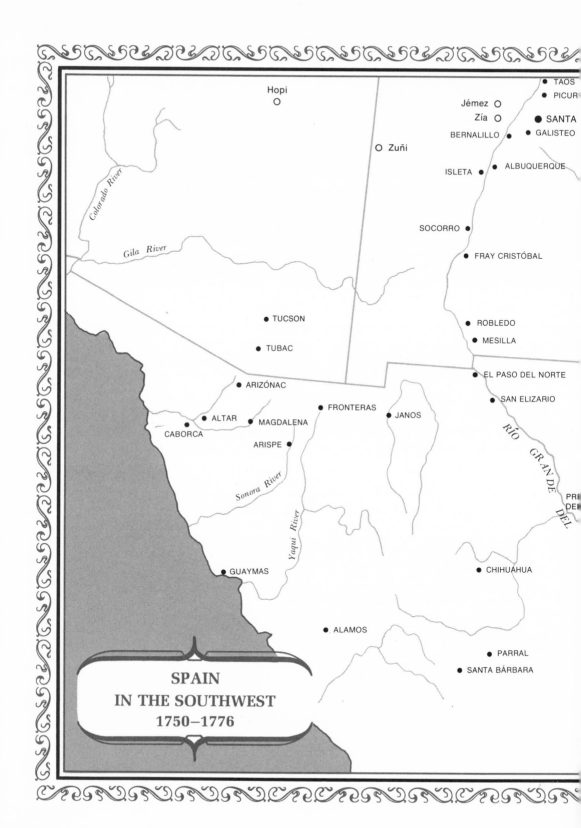

Hopi
O

Jémez O
Zía O
BERNALILLO ●
● TAOS
● PICUR
● SANTA
● GALISTEO

O Zuñi

ISLETA ●
● ALBUQUERQUE

Colorado River

Gila River

SOCORRO ●

● FRAY CRISTÓBAL

● TUCSON

● TUBAC

● ROBLEDO

● MESILLA

● ARIZÓNAC

● FRONTERAS

● ALTAR
CABORCA ●
● MAGDALENA

● JANOS

● EL PASO DEL NORTE

● SAN ELIZARIO

ARISPE ●

RÍO GRANDE DEL

PRI
DE

Sonora River

Yaqui River

● GUAYMAS

● CHIHUAHUA

● ALAMOS

● PARRAL
● SANTA BÁRBARA

**SPAIN
IN THE SOUTHWEST
1750–1776**

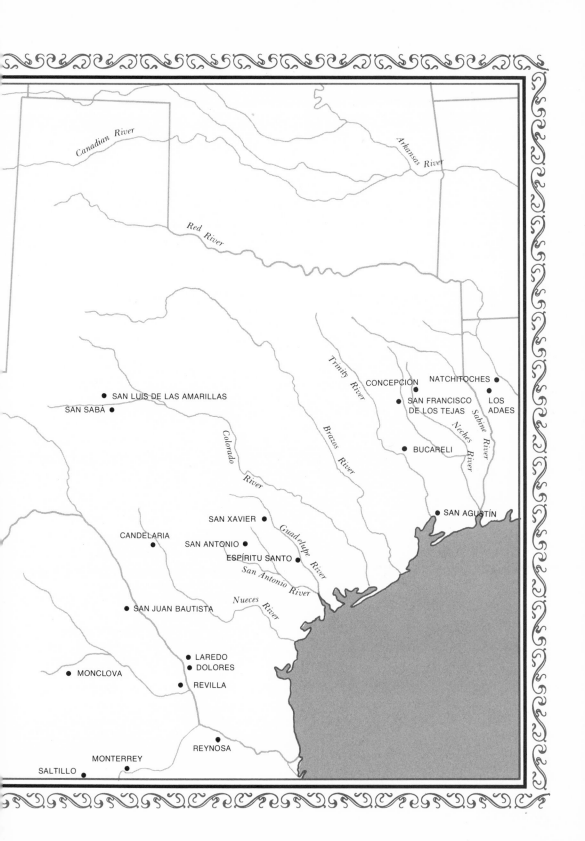

The whole weary enterprise in the north might wisely have been abandoned if Spaniards hadn't been made of tougher stuff. Centuries of unbroken medieval war between Moor and Christian had left a unique people on the Iberian peninsula. Though they were remarkably uniform in how they worshiped their God and obeyed their king, their character remained a mix rather than a reconciliation of opposites. In them extremes coexisted: pride and poverty, cruelty and compassion, idealism and cynicism, the highest purpose and the meanest means. Within them was a diamond-hard residue, a genius for enduring, for staying, and when finally gone, leaving behind with half-Spaniards, or quarter-Spaniards, or sixteenth-Spaniards, or those simply touched by the Spaniards' culture, an altered view of the world that was basic and lasting.

Even if New Mexico had not been a complete failure financially and a bad investment spiritually, even if holding onto the northern satellite had not been deemed indispensable to the defense of Mexico, Spaniards had another reason for staying after 1759. That was new hope born of the Bourbon influence out of France, where the new enlightened thinkers believed all was possible if men but applied their God-given reason. The optimism infected more than a few men on New Spain's northern borderlands. In 1776, at the height of the Indian agony, when the outlook was downright dismal, there was expansion — less in territory held than in furthering Spanish knowledge of the West. The Spanish presence in Arizona inched north that year when a presidio was moved from Tubac to Tucson, deeper into tormented lands controlled by the Gila Apaches. The settlement owed its existence to the indefatigable Father Garcés, who had laid out a pueblo there but was now gone, spending the first half of 1776 on an incredible walk of the West no white man had seen, from the San Joaquin Valley of California through southern Nevada and deep into northern Arizona. The inhospitable Hopis prevented Garcés from making it all the way east to New Mexico, but the resourceful Franciscan did manage to send on to Santa Fe the news that the journey could be made, and that only the maize farmers of the mesa tops were an obstacle to a land link between California and New Mexico.

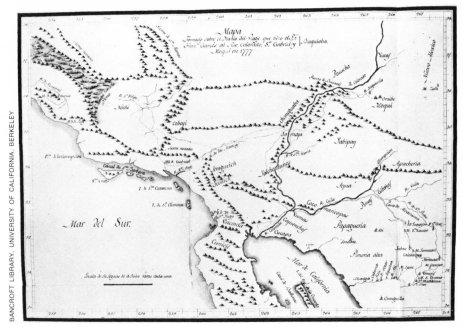

In 1776 and 1777, the fearless and tireless Father Garcés walked a vast stretch of the Southwest no white man had seen.

Garcés' letter, written in the waning hours of July 3, was studied with the greatest interest by Father Silvestre Vélez de Escalante in Santa Fe. Not the part about the contrariness of the Hopis — he, too, had visited them the previous summer and knew their ways — but the fact that Garcés had actually come from California, the destination of his own travel plans.

In 1775, doubtless on orders from Viceroy Bucareli, the New Mexican governor, Mendinueta, had asked the twenty-six-year-old priest for a report on how Monterey might be reached from New Mexico. Then, in the following spring, Father Francisco Atanasio Domínguez, the same citified newcomer who had made such a frank appraisal of the status of New Mexico's churchmen, invited Escalante to come from his mission among the Zuñis to Santa Fe, there to discuss the possibility of an expedition to California.

An air of conspiracy hangs about the two clerics. The father-visitor had been instructed to learn what he could about a connection between the interior and Monterey, and to forward any

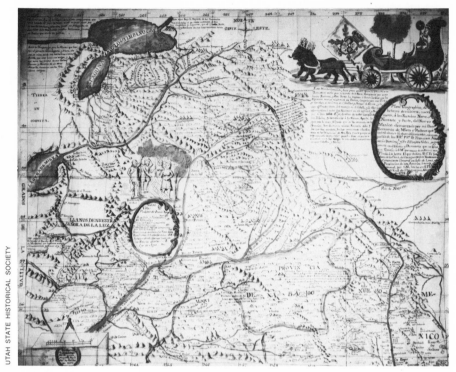

Modern Utah got feature treatment from Bernardo de Miera y Pacheco, a member of the Dominguez-Escalante expedition of 1776.

information on the work of Father Garcés, information that would please "both Majesties" (God and king). But, not unlike José de Gálvez before them, the young and eager pair seem to have taken matters into their own hands by actually doing as they did, which was to pick up and go west, not due west through Hopiland, but northwest in a great circle over lands theretofore unknown. Ironically, their departure had been set for July 4, but a Comanche campaign and then illness delayed them until July 29, when the two set out with eight other men on a fifteen-hundred-mile trek that would take them up western Colorado, across northern Utah below the Uinta Range, down onto the flats west of the Wasatch to Lake Utah, south into the juniper and sandstone country, across the deep gorge of the Colorado, and finally home. They returned to Santa Fe on January 2, 1777, alive and happy.

It was a stupefying achievement, equaled in courage and luck that year only by the lonely wanderer of the wastelands, Fray

Garcés. They did not make it to Monterey, however. In fact, the letters of Domínguez and Escalante reveal that neither thought they would ever reach California, their ostensible destination. For them the adventure was the thing, seeing new lands and new peoples, and—inevitably, overridingly—saving heathen souls. Prior to leaving, Domínguez wrote of hoping to reach the Cosninas (Havasupais) in the Colorado River canyon "in order to strengthen the people of this nation in their good intentions of becoming Christians."

Governor Mendinueta, who generously supplied the travelers with the horses and livestock and other necessities for their trip, expressed doubts about the wisdom of such enthusiasm. "If there are not enough fathers for those already conquered," he inquired, "how can there be any for those that may be newly conquered?" The pair might have answered the governor by recounting Christ's parable in which the shepherd left the ninety and nine alone in the desert to go after the one that was lost. For, upon returning, the two gloried in having brought back a single Indian convert, who joined them near Utah Lake. No, optimism had not vanished on the Spanish frontier in that year of war—that year of America's war in the East and Spain's war in the West.

A VETERAN SOLDIER, the Marqués de Rubí, was sent to the crumbling rim of nominal Christendom in 1776 by the king to report on its full breadth, from Texas to Sonora. He did not expect to see Russians or Englishmen lurking in the mesquite, but redskins, yes. Those he found everywhere, and they were on the warpath. Papagos were raiding the presidio of Tubac, then Spain's farthest penetration into modern Arizona. Far to the east, in Texas, Comanches and the tribes Spaniards referred to as the Indians of the North (Wichitas, Tonkawas) threatened to link up and destroy the sparsely populated and sadly strung out Spanish outposts. Everywhere in between—west, south, and east of New Mexico—there were Apaches: Lipans, Jicarillas, Faraones, and Natagés east of the Rio Grande; Mescaleros to the south on both sides of the river; and Gila Apaches in western New Mexico and Arizona.

Never had the Apaches been stronger or more brazen, now riding the best horses the Spanish bred, running off and feasting on Spanish cattle, and raiding Spanish supply convoys. So successful were these parasites that they threatened to do in their hosts. Father Garcés saw God's hand in the Apache mayhem. He thought the savages had been sent as a scourge to punish Spaniards for "having lapsed from that primal fervor of conquest of souls for God." If so, then the Spaniards compounded their sin of neglect by openly resisting God's vengeance; all-out war was to be waged on the Apache bands, just as soon as the Spaniards were strong enough to wage it.

Rubí reported his findings in 1769 at a council of war in Mexico City. Some military commanders on the northern frontier were cowards, he said, while others were peculators, cheating the men they led of their meager salaries. The troops were in rags, poorly armed, their morale as low as the spirit of the sorry nags the Apaches had left them. Rubí recommended reform and new martial blood in what was strictly a military solution. The defensive perimeter had to be shortened to conform with what he called the "real" rather than the "imaginary" frontier. Some posts should be abandoned, especially in Texas, where there was no longer a French danger and where his Most Catholic Majesty's subjects were too widely spaced for their own good. New presidios should be built to make taut the chain.

The recommendations were accepted and incorporated into the Royal Regulation of 1772, and Viceroy Bucareli appointed Don Hugo O'Conor commander-inspector to implement them. Four missions and two presidios were abandoned in east Texas, and their inhabitants forced to move to San Antonio which was, like New Mexico, an outpost north of the fifteen presidios that were to anchor a defensive barrier stretching from Espíritu Santo on the shores of south Texas to Altar in northwest Sonora. The uprooted Spanish-speaking settlers were so dissatisfied with San Antonio that the following year, under their leader Gil Ybaro, several hundred were permitted to return north and found the town of Bucareli on the Trinity River. In a few years the Comanches had them on the move again, not back south toward the presidial line as the *Reglamento* would have it, but east, off the open plains and into the protective fringe of the woodlands where, in the spring of 1779, the settlement of Nacagdoches took permanent root.

Meanwhile, General O'Conor had arrived on the northern frontier with more arms and reinforcements, and was immediately initiated into the shadow world of Apache war. For four years he campaigned almost continuously against the fugitive bands, absorbing some defeats but also achieving his share of victories — successful overall in rolling the Apaches back to the north. By 1776 conditions had become almost tolerable in Sonora and Nueva Vizcaya, but in New Mexico, where many of the Apaches had retreated and where the Comanches were as active as ever, there was no surcease from the violence. O'Conor, in failing health from the effort, asked to be relieved and given a less demanding post. In this he was rewarded with the governorship of Guatemala for his sterling — if incomplete — services.

The month after England's thirteen colonies formally declared their separateness, Spain's Council of the Indies separated the northern territories from the rest of New Spain into the *Provincias Internas,* a single governmental department under Commandant-General Teodoro de Croix, who was to attend first to reducing the hostile Indians. The French-born Caballero de Croix had served under his uncle in various capacities while the Marqués, Gálvez's pawn, was viceroy, had gone back to Spain with the senior de Croix in 1772, and now in 1776 had returned to the Americas to head up the Interior Provinces.

It was inevitable that Bucareli and Croix would grate on one another and clash as often as they did. The viceroy had just lost control of almost half of New Spain to the forty-six-year-old soldier with friends in high places. Croix, for his part, returned coolness with coolness during his nine-month "familiarization" stay in Mexico City; and even before he reached the lands he would administer, reports from the various governors of the northern provinces convinced him that he needed two thousand additional troops to carry out the king's will on the fifteen hundred miles of bleeding frontier. The fiscally conservative Bucareli was appalled at the six-hundred-thousand-peso annual cost of meeting such a request and brushed him off, saying he would probably change his mind once he actually inspected the provinces that O'Conor had tamed.

The ill feeling between viceroy and commandant-general then went into its long-distance phase. When Croix finally went north and made a partial inspection, he decided even two thousand troops would be inadequate. There were Indian uprisings — some completely out of hand — in all the provinces. He forwarded horrendous casualty and damage reports, adding that the governments were inept and corrupt, and that the military officers had sunk into "all the abominable excesses of drunkenness, luxury, gambling, and greed," setting bad examples for the troops. O'Conor, he clearly implied, had lied about the true state of things in the north.

An attack on O'Conor, Bucareli's appointee, made Bucareli burn, but with Croix regularly airing his dissatisfactions to Gálvez, the viceroy could only defend O'Conor by pointing out that some officers presently serving under Croix had filed encouraging reports. The commandant-general persisted in his demands for the two thousand troops which, even if they had been available, would never be sent. In February of 1779, Croix received a royal order to cease offensive war against the Indians and to try to win them over by gentle means. It was a heavy blow to Croix, followed by another in September when Gálvez informed him that Spain had gone to war with England. That meant no reinforcements, ever, and that he was on his own.

In truth, Croix had been pretty much on his own all along. Apparently a natural complainer but nonetheless an able officer, he had had his local successes along the impossible boundary that knew few silences between war whoops. He had organized local militias among the settlers to provide a defensive capability that would free presidial regulars for offensive war. As early as November of 1777, while Englishmen digested the debacle of Burgoyne at Saratoga, Croix convened the first of a series of war councils with his frontier commanders, mainly to decide what to do about Texas and New Mexico. Out of them evolved the resurrection of a divide-and-conquer policy. The Apache bands were to be split up — the Lipans to be warred on and the Mescaleros to be wooed with concessions. Where possible, the Spaniards were to ally themselves with the Comanches, who were themselves to be isolated from other tribes and set against the Apaches, their natural prey. The stratagem worked especially well in Texas, largely due to a man who was not a Spaniard. With their acquisition of Louisiana in 1763, Spain inherited from France Athanase de Mézières, an officer at Natchitoches, old post of the dashing St. Denis. Indeed, de Mézières had once been married to a daughter of St. Denis and, like his father-in-law, was Paris-born, educated, cultivated, successful as a trader, and possessed of that same uncanny skill in dealing with the red man. Through diplomacy, de Mézières had kept the Wichitas and Tonkawas from joining in permanent alliance with the Comanches. To Croix he was an invaluable adviser who refined the scheme to break the power of the eastern Apaches. In 1779, about to be rewarded for his services with the governorship of Texas, de Mézières died after being thrown from a horse.

Early that same year the Comanches assaulted the Lipans mercilessly, costing the Apaches three hundred of their number and sending the survivors to the Spanish, begging peace and protection. The Lipan humiliation was a windfall for the Spaniards in their plan to break the power of the eastern Apaches. How the Comanches could succeed where the Spaniards often failed points up not only the fighting heart and skill of the Comanches but the lack of the same for the Spaniards. The effectiveness of the common soldier or leather-jacket—so called for his multi-ply leather coat used as armor against Indian arrows—had long been disadvantaged by inferior weapons and poor training. Croix managed to improve both. But troops had to be led, and well led, by officers of courage and imagination; on the northern frontier there was a dearth of these, too. Fortunately for Spain, Croix had at least one—Juan Bautista de Anza.

After Anza's second trip to California in 1776, Croix put him in command of the armed forces in his native Sonora. In the year he was there, he gave further proof of his abilities by putting down a Seri uprising. Clearly a comer, in 1778 he became civil and military governor of New Mexico, appointed to that office by the king, not by Croix. Anza immediately inspected all the villages in the province, redesigning fortifications and laying plans to

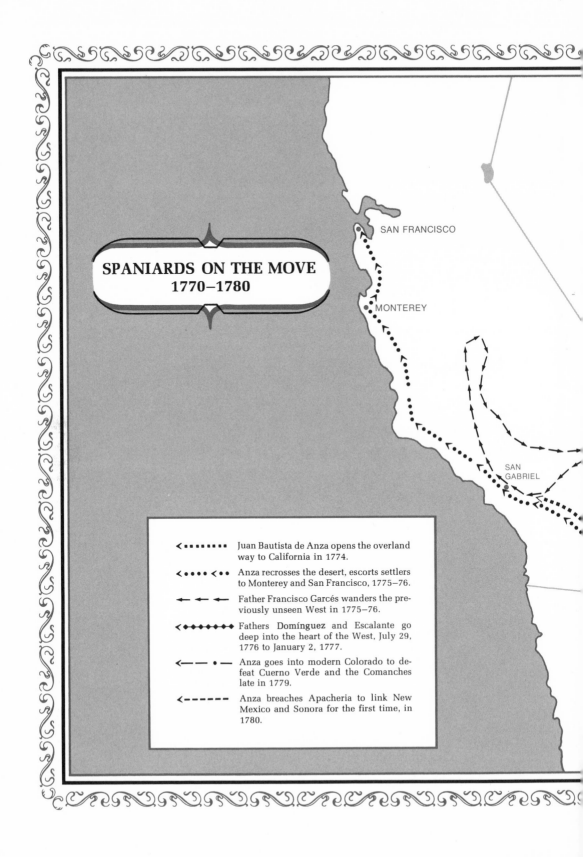

SPANIARDS ON THE MOVE
1770–1780

SAN FRANCISCO

MONTEREY

SAN
GABRIEL

< ••••••• Juan Bautista de Anza opens the overland
way to California in 1774.

< •••• < •• Anza recrosses the desert, escorts settlers
to Monterey and San Francisco, 1775–76.

← — ← — Father Francisco Garcés wanders the previously unseen West in 1775–76.

< ◆◆◆◆◆◆◆ Fathers Domínguez and Escalante go
deep into the heart of the West, July 29,
1776 to January 2, 1777.

← — • — Anza goes into modern Colorado to defeat Cuerno Verde and the Comanches
late in 1779.

< ------ Anza breaches Apacheria to link New
Mexico and Sonora for the first time, in
1780.

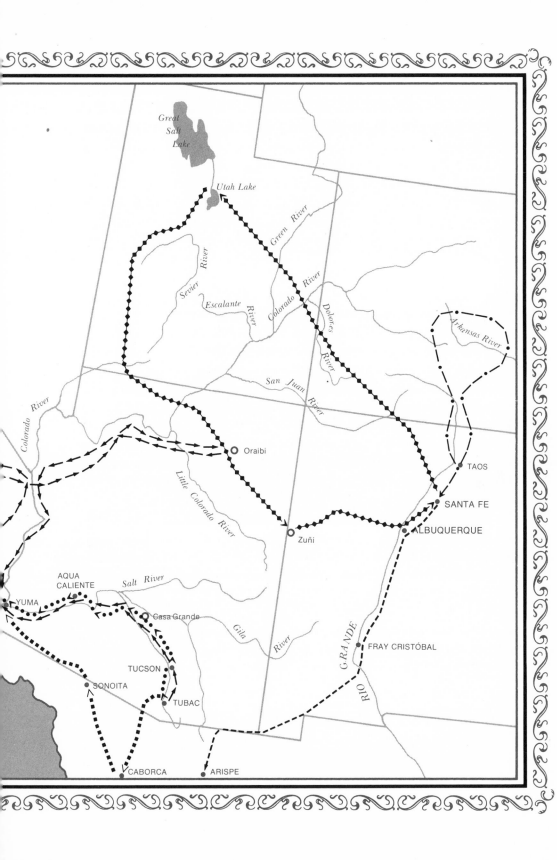

bring the settlers into defensible pueblos from their scattered fields, where they were easy marks for Apache and Comanche raiding parties. In his resettlement plan the governor was frustrated by the recalcitrant ranchers, who complained to Croix and anybody else who would listen.

In little else did Anza fail. In the cold August of 1779, he led six hundred soldiers, militia, and Indian auxiliaries north out of Taos on a little-used trail through Colorado's Front Range, to seek and destroy the notorious Comanche chief Cuerno Verde and his band, who had been terrorizing New Mexico for ten years from their Colorado sanctuary. Near modern Pueblo, Anza's force trapped the Comanches and killed Green Horn and his finest warriors, to the great relief of northern New Mexico.

Anza was more than an efficient bloodletter. The following September he went on a mission of mercy to the Hopis, decimated by drought on their mesa tops, and offered food and escort to those who wished to resettle along the Rio Grande. A few months later the proven pathfinder was off on a delayed project—that of finding a trail from New Mexico to Sonora, with hopes of stimulating needed trade between the two provinces and breaching the rugged homeland of the fierce Gila Apaches, the most exasperating of all the Apache bands. Anza left Santa Fe on November 9, 1780, and struck southwest from the Rio Grande at Fray Cristobal over the desolate crags of the Mimbres and Chiricahua mountains, entering Arizpe in mid-December. Though the route would not be the one later profitably used by the Spaniards through the Gila Apache country, Anza had again shown himself master of the possible.

While Anza served Croix well, the reverse was not to be true. Modest successes attended Croix's management of the frontier from Texas to Sonora. But the commandant-general had not gone farther west, and that was where disaster occurred. The Yuma revolt in the summer of 1781 permanently cut the land link to California. Croix needed a scapegoat and found it in Anza, who, so Croix said, had misled his superior by representing the Yumas as peaceable. Actually, Anza had warned that the tribe required tender treatment, and Father Garcés, who had stayed on at the Colorado River settlement to his martyrdom, repeatedly advised Croix of the deteriorating situation. Curiously, a few months before Croix blackened Anza's reputation, he had authored a report praising Anza for his exceptional gifts. No matter. Anza's career was capped. In 1783, the same year the other general war on the North American continent was officially concluded in Paris, Croix was promoted to viceroy of Peru. Succeeding him as commandant-general was the governor of the Californias, Felipe de Neve, who joined in the slander of Anza and meant to have him relieved of his command and his service record cleansed of honors. Neve, however, died a few months after taking the post. Anza stayed on as New Mexico's governor for another four years, weaning the Navajos away from an alliance with the Gila Apaches and cementing treaties with the redoubtable Comanches that gave New Mexico a generation of relative peace and prosperity. Then he returned to Sonora with the lesser title of provisional commander of the province's armed forces and captain of the presidio of Tucson. He died within the year.

The urge is always strong to scratch the past for good guys and bad guys, for successes and failures, for those who made history and those who were unmade by it. New Spain, resurgent at the time of the American Revolution, presents many opportunities. Some historians have singled out Croix for blame in the eventual failure of Spain on its far northern frontier; others, in defense of Croix, have disparaged Bucareli as a visionless bureaucrat. If responsibility must fall somewhere, perhaps it should be on the forceful brow of José de Gálvez, the ambitious man who in following his own lights expanded and thereby lessened Spain's already weak hold on the American West. Yet Gálvez was a man of vision. He made things happen. Those who write histories tend to remember movers and shakers kindly, even though external events often intrude on a man's dream and reshape it into a nightmare.

Croix, in reporting on Texas in 1781, said that not until the present Anglo-American war "is concluded can anything advantageous be done to keep the greedy nations of the Indians of the North content and quiet." The commandant-general correctly recognized the other war as the key event. He simply mis-identified those "greedy nations."

Chapter 14

The Wonder Worker

José was not the only Gálvez. He had a brother Matías, whom he appointed viceroy of New Spain in 1783. Matías had a son, and José a nephew, named Bernardo, a promising young officer who had performed well against the Apaches in Nueva Vizcaya and Texas from 1770 to 1772. Bernardo had as a friend Teodoro de Croix, nephew of the Marqués de Croix, Bucareli's predecessor as viceroy, who was, not surprisingly, a close friend of José de Gálvez. They made a cozy little circle—also a talented circle. Perhaps the most talented of them all was Bernardo. At least Americans would have reasons for remembering him with fond gratitude, just as the English were to rue the day the gallant Spaniard set foot on Louisiana soil. That fateful day belonged to the year 1776.

Schooled in military science in France and several times wounded on Spain's battlefields, Bernardo de Gálvez rose rocket-like in the Spanish army, from the rank of lieutenant during his Apache-fighting days to lieutenant colonel when he arrived in New Orleans to command colonial forces. He remained in that duty only a matter of months before, not yet thirty years of age, he was appointed governor-general of the colony, to succeed the retiring Luís de Unzaga y Amezaga. Having sponsors in high places had brought him far and fast; now he would have to draw on his own gifts in ruling fewer than twenty thousand non-Spaniards in a land without limits, while destiny's war raged east of the Mississippi River.

Actually, when Gálvez took over, the internal situation in Spanish Louisiana was almost stable, much improved from the years immediately after the 1763 treaty transfer. Some have said France was glad to pitch its useless burden off onto the back of poor-cousin Spain, and that the Spaniards—nobody's fools—had accepted it with the greatest reluctance, as a sop for the loss of their Floridas to England in the Seven Years' War. Why else the four-year hiatus from paper possession to token occupation?

More likely Spain did want western Louisiana, if for no other reason than to appease her inexhaustible national passion for defense—for one more layer of savage land with savage peoples betwixt the enemy and Mexico. Whatever the reason, the passing of the baton had been fumbled, to the embarrassment of both Spain and France. There was that nasty episode in 1768 when the latecomer Ulloa tactlessly provoked a rebellion that saw the governor and his shabby soldiers unceremoniously evicted. Then the following year General Alejandro O'Reilly arrived in New Orleans in force and promptly arrested the readers of radical European writers and had five of the ringleaders shot, thus ending a minority dream of a Creole republic.

Things turned around and got better after that. O'Reilly relaxed his hold on the governed and treated them justly; the plaintive strummings of the guitar became as pleasing as they were familiar to French ears on sultry summer evenings in old New Orleans. O'Reilly left in 1770, and the mantle of authority fell on the shoulders of the aging colonial administrator, Unzaga. Almost immediately Unzaga faced a war scare brought on by a Spanish-English dispute over the Falkland Islands in the far south Atlantic. British contingency plans called for an assault on Spanish Louisiana should war come, and Unzaga was ordered to defend the territory if he could; otherwise he should retreat to Mexico. But the danger passed, and the even-tempered governor got down to the business he was best at—conciliation. He was careful not to tread on French customs and perquisites. He cushioned the rage of hard-shelled Spanish priests, who found the French Capuchins voluptuaries remiss in even their basic religious duties. He looked the other way from the contraband trade—much of it with English ships anchored in the Mississippi—that was against Spanish law but vital to the colony's survival, cracking down on only the most flagrant offenders. Under Unzaga's

General Alejandro O'Reilly crushed the French radicals and their dream of making Louisiana a Creole republic.

efficient direction and tolerance the colony began to grow and to prosper as it never had under France.

Then came the split—the breakaway of the colonies to the east from their mother country, the dreaded England. An observation Unzaga had made four years earlier took on the weight of prophecy: "If they [Anglos of either political bent] possess these establishments fronting on the kingdom of Mexico without any other interposition than the Mississippi River, they will introduce to us commerce in time of peace and armies in time of war." Months before the Americans declared independence, the rebels informed Spain that it would be in her interest to support them. Otherwise, went the none-too-subtle blackmail, England would swallow the West. Unzaga found the official posture of "perfect neutrality" (which was, in fact, nakedly imperfect) uncomfortable, especially after conspiring in the secret shipment of gunpowder to the Americans. He was an old man who wanted out. He wanted to go home to Malaga, and his request was granted.

Enter Bernardo de Gálvez, a younger man and a soldier, better suited to meeting the danger from the east. Gálvez picked up where Unzaga left off in supplying the rebels. It was a role Spain as a nation assumed with little enthusiasm, committed to the task because France willed it and because Protestants divided were preferable to Protestants united. Carlos and his ministers were under no illusions. England had to be stopped; but the Americans were themselves noisesome upstarts setting the worst possible example for Spain's own awakening New World colonists. When all was said and resaid, Spain was faced with a Hobson's choice. At least that was how it looked at the royal quarters in Aránjuez, Carlos' retreat south of Madrid. Bernardo, though, did not see it that way. Youthful and attuned to the new enlightened thinking, his partiality to the Americans exceeded the dictates of cold-blooded statecraft.

Among Bernardo's instructions upon assuming office was to welcome non-Spaniards into his lands, provided they were Catholic and would swear allegiance to Spain. The motive was transparent. Spain lacked settlers and she had druthers for those who could be trusted. After the French ceded eastern Louisiana to England in 1763, Anglos began pouring into the lower river valley in intimidating numbers, many settling themselves flush against the Mississippi, where the commercial action was. What did Louisianans have facing them on the west side of the river? A census taken by Bernardo de Gálvez in 1777 gave statistical dimension to the Spanish dilemma: there were no more than eighteen thousand non-Indian subjects in all of Spanish Louisiana. Half of these were black slaves, and most of the rest were Frenchmen, whose loyalty—true for the moment—could not be considered absolute. Moreover, nearly half that total were not west of the Mississippi at all, but in the district of New Orleans; and those actually on the west side were clustered on the German and Acadian coast, around Natchitoches and in the neighborhood of Saint Louis, leaving gaping holes through which Anglos could penetrate at their pleasure.

The Anglo pleasure was indistinguishable from business, and it was trade that pulled them through the porous barrier and into the West. Early on they followed the lead of dead Frenchmen up the Missouri and the Arkansas. They even traded on the Neches and Trinity rivers, well behind Spanish lines, deep in the heart of Texas. Yet the greatest incursions took place in the far north, out of Prairie du Chien and along the Des Moines and Minnesota

Friend to Americans, foe to Englishmen, Bernardo de Gálvez brought glory to Spain during the Revolutionary War.

rivers, the fur-trade country that Englishmen, building on a French base but with superior merchandise and business acumen, quickly dominated. It wasn't as though the Spaniards were ignorant of what was taking place in the Upper Mississippi, or its ramifications. The first governor, the short-termed Ulloa, sent Capt. Don Francisco Ríu upriver in 1767 to build a fort at the mouth of the Missouri with a twofold purpose in mind: "The first is to keep the savages in friendship and alliance with the colony; the other is to prevent the neighboring English from entering the territories and domains of his majesty." The distinction was somewhat arbitrary, or at least the two purposes merged. Indians bartering with the English would not be predisposed to ally themselves with Spain in a showdown—at least not in the Iowa country and north, where Spaniards were conspicuously absent.

The failure to keep Englishmen out of the north derived from a shortage of money and manpower, not from any flaws in policy. In assuming control of western Louisiana, Spain showed herself enlightened and flexible. Instead of employing her traditional methods of Indian control—the mission and the presidio—she followed the French lead in distributing presents among the tribes to hold their favor. Indeed, she made heavy use of existing French contacts in trading with the red man and appointed able Frenchmen to high posts within the new colonial administration as well—moves that were to reap many dividends. Spain had never been much of a beaver-buying nation. But by licensing and encouraging the peltry trade in the vicinity of Saint Louis and Sainte Geneviève, she maintained her influence along the Missouri River as far as the Platte. That in itself was mighty far for a nation that was never at home on the Great Plains, a nation that throughout the Revolutionary War actually retired from the interior lands opened by the French.

When Bernardo de Gálvez took over, the neglect of the French West became more, not less. The governor-general spent the bulk of his time in New Orleans. A cultured man, he doubtlessly gave in to its charms—charms peculiar still to cities that are French. Certainly he surrendered to the charms of a beautiful French widow, whom he married, to the great joy of his French subjects. But aside from the comforts it offered, Bernardo had the best of reasons for being there: it was the colonial capital and it was closest to the danger—not even removed from it by so much as the Mississippi's breadth. As guardians of the West, Gálvez and his officers at the upriver posts crowding the river faced east, absorbed in the unfolding drama that would in a few years drag them into it. The morning shadows they cast were long over the West, where trails blazed by the Bourgmonts and du Tisnés were allowed to grow over with grass.

With the outbreak of the Revolutionary War, Anglo-American infiltration west of the river slowed. Yet they crossed it, less as outlaw traders than in a pathetic role as old as war itself—as refugees. Gálvez and his aides must have wondered at the bitterness between the two factions who spoke and looked alike and yet had turned the cis-Mississippi lands into a bloody hell. Gálvez was, among other things, a humanitarian. The suffering innocents of both persuasions (though most were loyalists) sought refuge on Spain's side of the river, where they were treated with the utmost kindness and solicitude.

That was the gracious and gentle side of Bernardo. In matters of state and politics, the young governor was hard-nosed. His country's interest and his personal sympathy lay on the side of the Americans, and soon after assuming office, he began a brilliant tightrope act on behalf of "neutral Spain." There was living in New Orleans at the time a well-to-do Irish-American trader named Oliver Pollock, who had been a close friend of O'Reilly. Pollock was also a dedicated believer in the American cause, and in the summer of 1776 he persuaded Unzaga to part with two shipments of the king's gunpowder for the insurgents' use.

When Gálvez took office, Pollock, in his capacity as agent for the colony of Virginia, found a kindred and cooperative soul. Together, with Pollock staking his personal fortune and Gálvez his nation's surface neutrality, they surreptitiously sent muskets and powder and bayonets and medicines up the Mississippi and Ohio rivers to the rebels—a risky business that did not escape English intelligence.

England had other reasons to be unhappy with Bernardo. In 1777 he implemented new trade regulations and started enforcing those already on the books against smugglers, which effectively cut England out of the lower Mississippi River trade. An even greater provocation was his opening of New Orleans to American privateers for the sale of spoils taken from British vessels. British protests were deflected by the glib Gálvez. If those buyers of arms and medicines were rebels, he said, Spanish authorities were ignorant of the fact. As for ships on the river, all were free to use it, but no hostile action would be tolerated by the king.

Gálvez was harder put to defend his actions during the second year of his administration. In January 1778, a hotheaded American patriot named James Willing, commissioned by the commerce committee of the Continental Congress to strike at loyalists on the Lower Mississippi, set off in that direction down the Ohio River in an armed boat called the *Rattletrap*. At the riverside settlements of Natchez and Manchac, Willing carried out his commission well enough—perhaps too well—looting and putting the torch to property owned by those who refused to take an "oath of allegiance" to the American Congress. The foray was destructive, aimed more at confiscating property than harming persons, and included

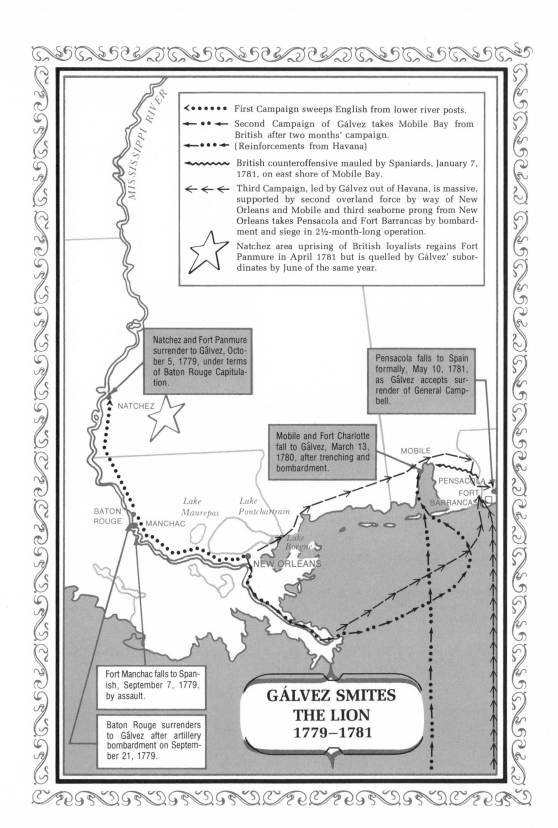

First Campaign sweeps English from lower river posts.

Second Campaign of Gálvez takes Mobile Bay from British after two months' campaign.

(Reinforcements from Havana)

British counteroffensive mauled by Spaniards, January 7, 1781, on east shore of Mobile Bay.

Third Campaign, led by Gálvez out of Havana, is massive, supported by second overland force by way of New Orleans and Mobile and third seaborne prong from New Orleans takes Pensacola and Fort Barrancas by bombardment and siege in 2½-month-long operation.

Natchez area uprising of British loyalists regains Fort Panmure in April 1781 but is quelled by Gálvez' subordinates by June of the same year.

Natchez and Fort Panmure surrender to Gálvez, October 5, 1779, under terms of Baton Rouge Capitulation.

Pensacola falls to Spain formally, May 10, 1781, as Gálvez accepts surrender of General Campbell.

Mobile and Fort Charlotte fall to Gálvez, March 13, 1780, after trenching and bombardment.

Fort Manchac falls to Spanish, September 7, 1779, by assault.

Baton Rouge surrenders to Gálvez after artillery bombardment on September 21, 1779.

MISSISSIPPI RIVER

NATCHEZ

MOBILE

PENSACOLA

FORT BARRANCAS

BATON ROUGE

MANCHAC

Lake Maurepas

Lake Pontchartrain

Lake Borgne

NEW ORLEANS

GÁLVEZ SMITES THE LION 1779–1781

the capture of the British warship *Rebecca* by Willing and other armed riverboats by other patriot-opportunists. The mischief done, Willing and the rest of the Americans retired into the sanctuary of Spanish Louisiana, where many faithful English subjects had also fled to escape Willing's terror. Gálvez sheltered all, and Willing was allowed to auction his plunder in New Orleans.

The British were incensed, and British anger had a way of manifesting itself in the appearance of warships, as Gálvez learned to his discomfort in March of 1778, when Capt. John Fergusson sailed up the Mississippi in the frigate *Sylph*. A brisk exchange of pointed letters ensued. Fergusson informed Gálvez that he was not comporting himself as an officer of a neutral power and that satisfaction was expected from the governor for the insults and confiscations in his jurisdiction, "to prevent the fatal consequences that may attend your giving more countenance to a lawless Banditti, than you seem to do to his Britannic Majesty's and liege Subjects."

Gálvez was in a ticklish spot. New Orleans was so poorly fortified as to be indefensible, and troop strength was insufficient to hold back any British attack of consequence. The only way to keep the English navy off the river was to stop them at Balize at the very mouth of the Mississippi, or at Fort Saint John on Lake Pontchartrain, the strategic link in the chain of lakes and rivers that connected with the Mississippi at Manchac and made an island of New Orleans. But that, of course, would be an act of war, and Spain was not ready for war. Neither was England, Gálvez could gamble. So the young Spaniard resorted to bluff, diversionary arguments, and legalisms. Spain was not responsible for foreign activity on the English side of the river above Manchac, he remonstrated. Only below that point, where Carlos III had control over the whole river and where fighting and seizures — by either Americans or Englishmen — would not be condoned. If wrongs had been done in Spanish territory, Spanish justice would right them, as indeed it already had, Gálvez pointed out, in several instances where loyalists had had their goods returned to them.

Early in April, Fergusson sailed away, but not before urging British loyalists to desert Spanish Louisiana or suffer possible dire consequences, and expressing to Gálvez his opinion that

"Nations . . . possessed of Colonies . . . should be cautious of setting a pernicious example in abetting, favoring or assisting by any means . . . such Subjects united in direct and open Rebellion." The governor's relief over Fergusson's departure was brief. Soon two more English frigates, commanded by Joseph Nunn, a man with a reputation for meanness, lay off New Orleans. Gálvez held his shaky, not-quite-middle ground. Against Willing's loud objections, he insisted on a restoration of prizes and plunder taken in Spanish territory. He also exacted an oath of neutrality from both Englishmen and Americans in New Orleans—a move that prompted a chorus of protests, from Nunn, Alexander McGillivray, the British commander at Natchez, and Governor Chester of West Florida.

Willing's rampage through the Lower Mississippi, while initially a success, backfired the following year. His severity towards British-leaning settlers had hardened them against his cause. Worse, England had responded by sending heftier garrisons to Manchac and Natchez, and the warship *West Florida* to Lake Pontchartrain, stationing other vessels off the subdelta to blockade rebel shipping up the Mississippi. It was all very deflating to American hopes. It was also an ominous semicircle that had formed around New Orleans and Gálvez.

The governor held to a steady course between the narrowing shoals. Willing and his men, who had abused Gálvez's hospitality by staying on indefinitely in New Orleans to enjoy the easy living and incite trouble across the border, were a growing embarrassment. When Willing balked at Gálvez's decision to return the prizes taken by the Americans in Spanish territory and in contravention of Spanish neutrality, and then declared that the Spaniard would have to be "answerable to My Masters the Honorable Congress for the Restitution of these Prizes," the governor let Willing know that his decision would remain the same even if the entire American navy put in an appearance. (There was no way that bluff would be called; wherever the English navy was, the American fleet would certainly be far distant.)

Gálvez was not alone in his dislike of the swaggering bully. Americans who knew Willing likewise perceived in the man and his followers an inordinate love of plundering masked in patrio-

Monuments to Spain's brief presence — the old Spanish cathedral and palace of New Orleans. (From a print, circa 1820.)

tism. Among them was Oliver Pollock, by now on the verge of personal bankruptcy (in part from funding Willing's "vacation"), but no less ardent in his support of the new nation. He lauded Gálvez to the Continental Congress as a true friend who boldly defied English power for the cause and wished Willing, whose conduct was counterproductive to American interests, gone from Louisiana. At last, in September of 1778, Willing's men crossed the Mississippi to the west bank and were led north and safely back to rebel territory. As for Willing himself, he subsequently shipped out of New Orleans, only to be captured by the British, then later released in a prisoner exchange.

Willing's departure did little to improve Gálvez's position anent the British, whose protests and encirclement continued. Not to be outshouted, the governor registered complaints of his own with Chester, his opposite number in British West Florida: an English corsair was interfering with domestic shipping on Lake Pont- chartrain; Englishmen and Chickasaw Indian allies atop the Chickasaw Bluffs were firing down on innocent traders and trappers coming down the Mississippi; and English traders had crossed the river and, in violation of Spanish regulations, were engaged in barter with the Indians of the Spanish West.

The letter of grievances was personally delivered to Governor Chester in Mobile by Maj. Jacinto Panis, along with gifts of wine and sugar. Chester was up to Gálvez's game of inflating excuses and brushing aside real issues. Lieutenant Burden, the perpetrator of the alleged depredations on the southern lakes, was under another's control; complaints really should be sent to his commander in Jamaica, though he, Chester, had asked Burden to refrain from harassing Spanish fishermen. As for the stated shootings from Chickasaw Bluffs, those men likewise answered to another authority. Those English encroachers on the Spanish West actually answered to no authority, being "Banditti, Outlaws, who have fled from Justice, out of some of the Northern Colonies, and live in a Savage Manner."

The exchanges were couched in elegant phrasing and accompanied by gifts and elaborate courtesies. Gentlemen presided in Lower Louisiana and British West Florida, and mutual generosity was as much a fact of life as political differences. When famine threatened West Florida, Gálvez sent grain across the Mississippi to the hungry. When floods dispossessed the citizens of Pointe Coupée, the British offered shelter to the needy on their side of the river.

Yet the tension between the two imperial rivals was drawn beyond relaxation along the river boundary that separated the East from the West. The actions of the Americans had only pushed forward the inevitable day of reckoning, and it was merely a matter of time before the taut river line snapped and opened the West to England or the East to Spain.

"THANK GOD THAT WE ARE ALL FIRM and relishing the opportunity to strike a blow against the Dons," enthused a letter from an English official to William Horn, the English commander at Natchez. Another from Maj. Elias Dunford, the commander of Fort Charlotte at Mobile, advised Horn to prepare for an assault on New Orleans, "which it is possible we shall be engaged in shortly." Both communications fell into Gálvez's hands and confirmed his suspicions. Now the governor knew the particulars of the planned invasion—the descent of a large force from Canada that was to link up with British regulars and German mercenaries at Natchez, Baton Rouge, and Manchac, while a British fleet from Pensacola would complete the pincer effect on the Spanish strength at New Orleans.

Spain had other advantages. Major Panis, who visited Governor Chester in 1778 with Gálvez's complaints, doubled as a spy, making a visual inventory of English strength in West Florida. The last and most telling advantage was in timing. For over two years the Spaniards had shied away from war with England, as had England, with greater reason, from Spain. When war was declared, Spain did the declaring—formally to the world on July 8, 1779, about a month after disclosing her intention of doing so to Spanish colonial administrators.

Gálvez did not get the word until late, but he was already preparing for the showdown. In July he called a war junta to discuss the none-too-heartening state of the colony's defense. The English buildup east of the Mississippi was estimated above a thousand, while there were only six hundred regulars—two-thirds of them untested recruits—in all Spanish Louisiana. The members of the junta overwhelmingly counseled caution and defense for New Orleans, the meager garrisons of the distant outposts to be written off as lost. Bernardo listened, but he shared with his uncle José an impatience with deliberating bodies. When the news of actual war reached him, he kept it from his subjects and from the uninformed English across the river, building small gunboats and busying himself with a mobilization that had all the outward look of being defensive. Then he made his bold move. On August 27, 1779, he led more than six hundred fifty men, including a handful of Americans, out of New Orleans and across the Mississippi, gathering additional militia and volunteers on the German and Acadian coast. Only after recrossing the river and nearing Fort Manchac did Gálvez tell his green and eager troops about war having been declared and their immediate mission.

The post fell to Gálvez like an overripe apple. It was undermanned because the English had earlier pulled many men out to build a better bastion upriver at Baton Rouge. With little delay

Gálvez marched with his inspired men to the greater redoubt and a more meaningful test. Choosing not to waste his men in an assault against cannon, Gálvez set up a diversionary commotion under cover of night while quietly digging a trench toward the fort, where, undetected, he emplaced and protected his own cannon. The next morning, September 21, 1779, the Spanish guns pounded Baton Rouge into submission. The surrender by its commander, Lieutenant Colonel Dickson, was accepted, but on condition that Fort Panmure at Natchez be included in the capitulation. Dickson assented, and the English defenders of Natchez became prisoners of war before they knew there was a war, and without an angry shot being fired at them.

For Bernardo it was a glorious success. The three cornerstones of English power in the lower Mississippi Valley were now Spain's at a negligible cost, and some six hundred English regulars were taken to New Orleans as prisoners—a status that under the always lenient and charitable Gálvez was not half-bad duty, as word quickly got around. The young governor-commander could not help gloating to his superior, Diego Joseph Navarro, the captain-general in Havana who had discouraged him from taking any rash action: "I believe that you will not disapprove my resolution to attack them first, taking advantage of their ignorance of the declaration of war; for if this opportunity had been allowed to pass, and they had had time to put their plan into execution, there is no doubt that there would have been a very different outcome for our arms in this province."

Worldwide, Spain might have been a lightweight matched with a heavyweight, but at the time England was distracted by too many challengers, and at the place—the lower Mississippi that separated her from New Spain and the West—she had been caught flat-footed with a string of lightning-quick jabs from which she would never fully recover. England's plan to push Spain out of the near West did stumble awkwardly forward for a brief time. That was in the Spanish Illinois Country, where a succession of lieutenant-governors of Louisiana, quartered in Saint Louis, attempted to protect the national interest with seat-of-the-pants decisions. Fernando de Leyba, appointed lieutenant-governor in 1778, sided with the Americans and openly aided George Rogers

Clark, the American hero of campaigns east of the Mississippi. That same year de Leyba requested from Gálvez the authority to establish a fort with two hundred men at the entrance to the Des Moines River, where Englishmen were violating the border with impunity. Gálvez vetoed the idea, pleading a lack of authority and money; England kept its leverage in the Upper Mississippi. In May of 1780 a British army of mostly Indians marched down from Canada, only to be stopped and repulsed at Saint Louis, chiefly by French defenders.

The defeat at Saint Louis dashed English hopes to extend the war into the trans-Mississippi West, but welcome as it was, Spain remained absorbed in the south, along those warm-water shores Ponce de León and de Soto had given her long before there were *Norteamericanos* with pale skins.

José de Gálvez succinctly summarized the royal wishes in a message to Captain-General Navarro in August of 1779: "The king has determined that the principal object of his forces in America during the war against the English shall be to expel them from the Gulf of Mexico and the banks of the Mississippi where their establishments are so prejudicial to our commerce and also to the security of our valuable possessions." His nephew had seen to the latter wish before the war was three months old. Now he was itching to follow through on the former. Though timid bureaucrats and naval officers in Havana would prove a constant drag on his ambitions, Bernardo was not about to be stopped by anything less than a royal order to desist, and with his uncle calling the shots, that would never come. After the humiliation of the English on the Lower Mississippi, Bernardo began assembling a small fleet that was to sail for Mobile with 754 men, a mélange of Spanish regular soldiers, loyal French Creoles, free blacks, and Anglo renegades. On January 11, 1780, they embarked on a voyage that the winds would not help and that sandbars at the mouth of the target bay would arrest. Undaunted, Gálvez landed his forces and began to move on Fort Charlotte and Maj. Elias Dunford's defenders. The two-week-long siege was marked by chivalric exchanges. Gálvez sent Dunford wine and fruit and cigars and flowery compliments; Dunford sent Gálvez wine and bread and mutton and flowery compliments. All the while Dun-

ford waited for a rescue force from Maj. Gen. John Campbell at
Pensacola that was slow in coming. Gálvez, made aware of the
imminent relief, pressed his advantage and by means of trenching again reduced an English fort. Dunford surrendered himself
and more than two hundred of his countrymen to Gálvez's renowned mercy, and on March 12, Spaniards took up positions in
Fort Charlotte. The tardy Campbell retreated to Pensacola with
eleven hundred men to await the follow-up attack Spain was sure
to launch. To his relief, there was none—for a while. The faint-
hearted Captain-General Navarro had failed to send reinforcements from Havana, receiving a reprimand from the Crown for it,
while Bernardo was elevated to the rank of field marshal of
Spanish forces in America.

Campbell was breathing more easily by summer. The Spanish
attack had not come, and the protector of Pensacola had cause
to hope for reinforcements of his own that would allow him to retake the lost territories "and to add Louisiana to British dominion."
That same summer Gálvez personally went to Havana to assem-
ble an expeditionary force. The obstructionists stepped aside for
him. You couldn't argue with success, and you really shouldn't
argue with José's nephew. But this time it was nature rather than
man that upset the governor's plan to take Pensacola. A hurri-
cane in mid-October struck his flotilla of sixty-four ships carrying
nearly four thousand troops and scattered them all over the Gulf
of Mexico. The British rejoiced at the news, and in January of
1781 Campbell went on the offensive, briefly, sending a force out
to recapture Mobile. Though greatly outnumbering the Spanish
defenders, it was mauled and fell back.

The initiative quickly reverted to Gálvez. He would not abide
by the Havana junta's opinion that the next try be delayed until
a milder season. On February 13, he sailed again with many
fewer ships and men, arranging for other Spanish forces from New
Orleans and Mobile to join him in the humbling of Pensacola. It
was the largest-scale battle Gálvez would fight, involving nearly
7,000 men on the Spanish side before it was over, and it would be
of the longest duration—two months. Yet the result was the same.
On May 8, after a Spanish hit on a British powder magazine, the
English ran up a white flag over Fort George and General Camp-

bell entered into negotiations on the terms of surrender. Spanish casualties numbered over 300; of the enemy, 1,600 had been killed or taken, but the more grievous loss to the British was all of West Florida.

To the vanquished, Gálvez was his usual gracious and considerate self. To his king he was a godsend, the man who mostly on his own had expelled the English from the Gulf of Mexico, "where they have so prejudiced my vassals and my royal interest in times both of peace and of war," and for this most recent feat he was promoted to lieutenant general and made governor of West Florida in addition to Louisiana.

The war was now winding down but not quite over. While Gálvez was hammering at Pensacola, there had been an uprising in Natchez by English loyalists, most of whom had been present when the district fell to Gálvez and had sworn an oath to bear no arms against Spain. The Natchez settlers were confident that the Spanish would be trounced by Campbell, and when the reverse proved true they were in a quandary. The Spanish quickly crushed the rebellion and captured many of its instigators, who by their treachery had legally earned themselves a place on the gibbet. But Gálvez mercifully spared them and, with the conclusion of the war, released them. The gestures were characteristic of the young man beloved by the French he governed, respected by the Englishmen he defeated, admired by the Americans he aided, and valued by the Spaniards who would have been in a bad way without him.

Bernardo de Gálvez's career continued glorious, though it would be short-lived. He went to Spain in 1783 and the following year arrived in Havana with the added title of captain general of Cuba. There he shortly learned that his father, Matías, had died and that he was to succeed him as Viceroy of New Spain. In the year and a half of his viceregency, he endeared himself to the Mexican *capitaleños* by his open-handed generosity in a time of famine, before dying suddenly in an epidemic in 1786 at the age of thirty-eight. New Spain mourned its magnanimous man.

Bernardo de Gálvez left behind more than good deeds done. Through his actions he had won for Spain West Florida and a strong hand at the peace table, where England coughed up East

Florida as well. As for the West — the buffer land interposed between the Anglo-Americans and the Pacific — it was as secure as it had ever been. One might add that it was as secure as it would ever be. There had been a realignment of players east of the Mississippi, but the game was the same.

The aging Count Aranda, Carlos III's ambassador to France, discerned a new danger in that year of peace, 1783:

> This federal republic is born a pigmy. . . . It has required the support of two such powerful states as France and Spain to obtain its Independence. The day will come when she will be a giant, a colossus formidable even to those countries. She will forget the services she received from the two powers, and will think only of her own aggrandizement. The liberty of conscience, the facility of establishing a new population upon immense territory . . . will attract the agriculturists and mechanics . . . for men ever run after fortune, and in a few years we shall see the tyrannical existence of this very colossus of which I speak.

Bernardo de Gálvez might have been a savior; and the count was at the very least a prophet.

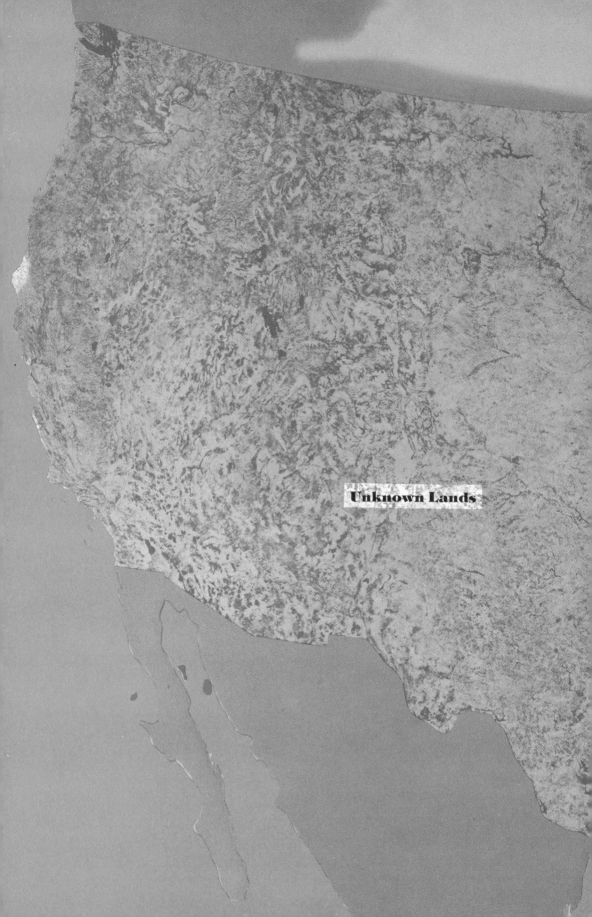

Unknown Lands

PART V: THE DIVISIBLE EMPIRE

Explored Lands

Known Lands
(Settled)

The
Anglo-American Presence
1776

PART V
THE DIVISIBLE EMPIRE

July 12, 1776. The green of England fell away as the three-masted sloop *Resolution* slipped out of Plymouth Sound into the blue-gray of the English Channel. On deck stood a tall man in gold-trimmed blue coat and tight white knee breeches, watching intently while the hoarse cries of deckhands sang out and farm beasts lowed and bleated loudly from the hold. His face was long and angular, weathered by too many years at sea, its features a curious frieze of kindness, patience, and determination. No doubt he wondered whether he would see his native land again, and no doubt he worried about his wife Elizabeth and their children, of whom he had seen so little. But he was glad to have brine air in his nostrils again and a horizon of water in view, and more than glad to leave his tedious desk job.

James Cook was an up-from-the-ranks captain now, promoted after returning from his second triumphant voyage of discovery only the July before. Behind him were three years of sailing the icy waters of the far south, back and forth across the Antarctic Circle before satisfying himself there was no "lost" continent as had been widely supposed. More to his immediate credit, the seventy-thousand-mile voyage had been made without the loss of a single seaman to the killer scurvy—thanks to the skipper's insistence on heavy rations of citrus juice, sauerkraut, and fresh greens whenever in port. These achievements set nicely on the earlier ones of his first voyage: the circumnavigation of the two islands of New Zealand in 1769 and 1770, the later mapping of two thousand miles of Australia's previously unseen east coast, and the sailing through Torres Strait that proved New Guinea an island.

England had taken Cook to her heart—"the ablest and most renowned Navigator this or any country hath produced," he was. With the encomiums and the promotion came the Copley Gold Medal, the Royal Society's highest tribute for intellectual achievement, and the cushy appointment as captain general of the Greenwich Hospital. Not bad for a poorly schooled, self-made son of a humble Yorkshire farmhand. But when Cook learned the Admiralty was planning a new expedition of discovery, he let it be known that he was available. At a dinner party with Lord Sandwich, first lord of the Admiralty, on February 9, 1776, the restless seafarer offered to captain the *Resolution* and head up yet another girdling of the globe.

On the following day his offer was formally accepted, and by June 8, Cook's sloop was nearly ready for sailing. That night he entertained Lord Sandwich, Sir Hugh Palliser, and assorted "noblemen and gentlemen" at a gala dinner on ship, giving his guests a seventeen-gun salute both as they came aboard and upon their departure. Exactly one month later, on July 8, Cook received his secret instructions (which in fact he had helped draft), signed by the Earl of Sandwich and giving words to the king's wish "that an attempt should be made to find out a northern passage by sea from the Pacific to the Atlantic Ocean." Since the putative strait had for two hundred years eluded seekers in the north Atlantic, a try from the other side, the little-known north Pacific, was in order—to prove, if nothing else, the fabled Anian's nonexistence.

The instructions were explicit: Cook's search should begin on the coast of "New Albion" at forty-five degrees north latitude, and he was not to "touch upon any part of the Spanish dominions on the western continent of America, unless driven thither by some unavoidable accident, in which case [he was] to stay no longer there than . . . absolutely necessary, and to be very careful not to give any umbrage or offense to any of the inhabitants or subjects of His Catholic Majesty."

On its face, the mission was no more demanding for the first mariner of the world than those before. But this time things were different. Cook's vessel could have stood lengthier repairs after its three years of dodging Antarctic ice floes. Then there was his own disposition, or rather indisposition, an intestinal problem, a "billious colick" that had not cleared up from the last voyage and made him irritable. Finally, there was this unsettling business with the colonies—political problems that had nothing to do with seamanship and discovery. But they were a bother all the same, and the potential for division was there among his own crew, some of whom had been born in America. All in all, it was not the best time to go a-sailing.

Captain Cook spent a rather uneventful year crossing the Atlantic and Indian oceans, revisiting old friends in the South Pacific, until in December of 1777, with Capt. Charles Clerke of the companion sloop *Discovery*, he headed into the mysterious north Pacific. The route he took was direct, a new one, and for that, as in voyages past, he was rewarded with discovery. He found a beautiful archipelago that he named the Sandwich Islands in honor of his friend and sponsor, and the always benevolent and forbearing Cook was hospitably received by the natives, who supplied him with pigs and yams and helped him take on fresh water. He thought highly of the Hawaiians, commending them for their "frank, cheerful disposition," faulting them only for their "propensity to thieveing."

On February 2, 1778, the *Resolution* and *Discovery* continued on their way to the western coast of North America, still enveloped in a shroud of geographers' conjecture nearly three hundred years after Columbus. A month later, at the latitude of Oregon's Cape Foulweather, which Cook named for the inclement days to follow, he began his northern run along the coast. The Englishmen rested for a time at Nootka Sound. Here they learned that Spaniards had come before them, and here they conducted a brisk trade for sea-otter skins they did not yet know would be as prized as gold in China. Then it was time to return to duty. For four months Cook nudged the coast for sign of a strait, compelled to sail west again as the shoreline curled outward. He followed the Aleutian arm, then cut north through it and the Bering Strait to nearly sixty-nine degrees before the lateness of the season and a barrier of ice turned him back. He doubted there was a Northwest Passage, but he would return the next summer for another try.

For winter quarters Cook headed for the island of Hawaii, where his luck and his welcome ran out. He took too long getting provisions. The patience of the natives wore thin. There were frictions, then incidents, culminating in the theft of a cutter from the *Discovery*. Cook's attempt to retrieve it brought a confrontation that on February 14 erupted into violence and claimed, among other lives, that of the great captain. In his fiftieth year, Cook was stabbed and clubbed to death in the Hawaiian surf as he pleaded for peace between Englishmen and Polynesians.

The ill-fated third voyage was resumed without Cook, and six months later without Captain Clerke of the *Discovery*, who succumbed to tuberculosis. Another look for the Northwest Passage fizzled, followed by a long voyage home to England. One significant stop was made on the way back. At Macao those sea-otter pelts so casually acquired in Nootka were a sensation among well-heeled Chinese with an eye to luxury, bringing as much as one hundred Spanish dollars a skin. The crews came close to mutiny when their requests to return to Nootka for more furs were overruled. But the word spread rapidly among sea traders, and that far and little-known timbered coast would never be so far nor little known again.

Resolution and *Discovery* brought home some notable survivors. Among them was William Bligh, later to have his mutiny on the *Bounty*. There was George Vancouver, who in twelve years would carry on the tradition of Cook in exploring America's northwest coast for England. There was Joseph Billings, an Englishman who sold his services to Russia and later commanded two of the Tsarina's ships in Unalaska. Then there was John Ledyard, a restless young American in love with adventure who later on in Paris, of all places, would fill the head of a fellow American named Thomas Jefferson with a scheme for exploration of those obscure lands west of the river Mississippi.

The loss of Cook was a loss for the scientific world, but for England it was more bad tidings in a very bad year. The war with the colonies, fresh when Cook left for the Pacific, was stale and dragging on, the outcome uncertain, the prospects dim. Worse, the "enemy" had multiplied— France joining the fray in 1778, Spain in 1779. Now few friends were to be found, thanks to French conniving on the Continent, where Russia, Prussia, Sweden, Denmark, Portugal, and the German states were about to join a pact of "armed neutrality," which made it clear that English interference with "free ships carrying free goods" would not be tolerated. Britain, so triumphant after the Treaty of Paris in 1763, Britain with the globe on a leash, had in a brief decade and a half found herself alone, besieged, her empire crumbling. What had gone wrong, and why so soon?

In Europe the time-honored principles of statecraft dictate an alliance of the weak against the strong in the interest of equilibrium. The crafty Duc de Choiseul, who made the humiliating peace with Britain in 1763, knew that mighty England had a mighty weakness in her North American colonies, in their growing estrangement from the mother country. His successor as foreign minister, the Comte de Vergennes, promoted the split by sending spies to encourage revolt in America while pursuing a diplomacy to part England from potential allies in Europe. It worked.

French skullduggery and the stars aside, fault was also to be found in England and her underlings. The obstreperous Americans, whom the England of George III looked on as its own, were not really treated as its own. Politically and economically they were second-class Englishmen, plantation managers ideally, who would follow mercantile orders. Some at home perceived the danger of this policy and its possible consequences, but they were outnumbered by shortsighted merchants and political hacks. With his acid pen, Jonathan Swift had earlier warned against those who "with the spirit of shopkeepers tried to frame rules for the administration of kingdoms." Men of broad vision were needed to run a great empire, and in England between 1763 and 1783 such men happened to be in short supply.

London subscribers to the *Evening Post* who read the delayed reports of reversals at Saratoga and the second battle of Stony Point could only shake their heads in unhappy wonderment and look back with sore nostalgia on what were already known as the good old days of '63.

Chapter 15

Snatching Defeat
from the Jaws of Victory

"THERE IS SOMETHING ABSURD in supposing a Continent to be perpetually governed by an island," wrote Thomas Paine in 1776. "In no instance hath nature made the satellite larger than its primary planet." Citizen Tom rested his argument on the spongy ground of "natural law," but the tone of *Common Sense* is one of moral outrage — Britain's dominion over her transatlantic colonies was an offense against any self-respecting radical republican's sensibilities. Still, the core of his argument remains when slightly rephrased. *Could,* not should, an island rule a continent? Or could it even rule the vast half of one that had fallen in its lap at the end of the Seven Years' War? Could a maritime nation reliant on sea trade hold its own in the recesses of a mostly dark continent? Wasn't "going west" going to ruin?

That possibility was argued in Parliament even before the Paris treaty was signed in 1763. William Pitt, the architect of the victory, saw danger in the terms of the peace: "Some are for keeping Canada; some Guadeloupe; who will tell me which I shall be hanged for not keeping?" Behind the irony of his question posed to the House of Commons was the knowledge that France had already been stripped of colonies around the world, and to get both the little Caribbean sugar island and Voltaire's big block of ice was out of the question, unless the hostilities were to be prolonged — certainly not what the war-weary majority wanted.

Some shrewd heads pointed out that it was neither Guadeloupe nor Canada that was most desirable, but Louisiana, the "West," which was said to be rich and if not taken would leave that raw frontier exposed and hard as ever to defend.

SNATCHING DEFEAT FROM THE JAWS OF VICTORY

Cassandras of conservative stripe warned against absorbing either Canada or Louisiana. Take Guadeloupe with its canefields and let the rest go, they said. Otherwise England would repeat the same mistakes of Spain, becoming colony-rich and treasury-poor. Moreover, went another more prescient argument, if England accepted Louisiana or Canada, it would only encourage the restive colonials to move west, increase their numbers, become strong, and lose their dependence on the motherland. Let France keep her countless unimproved acres. "A neighbor that keeps us in some awe is not always the worst of neighbors," observed William Burke in support of the minority view.

But the expansionistic majority ruled, leaning toward Pitt on this issue. Good imperial sense dictated a "rounding out" of the holdings on the North American continent to protect those valued colonies from foreign threats. The mercantile argument against the acquisition got a mercantile rebuttal—baldly specious in hindsight. More territory would mean more cheap land, and more cheap land would mean more farming and forestall that day when the colonists might be tempted to manufacture in competition with England. Not only that, an increase in colonial population would also mean a greater number of consumers of English goods.

The national will had what at first seemed a perfect day in Paris. France gave, but without buckling. Canada went to England, as did all Louisiana east of the Mississippi except the "island" of New Orleans. Spain, a well-thrashed latecomer to the peace table, had to cough up the Floridas to further round out English holdings, bribed to do it by the Duc de Choiseul with the secret cession of trans-Mississippi Louisiana to Carlos III. England would find that out a little later—and the discomfiting fact that the "island" of New Orleans, key to the river that was key to the continent, was still in the Bourbon enemy's keep.

Some Englishmen were delighted with Choiseul's Trojan horse. "We are now in the heart of their favorite Louisiana, masters of all that mighty project of uniting by traffick, the lakes and the Ohio, the sources of St. Lawrence and Mississippi, and of cloathing unnumbered nations with our manufactories," enthused one ministerial mind, who very likely had his pounds in the wool industry. Translations of the early French works on Louisiana were read avidly by politicians and speculators. Charlevoix's *Journal* and du Pratz's *History of Louisiana* were available in the 1760s. Bossu's *Travels in the Interior of North America* could be bought in English translation in 1771. Even the fork-tongued Baron Lahontan had his lies resurrected for Englishmen. Of course, none of those Frenchmen had been to Louisiana lately, and what they had written wasn't exactly gospel.

When hunger for land becomes hunger for land's sake, there are problems of digestion, and when you conquer a country you have to do something with it. England, who had always been more intent on the mysteries beyond the point of a ship's prow than where a stream or an Indian trail might lead, was forced by the narrow logic of imperialism to move forward, northward, and westward, after 1763, leaving behind the tidewater and the piedmont, crossing the mountains into the forests primeval—and out of her element.

To secure the new boundaries against potential enemies (Frenchmen now separated from France, Indians whose hearts

Changing the colors: When England occupied Fort de Chartres on the Mississippi, October 10, 1765, she seemed the winner of the West.

had been poisoned against Englishmen by their French friends, and Spaniards ensconced on the opposite side of the dividing river), England sent garrison troops to forts from the Saint Lawrence to the Gulf of Mexico, from the Alleghenies to the Mississippi. Along that river of commerce redcoats were stationed at Natchez, old Fort de Chartres, and Kaskaskia in the ever-attractive Illinois Country. England's west, of course, was the cis-Mississippi west, but the imperial appetite didn't stop at the river. Many letters and memorials reveal an ill-disguised contempt for Spain and a belief that when the opportunity presented itself the Spaniards could be easily run out of their Louisiana and the port of New Orleans. Indeed, one Harry Gordon, a captain sent from Philadelphia to Fort de Chartres, wrote in 1766 that the Mississippi frontier forts were themselves unnecessary. Troops from New York and a sizeable fleet based in the Gulf of Mexico would be sufficient when the moment of decision came to "spit upon Spain." He predicted that Carlos would "lose Mexico in a twelve months' war."

Britain soon had legitimate if hypocritical complaints against her new neighbor in the West. Frenchmen in Saint Louis were still crossing the river boundary to trade with the tribes of the Great Lakes and along the Illinois and Wabash rivers. Pelts taken on English land were going down the river to New Orleans and winding up in Madrid instead of in London and Glasgow, where they belonged. It had been expectations of monopolizing the fur trade that gave solid support to expansion in the first place. Without that inducement, the West was not nearly so attractive.

While eighteenth-century Englishmen stood second to none in the promotion of maritime trade, it took them four years to wise up to the ways of the fur trade. In the imperial plans initiated by Lord Shelburne in 1763 and spelled out in 1764, traders were to set up their posts near English settlements and wait for the Indians to come to them; it had worked well enough up in Hudson's Bay—red men hoofing and paddling hundreds of miles to get their blankets and baubles at the company store. It did not work in the heartland where, for a century or more, Frenchmen had taken their portable stores onto tribal lands to make the exchange. Under that same decree of 1764, two Indian superintendents were appointed, one for the north and one for the south, and all traders were to be licensed by the Crown and confined to pre-scribed posts in order to protect the Indians from abuses. Like previous French attempts at regulation, such rules proved un-workable. French traders operating from Spanish Louisiana were under no such restrictions, and they had the corner on the traffic. Adjustments were called for and made in 1767. Traders were henceforth allowed to roam as they wished.

Other adaptations followed. Frenchmen in the Illinois Country, who were made to swear allegiance to their new political masters, and Frenchmen in Canada were absorbed into the middle and lower echelons of an efficient system that employed mostly shrewd Scotsmen at the top. English goods were superior goods, and smart Protestant managers knew how to maximize profits. But the addition of French *coureurs de bois,* field managers, and clerks was just what the business lacked: men who knew the In-dians and were tolerant of their ways, who were more reliable and loyal to their superiors and less given to criticizing than English-men, men who were physically tougher and better able to travel into little-known lands where pelts were invariably cheaper.

Within ten years the imbalance had shifted. The supply of furs going down the Mississippi dwindled as those reaching Montreal increased, bound not for France as in days of yore, but for the merchants of London. Most "border violations" were now by the "Montreal peddlers" and their agents who came down from Can-ada and crossed the river into the Upper Mississippi—the Spanish Illinois—via the Iowa, Turkey, and Des Moines rivers. The pre-mium beaver and otter skins were found in the north, and it was in the north that England ingratiated herself among the Sioux, the Iowas, even the Little Osages from the Missouri country. With gifts, flattery, and bargain prices, she soon had Spain on the defensive.

The Spaniards did put up resistance. They entered the bribery contest, and though their wares were inferior to those of the British, they managed to hold the allegiance of the Sauks, the Foxes, the Wichitas, and the Missouris. In 1767 they even raised Fort Carlos III at the confluence of the Missouri and Mississippi rivers and manned it with eighteen troops and five cannon. It was a lonesome and ineffective station, a solitary point dwarfed by a universe of woodlands and plains. Upriver at Prairie du

Maj. Robert Rogers had designs on the West. He also had problems with his English superiors.

THE BETTMANN ARCHIVE

Chien, on a flat stretch of land where the Wisconsin River spilled into the Mississippi from the east, the English traders enjoyed themselves as they reaped their profits. Spring and fall offered games and roistering at the great rendezvous of traders and red men from all over. Peter Pond, an American eyewitness to the 1773–74 gathering, said the camps of the Indians "exceaded a mile and a half in length." Spain's slight sway above Saint Louis was eroding fast.

Besides ordinary fur men, England had a few dreamers loose on the landscape whom La Salle and the Vérendryes would have recognized as brothers under the skin. One, Robert Rogers, came out of the Seven Years' War a hero, the daring commander of Rogers Rangers who was with Wolfe at the fall of Quebec and later accepted the French surrender of Detroit. He was an ambitious and a west-thinking man. When he arrived in London in 1765 to bask in glory and publish his *Concise Account of North America* (in which he made the encouraging revelation that "the further you travel westward, the more mild and temperate it grows"), he also petitioned the king for backing of an expedition to cross the continent and find the Pacific Ocean. It was Northwest Passage time again: time to locate that fabled River of the West and ride it right out to the big briny.

Instead of a subsidy, the Massachusetts-born Rogers got an appointment as commander of the post at Michilimackinac, where he began outfitting an exploration on his own. To do the legwork, he tapped two former officers who had served under him in the Rangers — Jonathan Carver and James Tute, both New England colonials like himself. Eager Jon Carver was at Prairie du Chien in October of 1766, much pleased with what he saw. The Indians, he was convinced, could be won over to the English side with presents and coaxing, away from dissembling Frenchmen who were scattered about and preaching a French return. Carver then traveled north up the Mississippi and west up the Minnesota, where he wintered in 1766–67 among the Sioux. Come spring, he headed down river to pick up trading goods promised by Rogers, only to meet Capt. James Tute and his party, whom Rogers had sent "to find out the great river Ouragon that runs into the South Sea and a Northwest Passage if possible." It was not possible. Carver joined Tute and headed for the planned winter bivouac on Lake Winnipeg, but the trinkets Tute carried were soon exhausted in trying to outdo the French traders, and they decided that they should go to Lake Superior to pick up more goods promised by Rogers before crossing Sioux country. Of more there was nil. Rogers had tumbled from favor and was shortly to stand trial (and be acquitted) for treason.

His backer gone, Carver began his pathetic private quest, first to deaf-eared Boston, then to London where his *Travels* was doctored and sold widely while he starved to death. His description of fertile lands and signs of copper and lead piqued the interest of a few influential men, as did his patriotic complaint that "had the English made themselves masters of the west side of the Mississippi we might now have the advantage of [the fur] trade with more Indians than double the number we have a right in all our extensive dominions." One member of Parliament went so far as to propose that Carver lead a party west to the Pacific, but the pall of impending war in the colonies put an end to that—and to Carver's dream of an inland empire. The first Englishman to get across the Mississippi and write down in detail what he had seen was in the right places but at the wrong times.

Spanish officials had no way of knowing how far west Englishmen had gone, so their worries had a lot of ground to cover. Ten or more English vessels were continuously on the Mississippi after 1763, operating as "floating stores" for Spanish planters and supplying the Anglos of Manchac and Baton Rouge, which were bidding fair to eclipse New Orleans as the first town of the river. As ominous as the fleet's presence might be, it was not illegal. What was illegal was the trespassing—the Englishmen who were sneaking up the Arkansas River, those from Prairie du Chien who were moving freely about on Spain's side of the river, those said to be even farther north in Upper Louisiana trading with the Sioux.

The administrators of Spanish Louisiana fired off letters of protest, which British officials artfully dodged. Those Englishmen on the wrong side of the river were there without authorization—a bad lot of vagabonds—little more than banditti really. In a sense the official line was correct. Save possibly for Carver, those who crossed the Father of Waters were neither Pittite expansionists nor a fifth column sent by King George. They were free-lance hawkers whose personal politics, even after 1776, ran a distant second to turning a profit in the Indian trade. And yet, in a roundabout way, those gritty Protestants who had tracked into the trans-Mississippi West were the vanguard of forces that would in time push Spain back toward her precious Mexico.

THAT WAS THE GOOD NEWS. For expansionists there was much more bad news attending the English plunge west. Hardly was the ink dry on the 1763 Paris treaty before the Ottawa chief Pontiac forged an alliance of tribes and struck the new intruders on the ancestral lands. From Michilimackinac to the upper Ohio River fell the fury of red men who felt keenly the loss of their French friends and by now had their first taste of Anglo-Saxon land-grabbers and chicaning traders. Detroit and Fort Pitt withstood sieges, but most other northwestern posts went under before Gen. Jeffrey Amherst launched a counterattack to suture the torn frontier. Not until English troops finally reached Fort de Chartres in October of 1765 was the Pontiac rebellion ended. For England it had been a sobering welcome to the core of the continent.

Britain's problems were largely people problems: disunity at home; disagreements with the Amerind in the transmontane west; but mainly discord in the thirteen colonies, where those who were once proud to call themselves Englishmen were behaving like anything but. Many reasons have been advanced for the Anglo-American rift, but one of the earliest if not the most divisive had to do with the trans-Allegheny West: quite literally, *what* to do with it. Colonial fur traders wanted free run of the territory. Colonial farmers were equally dead-set on pushing the Indian off and putting the plow in. Colonial speculators (among them such worthies as George Washington, Benjamin Franklin, and Patrick Henry) sought to obtain and hold parcels until they could be, well, subdivided.

English politicians looking at the big imperial picture couldn't agree on what to do. But when word of Pontiac's uprising reached London in August, opinion soon crystallized into the Proclamation of 1763, signed by George III on October 7. As if to solve all their immediate western problems with one stroke of the pen, the British forbade the colonists to purchase any land or settle anywhere west of the Appalachians. Instead, they were urged to move to the three "safe" new colonies of East Florida, West Florida, and Quebec. All those forests, valleys, and plains beyond the Proclamation Line were to be considered temporarily the property of the Indians and the preserve of the fur traders.

The colonists were outraged. George Washington expressed their sentiments precisely when he said that he could not view the proclamation as anything more than a temporary sop to the Indians. "Any person, therefore, who neglects the present opportunity of hunting out good lands and in some measure marking and distinguishing them for his own will never regain it." The truth was, England herself recognized it as only a momentary expedient that might delay awhile the inevitable. Of the Americans and the imaginary line Edmund Burke would say, "over this they would wander without possibility of restraint."

Had England made a stick-point of the proclamation, there might have been instant upheaval. But she did not. She turned her head while the colonists went their western way, sharping Indians out of their lands and then bracing themselves for the follow-up war cries and the tomahawk.

There was something far more rankling than colonial land-grabbing in the English mind. That glorious victory of 1763 had not come cheap. The wages of success had been debt. Before the French and Indian War, the Seven Years' War (what historian Lawrence Gipson calls the Great War for Empire), England had spent £11,000 a year to keep troops in America. What with subsequent costs of garrisoning the West and keeping order between aggrieved Indians and their own wandering subjects, that sum had now trebled. Worse, financing the war had jacked the national debt to a numbing £130,000,000, the yearly payment to retire it running to a cool £4,000,000. The money had to come from somewhere, and that somewhere could not be the at-home tax-payer, who was already paying many times what his transatlantic brother was. It was time to end salutary neglect, time for those across the sea to shoulder their fair share of the burden, particularly when so much of the expense went to defending those colonists who, as was proved once again in the Pontiac trouble, were incapable of defending themselves.

What followed from this thinking is the well-known drama of successive acts: the Revenue Act, the Currency Act, the Quartering Act, and the odious Stamp Act, which riled colonists to a congress and the sending of a petition to king and Parliament. The Stamp Act was rescinded but followed by the Declaratory Act. And so on.

The British were at first puzzled by the colonists' resistance to what seemed more than equitable. What did those people want, anyway? And what was a mother country to do? Mostly it dithered and floundered, but in 1768 a major decision was made regarding the West which cracked open the gate to colonial expansion. A year before, Lord Shelburne had proposed that the entire Mississippi Valley be opened to settlement, that the colonies be left to handle their own Indian problems and regulate trade, and that troops in the West be reduced and placed at Fort Pitt, Natchez, Fort de Chartres, and a new post on the Iberville River. In a matter of months Shelburne lost his job to the conservative Lord Hillsborough, who, partly on a variation of the guns-and-butter theme, amended the plan. Let the colonists run the fur trade, yes. But new colonies for the river valley were out; instead the Proclamation Line of 1763 was grudgingly moved somewhat west. Garrisons would be sharply curtailed and maintained only at the strategic Great Lakes posts of Niagara, Detroit, and Michilimackinac lest the French get any ideas again. Gen. Thomas Gage, commander of British troops in America, gave the policy his blessing: "Let the savages enjoy their desarts in quiet. . . . I am of opinion, independent of the motives of common justice and humanity, that the principles of interest and policy should induce us rather to protect than molest them. Were they drove from their forrests, the peltry trade would decrease, and [it is] not impossible that worst savages would take refuge in them; for they might then become the asylum of fugitive negroes, and idle vagabonds, escaped from justice, who in time might become formidable, and subsist by rapine, and plundering."

Such sweet lemons! Behind the humanitarian facade was an economy move and a desire to be totally rid of the distressing frontier problem by leaving it to the colonials, who would never be stopped by any line drawn on a map in Westminster anyway. At least the fur trade would go on. Thus was a pullback of British strength begun, to be relocated on the seaboard, where, if things continued as they were, the men would be needed.

In 1770 an incident occurred that caused the lion to pause and momentarily turn with menace. A dispute between England and Spain over the south Atlantic Falkland Islands threatened to break out in general war. General Gage was ordered to prepare to take New Orleans. But the threat evaporated. Fort de Chartres and Fort Pitt were per royal wish abandoned — removes that would have a bearing on another war, far more important in its consequences, that was not far away.

Parliamentary tolerance for ungrateful colonials stiffened in 1767. The new Townshend Acts were resisted, and brought on

George III was not the fool some Whig historians have made him. But neither was he on history's side.

boycotts and, in 1770, violence in Boston. Though most levies were repealed, George III and Parliament were dogged in maintaining the right to tax distant subjects. An odd thing was happening in England. The people who gave the world few isms, other than utilitarianism, art-of-the-possiblism, and business-as-usualism, now obstinately stood on pride and principle. Imperial patience was exhausted. The malcontents were to be brought into line.

England has produced as many great and gifted leaders as the next nation, but not between 1763 and 1783. On the crest of empire, she had a dearth of those who could direct it. Of course, there was William Pitt, but the Great Commoner who became Lord Chatham was physically ailing and showed it during his last crucial administration. His radical follower, the Earl of Shelburne, had liberal views on how to handle the colonists and their West, but he was rarely in power for long. Then there was Edmund Burke, the Old Whig sage who chose humanity over principle and imparted political wisdom to ages beyond his own. But there were also scads of middling sorts, mediocrities who failed to follow through on the possibilities of '63. They collected in political fragments — Old Whigs, Bedfordite Whigs, Grenville Whigs, Rockingham Whigs, Tories, and "King's Friends." What divided them was not ideology or party platforms but personal ambition and offices in the government that brought prestige and the whiff of power. Under the stress of what to do with America and its West, ministries rose and fell with the regularity of a summer thermometer in an arid land. Presiding over it all was the Hanoverian George III. Recent scholarship has shown him to be neither the fool nor the knave that Whig historians have made of him. Neither was he a king for his time. The center was not holding; things were shortly to fall apart.

A deep-rooted arrogance toward Americans stuck in the minds of some Englishmen. The New World had, after all, been peopled in part with felons, tarts, debtors, and expendable and exportable scum. Benjamin Franklin had confirmed this by offering to repay the home country for the human resources it sent by exporting a shipload of rattlesnakes. And then, two French philosophers, the Comte de Buffon and the Abbé Raynal, had remarked on how European animals degenerated on the other side of the Atlantic. One couldn't hold one's breath waiting on human genius to spring from such a barbaric soil.

There was another contemporary crosscurrent of thought that bred a sense of fatalism among some Englishmen. Bishop Berkeley had put it into a potent quatrain way back in 1720:

> Westward the course of empire takes its way,
> The first four acts already past.
> The fifth shall close the drama with the day,
> Time's noblest offspring is the last.

To the degree that men believed, and they did believe if sometimes only viscerally, it was a self-fulfilling prophecy. Greece, Rome, Spain — they were all behind the now-supreme England. Had nature chosen this time to open the fifth act in America? An amusing skit popular in London in 1774 portrayed two urbane Americans visiting the quaint ruins of London in the year 1974, as eighteenth-century Englishmen might have paid their respects to Athens.

America kept some distinguished friends in England right up

Benjamin Franklin was in London in early 1774 as agent for seething Massachusetts. The Privy Council was not sympathetic.

to, and even through, its rebellious war. In 1776, George Grenville observed to his audience in the House of Commons that the "seditious spirit of the colonies owes its birth to factions in this House." William Pitt, though an iron-fisted imperialist, saw justice in the slogan of no taxation without representation. "America," he declared, "being neither really nor virtually represented in Westminster, cannot be held legally or constitutionally or reasonably subject to obedience to any money bill of this kingdom." Edmund Burke said that he did not choose to disown America or its spirit because it was the spirit of his native land. "An Englishman," he said "is the unfittest person on earth to argue another Englishman into slavery." The effete old wit Horace

Walpole also had waspish words for his countrymen and his Parliament, which he accused of childishly "smashing an empire to see what it was made of." Yet the aging Whig kept a supercilious distance. "One has griefs enough of one's own," he wrote, "without fretting because America has eloped with a Presbyterian parson."

It is impossible to say at what point the rupture between England and her colonies became irreparable. But if a gun were at one's head to produce an answer or else, then the Quebec Act of 1774 would be as good a lifesaving guess as any. What it was meant to do was to right wrongs already done. The same Proclamation of 1763 that tried to stem the westward push of colonial plowmen had made a botch of right-rule in Canada, where seventy-five thousand Frenchmen had overnight become wards of imperial England. French Roman Catholics were all but locked out of the governance of their lands. By religion they were forbidden to practice law; and the new English law, the proceedings of which were in a language strange to them, was different from the law they were used to — particularly in its harsh treatment of debtors, who found prison one's destination instead of the western frontier. Carpetbaggers arrived from England and the lower colonies to assume positions of authority. They did well by themselves, seizing control of the fur trade and relieving the *habitants* of the little they had, within and sometimes without the new English law. The abuses were so flagrant that James Murray, the first English governor of Canada, complained to Lord Shelburne in 1766 that "the improper choice and the number of the civil officers sent over from England increased the disquietude of the colony. Instead of men of genius and untainted morals, the reverse were appointed to the most important offices, under whom it was impossible to communicate those impressions of the dignity of government by which alone mankind can be held together in society."

The injustices in Canada gnawed at the consciences of England's ministers, who hesitated to offend a Protestant constituency. But the momentum continued to build until, in June of 1774, Parliament with a rare display of courage passed the bill in which an enlightened George III concurred, saying that it was "founded on the clearest principles of justice and humanity; and will, I doubt not, have the best effect in quieting the minds and promoting the happiness of my Canadian subjects."

The Quebec Act extended religious toleration to French-Canadian Catholics. It also extended the boundaries of Quebec to those lands between the Ohio and the Mississippi which happened to be, by the way, good fur territory and convenient to Montreal. The howl from the lower thirteen colonies crossed an ocean. Now a long-time colonial with backbone knew where he stood: well down on the list of the most favored. Why else would the choicest West be taken from flesh and blood and be turned over to a bunch of contemptible French Papists who had been until recently the sworn enemy of them all? A year down the road was Bunker Hill. After that, the break could not be mended. England, alone and befuddled, had lost her best chance for the trans-Mississippi West. Still heavily in shadow, it awaited a fourth imperial claimant.

Chapter 16

Intimations of a Destiny

F. SCOTT FITZGERALD at the close of *The Great Gatsby* rhapsodizes on what must have gone through the minds of the first white men who set foot on the east coast of North America, how for a fleeting moment they were confronted with a virgin continent commensurate with their capacity for wonder. His words are moving. But it was probably not what was on their minds at all—at least not the first Englishmen, for whom the overwhelming fact of life was loneliness, the feeling of being at the end of the earth.

In the beginning the New World was a frightening place. The new arrivals clung to tidewater where they worshiped God in their unpopular way or behaved as obedient second-class citizens and played their subservient role in the mercantile scheme of things. Tobacco was the first cash crop they sent home to their betters. In time would be added rice and indigo and hemp and "ships stores"—timber and turpentine and pine pitch lacking in the home country with the peerless navy. Looking to England, the West was behind them—the direction of darkness, the direction of terror, a "Devil's den" in the words of Michael Wigglesworth, who described it in 1662 as

> A waste and howling wilderness,
> Where none inhabited
> But hellish fiends, and brutish men
> That devils worshipped.

Terror became suspicion as the transplanted Englishmen—humble free farmers, indentured servants, religious separatists, decaying gentlemen, and all-or-nothing gamblers—slowly filled the littoral and backed into the continent. In no way did they

316

"Daniel Boone's First View of Kentucky" is the title of this painting by William Ranney. Eden would soon become a bloody hell.

resemble in mobility or daring contemporary Frenchmen or Spaniards with the fur itch or the gold itch, who wandered far into the continent in small numbers. Instead, they clustered and, befitting planters, put down roots, thus becoming many and strong in their prosaic way. Now the West showed flickers of light. It was where the supplanted native Americans went. Where the Frenchmen now were, it was said, and beyond them where the undeserving Spaniards were rumored to be in yet another of their El Dorados. Years passed. Children were begotten and they in turn begot. The West that had been the direction of attack became merely a direction, then a direction to go — where there was cheap and productive land, a refuge for debtors and those in need of a second chance — ultimately a mythical idea in the minds of northern Europeans with adumbrations of the biblical garden, of the New Canaan, the land of milk and honey.

There was a time — or perhaps not a time at all in the sense of a frozen moment, month, year, or even generation—when those in the thirteen colonies were no longer Englishmen, when they were transformed into something new, a variant strain. Maybe it was 1750 or thereabouts. At any rate, a people who proclaimed until the year 1776 that they were mistreated loyal subjects of England had undergone a metamorphosis that even the most self-aware of them could barely fathom. The natural environment may not be the straitjacket that some would make it, but certainly landforms and woods and rivers and weather and soils and horizons have a shaping effect on those who are familiar with them and ignorant of their opposites. For one thing, they demand adjustments, ways of doing things that keep one around for tomorrow's hunt or the next spring's planting. The New World was not sane and settled England, manicured and medieval still in its visible relics. On the contrary, it was, in a word, wildness, with strange beasts and trees and food plants that could be cultivated to one's sustenance.

Stranger still were the aboriginal peoples, sometime friends and sometime enemies who, as surely as the sun set in the west, had to be dispossessed of the West. Yet they had traits and ways that were picked up and absorbed into the tissue of the colonists: generosity in sharing what one had with another; a reverence for an extravagant nature, which alien influences from overseas insisted on reducing, subduing—a task so well-performed that it would leave, long after, guilts and scars. From the red man also came impulses to be antic, uninhibited, and violent. Those who took musket, knife, and tomahawk with them to the fields to do what they had to do became proficient in their use, and soon they were using them in deeds they did not have to do.

In the mid-eighteenth century the glacial movement west melted and released a torrent. Communication with England was never better than poor. To cope with the demands of a raw continent, the colonists made do, improvised. They became self-reliant, then sure of themselves, then even cocky. Because they had come from the middle and lower classes, they resented those who put on airs and invoked bloodlines rather than their individual record. *Levelling* was the English word for the phenomenon, and it crossed even the inviolable lines of the sexes; since women were in short supply, they were more valued and held in greater esteem than their sisters in England. The nearer to the frontier, the greater the levelling, and even in 1770 about a third of all Americans spent at least part of their lives on the frontier.

Separated for so long by so much water, language went in separate directions. Americans borrowed words from the Dutch of New Amsterdam and from the Indians, and made up some of their own to describe the new flora and fauna and that direction again—the "backwoods," the "backcountry." More critical for what was to happen in 1776, words acquired different shades of meaning on the two sides of the Atlantic. "Constitution" to an Englishman meant the accretions of law, precedent, and practice that were elucidated in Parliament. To the American, "constitution" meant a written document that governed the relations of king and subject, and that admitted no changes. Other terms relating to government—which under a policy of salutary neglect meant the evolution of satisfactory self-government, thank you— were open to varying interpretations.

After 1750 colonists started referring to themselves as Americans rather than Englishmen. When they went to visit the old country, as those of means sometimes did, they found it strange, cramped, its people morally decadent. They resented hearing *their* country referred to by Englishmen as "our" country. They missed "home" and its wide open spaces. As provincials, they were pleased with themselves and did not like being patronized. What no one else knew, but they at least sensed, was that they had come of age.

England was bewildered by it all. Indulgence had been repaid with ingratitude, and by the year 1768 dismay had given way to a mood of anger and the tardy putting-down of the parental foot. Enough was enough. Hadn't England just concluded a long war on America's behalf? And hadn't Americans throughout that war actually traded with the enemy in the French West Indies for sugar to make their rum, which they took to Africa to barter for slaves? Hadn't they flouted the Navigation Acts, which prohibited such conduct even in peacetime? Hadn't they spurned laws meant to maintain British naval strength, which alone assured their protection? As for this "no taxation without representation" hypocrisy, hadn't the South Carolina Commons House of

Assembly and the Virginia House of Burgesses in 1765 said no to representation when it was suggested? Hadn't the rabble-rousing colony of Massachusetts in the year 1768 turned up its nose at the same offer? As for this insatiable appetite for western lands where they only made trouble with the Indians, why, if you gave them a mile they'd take a river valley! The time had come to end the permissiveness. Now it was time to think as a family — imperially.

Filial greed and ingratitude were indisputably a part of it. What have you done for me lately? was a question implicit in every step toward separation. But the heart of the matter went deeper than that. The economics of England were still mercantile; those of her colonies were not — at least not by volition. Mother supplied capital and protection, and in return the wards were to provide labor and raw materials and, when it came to that, a market for surplus finished goods. That was the way it was and had been from the beginning — because it worked. Well, almost worked. In some places. Not in New England, of course, which had little that England lacked and seemed bent on producing in competition. A cardinal precept of the mercantile dogma was that there was a finite amount of money or controllable wealth in the world, and that competition within an extended nation was counterproductive. It upset the balance of trade between colony and home, and allowed foreigners a bigger slice of a small pie. Adam Smith would slay this senile dragon by showing that the universe of business was larger than supposed and unbridled competition was good, but too late. The *Wealth of Nations* first appeared in 1776, but even if George III and every member of the House of Lords had had the time to read it, it would have been too late.

Americans were no longer content as junior partners in the enterprise, nor would they entrust their well-being to the chance of whether a ship made it from England across three thousand miles of unreliable ocean. Even economically they were a new breed. Four out of five were farmers, and they had more than hemp and tobacco to sell to London merchants. They'd become agrarians on a grand scale, and what made it grand was the abundance of good cheap land that the lowliest man could buy after a few years' working for the high wages in the chronically labor-short colonies. With fertile fields and fertile women there was natural increase, a steeply rising population augmented by land-hungry immigrants, largely Scotch-Irish and Germans, who would go west to get theirs. After 1750 most arable land east of the mountains was either under cultivation or being held back by land speculators. Now more than ever west was the direction of making it, and when the defeated French were made to surrender land beyond the Appalachians, west was the only way to go.

Over in England, that land of crofters and cheap labor, Dr. Samuel Johnson belittled the cession as being only the "barren parts of the continent, the refuse of the earlier adventurers which the French, who came last, had taken only as better than nothing." The learned doctor Sam was in this case ill-informed, as any illiterate Presbyterian frontiersman could have told him. There was land out there, virgin land, and it wanted turning.

The restraining line of the 1763 proclamation sagged for five years, then snapped and all but vaporized. Settlers had been over the mountains before the French and Indian War, and now they were back in growing numbers, risking even the death penalty to root themselves on Indian lands. Besides the solitary buckskinned men who picked up rifle, hoe, and family, and struck out west, there were the many land companies with speculative capital, which continuously lobbied with their own colonial governments and made under-the-table stock offers to England's peerage for favorable handling of their petitions. They were a counterbalance to the fur interests that wished the West left alone. Many great fortunes in the colonies had been made in land speculation.

The western land schemes were many, and as backers they had men of highest rank on both sides of the Atlantic. The Ohio Company was the oldest of them, dating back to 1747, when Virginia nabobs put it together. It had its ups and downs, to be reorganized in 1769 as the Grand Ohio Company. Pennsylvanians got into the act in the mid-1750s with the Vandalia Company, of which Benjamin Franklin was a leading member. There was also the ambitious Mississippi Company, which had among its prime movers no less than George Washington, and which in 1763 sought parcels at the mouth of the Ohio along the Mississippi in partial payment for soldiers who had served in the late war.

There were dozens of other companies put together before, during, and after the war, and some that never quite got put together — such as that of a Philadelphia merchant named Samuel Hazard. All he was prepared to ask for was that territory west from Pennsylvania down to South Carolina and "thence [to] extend one hundred miles to the westward of the River Mississippi; and to be divided from Virginia and Carolina by the great chain of mountains that runs along the continent from the northwestern to the southwestern parts of America." Hazard intended to allow only Protestants on his land, which happened to include a few hundred thousand acres of the French and Spanish Wests. Unfortunately, he dropped dead just as he was about to sail to England with his petition, having earned himself an A for effort and an F in geography.

Most of the land schemes were bubbles — to pop, come to nothing. Pontiac's War and the proclamation of 1763 made England go slow in approving anything. Renewed hopes and new petitions came after 1768, when the line of settlement was moved west. But the whole British handling of western lands left a bitter taste in colonial mouths. Massachusetts, Connecticut, North and South Carolina, Georgia, and Virginia had claims to the West based on their original sea-to-sea charters. The most expansion-minded was populous Virginia, the Old Dominion, whose governor, Robert Dinwiddie, way back in 1755 had informed England's Board of Trade: "Virg'a resumes its ancient Breadth, and has not other Limits to the West y'm w't its first Royal Charter assigned to it, and y't is to the So. Sea, including the Isl'd of California."

Whether with plots legitimately bought from land companies or illegally staked out on their own, a flood of settlers left the East and aimed in the same direction Cabeza de Vaca had two and a half centuries before, in unknowing agreement with the Spaniard who wrote, "We ever held it certain that going to the sunset we must find what we desire." Some eighty Pennsylvanians headed for Natchez in the far southwest, following the Ohio and Mississippi rivers. In 1772, Capt. Amos Ogden brought more settlers to the river town from New Jersey, who were in turn joined by still others from New Jersey, Pennsylvania, and North Carolina. The

A wilderness farm of the eighteenth century. Such use of the earth outraged the Indian, who gave up his hunting land grudgingly.

largest group, four hundred families, left Connecticut in 1773 and 1774 under the leadership of Phineas Lyman. By 1776 twenty-five hundred whites with six hundred slaves were located in the neighborhood of the West Florida communities of Pensacola, Mobile, Manchac, Yazoo, and Natchez, looking down Spanish throats. It was right in keeping with English imperial policy, and it made good mercantile sense to those who believed in southern tropical colonies.

The big push, however, was directly west from the middle colonies. Land purchases from Indian tribes, negotiated by Indian superintendents but strongly influenced by speculator-lobbyists, helped pave the way. The Treaty of Hard Labor with the Cherokees in 1768 opened up some of backcountry North Carolina and much of West Virginia. In the same year, the Treaty of Fort Stanwix saw the Iroquois sell off dubious claims to lands in southwest New York, western Pennsylvania, and parts of West Virginia, Kentucky, and Tennessee. When every grasping hand was done fashioning the treaty, much of the communal hunting ground of the powerful Shawnees, Delawares, and Cherokees was gone. In the 1770 Treaty of Lochaber, Virginia paid off the Cherokees for another big bite of land in what is now Kentucky. Before long, in the employ of Richard Henderson of North Carolina, Daniel Boone found the famous shortcut, hacked out the Wilderness Road, and opened up Kentucky to settlers who soon established Harrodsburg and Boonesborough and Saint Asaph's on ground that Chief Dragging Canoe had warned would be "dark and bloody." The provocations of white men hastened that day of reckoning — or years of reckoning, because one battle or one war would not settle the issue.

The first round went to Virginia in 1774 in what is called Lord Dunmore's War. From the upper Ohio to Kentucky red men and white men killed each other until, in October, a Shawnee force was beaten at Point Pleasant and the chiefs were made to give up

Artist George Caleb Bingham titled this "The Concealed Enemy."
Woodland Indians used white men's weapons with red men's tactics.

Bingham also painted Boone escorting settlers through the Cumberland Gap. War awaited them west of the Appalachians.

Kentucky forever. Feeling ever safer, frontiersmen followed the rivers and cut through the gaps and plopped themselves down in lonely woodland stations around the Forks of the Ohio, eastern Kentucky, and even eastern Tennessee. By 1776 bitter seed had been sown in the bluegrass country, and it would not be long before the first bloody harvest came in.

IMPERIAL-MINDED ENGLISHMEN had the longer look west than those farmers who put one foot in front of the other and crossed the eastern mountains. The West beyond, the dark three-fifths of the continent that palsied Spain held on to, was tempting to those who would have a monopoly of the peltry trade. But the pull from the continental center was also felt by certain colonials who were neither frontier farmers nor London fur merchants. They were few, yet influential—those who, in Bernard De Voto's words, "had the unconscious feel of a continent, the continental will."

John Adams, a stripling of twenty just matriculated from Harvard, read the future before the war with France had turned in the Anglos' favor: ". . . if we can remove the turbulent Gallicks, our people, according to the exactest computations, will in another century become more numerous than England itself. Should this be the case, since we have, I may say, all the naval stores of our nation in our hands, it will be easy to obtain the mastery of the seas; and then the united force of all Europe will not be able to subdue us."

The exclusivity implied in the pronoun *we* reads unconsciously seditious for that early year. Or was it a mere slip of the tongue? Benjamin Franklin, who spent the years prior to the Revolution in England, professing loyalty while looking out for his western land schemes and watching his tongue, was so upset by the passage of the Stamp Act that he sent an impolitic letter to Lord Kames in 1767 on behalf of his put-upon America:

> She may suffer at present under the arbitrary power of this country; she may suffer for a while in a separation from it; but these are temporary evils that she will outgrow. . . . America, an immense territory, favoured by Nature with all advantages of climate, soil, great navigable rivers, and lakes, & must become a great country, populous and mighty; and she will in less time than is generally conceived, be able to shake off any shackles that may be imposed on her, and perhaps place them on the imposers.

What Franklin also told mercantile Englishmen, though there is no evidence that they were listening, was that Americans were an agrarian people who with new land to tend would raise both the station of the landless poor and the birthrate, until, within a century, more "Englishmen" would live west of the Atlantic than in the Scepter'd Isle. Franklin, of course, was a practical man, and practical men usually keep their fantasies under wraps. Poets do not. Philip Freneau and a Princeton classmate wrote a poem in dialogue for the commencement in 1771 entitled "The Rising Glory of America."

> What empires yet must rise,
> What kingdoms, pow'rs and states where now are seen
> But dreary wastes and awful solitude,
> Where melancholy sits with eye forlorn
> And hopes the day when Britain's sons shall spread
> Dominion to the north and south and west
> Far from th' Atlantic to Pacific shores?

The response to the burbling query is no less grandiose in vision:

> I see, I see
> A thousand kingdoms rais'd, cities and men
> Num'rous as sand upon the ocean shore;
> Th' Ohio then shall glide by many a town
> Of note: and where the Mississippi stream
> By forests shaded now runs weeping on,
> Nations shall grow and states not less in fame
> Than Greece and Rome of old . . .

Freneau, who became a super-patriot and a hater of Englishmen nonpareil, later revised "Britain's sons" to read "we," and in 1782, before the Revolutionary War flamed out, he returned to speak of the West, this time in unfettered prose. A land of ineffable beauty and fecundity it was, with a thousand rivers feeding the Mississippi. That "Prince of rivers," he said, made the Nile no more than "a rivulet and the Danube a mere ditch." The river is masculine and coming from an unknown source gathers "his remotest waters, rolls forward through the frozen regions of the north, and stretching his extended arms to the east and west, embraces those savage groves, as yet uninvestigated by the traveller, unsung by the poet, or unmeasured by the chain of the geometrician," before heading for the Gulf of Mexico and "laving the shores of many fertile countries in his passage, inhabited by savage nations as yet almost unknown, and without a name."

Freneau's words reflect the prevailing ignorance of Americans about what was beyond the Mississippi, and Freneau was not being quite fair to Frenchmen and Spaniards who had been as far as the Rockies, and along the Pacific shore. They knew those "savage nations" all too well in some cases and had even given them names. But then patriotism is patriotism, and it has a rhetoric of its own. What Freneau gushed about, Thomas Hutchins, a surveyor of lands extending west to the Mississippi who was later appointed "Geographer to the United States," put in hard-boiled terms. He viewed the continent as a whole and the Spanish claims to the West as no hindrance. "If we want it, I warrant it will soon be ours." So would the dominion of the seas, so rich and secure was the coming seat of empire. "North America," Hutchins predicted, ". . . as surely as the land is now in being, will hereafter be trod by the first people the world ever knew." The term Manifest Destiny was not coined until the 1840s, when the United States went to war with Mexico, but there it was, larger than life-size and smelling just as sweet, way back in 1784.

Words aside, neither Freneau nor Hutchins were larger than life-size in doing anything about the West. But behind them, and for that matter behind Adams and Franklin and Washington (who preferred a slow digestion of land in that direction), was the towering presence of Thomas Jefferson, that wonderfully complex man and gifted dilettante who would make scrupulous weather observations for five years at Williamsburg, catalog birds and plants and Indian tribes as though he were a one-man encyclopedia, and demolish Buffon's contention that New World life forms were inferior in size and quality to those of Europe. He would never go to the West, but he had a mind to encompass it. He would be the chief architect of its acquisition, and he would leave his mark on it and on his nation more than any other one man.

As a boy at his father's Shadwell plantation in Virginia's Albemarle County, Jefferson listened to family friends telling what they knew of it—the interior, the far beyond. A Northwest Passage might be there. Surely prodigies, wonders unseen. The boundless and systematic curiosity sucked it all in. Doubtlessly he took notes. When he drafted the Declaration of Independence, he included a protest against the proclamation of 1763 that tried to keep Americans from going in that direction. In his *Notes on Virginia,* begun in 1781 when he was governor of that brahmin colony, he imparted an astonishing accumulation of information: where Santa Fe was, how far Santa Fe was from Mexico City, how far

Of all Americans, the most west-thinking was Thomas Jefferson.

New Orleans was from Santa Fe, what tribes lived along the Missouri, which he rightly theorized came from a higher altitude than the Mississippi because it rushed in cold and crested later.

In his collecting he'd also netted some misinformation. He guessed that the Blue Ridge Mountains were most likely the highest in North America. He also passed along a howler from one Mr. Stanley, who claimed to have been captured by Indians and shuttled west from tribe to tribe to beyond the mountains where the Missouri was born. Here the aborigines reported real live elephants stomping around the country to the north of them. While Jefferson discounted the presence of elephants in such northern latitudes, the previous existence of mammoths he knew to be fact from the bones found at saltlicks on branches of the Tennessee River. Jefferson had some of those very bones in his private museum, having obtained them during the din of war from his friend, the American hope in the West, Gen. George Rogers Clark. While bones and antiquities occupied Jefferson's mind, there was also room to worry about the geopolitical here-and-now. In December of 1783, shortly after hostilities with England had been concluded, he wrote to Clark:

"I find they have subscribed a very large sum of money in England for exploring the country from the Mississippi to California. They pretend it is only to promote knowledge. I am afraid they have thoughts of colonizing into that quarter. Some of us have been talking here in a feeble way of making the attempt to search that country but I doubt whether we have enough of that kind of spirit to raise the money. How would you like to lead such a party?"

Nothing came of the English design or the offer to Clark, and the following year Jefferson went off to Paris, where he would succeed Franklin as minister to France, make a hit with French intellectuals, and listen for a beguiling while to a young American with a wild dream dear to both their hearts. John Ledyard was back from Captain Cook's last voyage. He had deserted the King's navy by jumping ship off Long Island and had written his own account of the journey. With the cerebral Virginian he discussed the pregnant possibilities of America's future in the Northwest — Nootka and the sea-otter skins and China . . . and the pure adventure of it all! The mad young man planned to make his way across the waist of Russia to the Bering Strait, and somehow get himself across on a peltry ship that would drop him on the Northwest Coast. Then he would hike across North America from the other way — west to east!

Jefferson could only have listened and smiled and nodded at such a farfetched itinerary. Ledyard, to anyone's everlasting wonder, actually made it to Yakutsk deep in Siberia, where in 1788 he was arrested as a spy inimical to Catherine's own impending expansion in the Pacific fur trade. Deportation was his punishment, and within a year he died in Cairo while on yet another harebrained exploration, this time into darkest Africa. There would be other candidates who failed to cross Jefferson's continent, including the French spy Michaux, before, years later, Merriwether Lewis and William Clark, the youngest brother of fellow Virginian George Rogers Clark, did the third president's bidding. That, of course, was in the future, at the dawn of the nineteenth and America's century, long after those revolutionary days when a handful of men turned the world upside down.

The even smaller handful of men who between the fall of Quebec and the surrender at Yorktown saw the West in their future were mainly of the elite. Neither Jefferson, preeminent among them, nor Adams nor Franklin nor Washington would ever watch August cumuli build on the far horizon of the sub-humid buffalo plains. But Jefferson would have heard about it. He was the bridge. Only he of the four of them adopted as his own the egalitarian unwashed on the frontier. They were his kind of people — in the abstract, of course, not as tablemates at Monticello. They were land tillers, socially and physically mobile, self-reliant individuals who could cooperate with one another in raising a barn or bringing in the corn, but who remained lovers of liberty with radical republican inclinations. They were the blade edge of the thrust west.

Those on the Mississippi side of the eastern mountains also had shortcomings. They tended to be shiftless and disorderly, bigoted and randomly violent. Moreover, as independence swelled from a passing thought to a compulsive need on the eastern seaboard, those in the hinterlands were largely unaffected. Down south, in the backwoods of Georgia and in the West Florida settlements fronting Spanish Louisiana, the political makeup was decidedly loyalist. Those farther north, in the valleys of Tennessee and Kentucky, and along the beautiful banks of the Ohio and its tributaries, though Whigs of a type with their woodland democracies, had less of a beef with Britain than with the old colonies. It was there that they were underrepresented and neglected. There in settled comfort lived the big-money wheeler-dealers in western lands who, no friends of the poor man, were after his piece of the bountiful interior garden.

The population of the colonies in 1776 stood in excess of 2.5 million, well over a half-million of them occupied with rolling back the western wilderness. Many of the westerners were Scotch-Irish and Germans who had come in the first part of the eighteenth century. Another infusion of those hardy peoples occurred between 1769 and 1773, when crop failures beset Europe; Irish, Italians, Greeks, Scots, and Minorcans also arrived then in modest numbers. America, the land of opportunity, was beginning to work its magic. America, the melting pot, however, was still a phenomenon for the future. The majority of the colonists — by estimates, between 65 and 70 percent — traced their descent from England, and after the close of the French and Indian War they enjoyed more security and prosperity than they ever had before. Nevertheless, they were ready to close their jaws on the hand that had fed them.

Revolutions are launched by those with appetites that have been whetted without being sated, not by hungry men scratching for their daily bread. For revolutions to succeed, there cannot be one cause; it takes many men of ardor to pull it off, and rarely if ever do they agree on what is worth their passion. Only when a sufficient number espousing diverse causes identify a common foe or frustrator do they get together and do the deed. That happened in 1776.

There were the radical demagogues like Tom Paine and James Otis, who decried injustice on the grandest scale and, speaking in the name of mankind, urged turning everything over and starting anew. They were a factor, but "their" revolution would take place thirteen years later in France. There were merchants, well-off, but wanting to be better-off, who regarded British mercantile restraints as intolerable. In economics they were *laissez faire,* and they were a potent factor. There were Anglophobes, who wanted to see the mighty humbled. There were Anglos who were Puritans or from Puritan stock and objected to an established church that had not cleansed itself of Papist trappings and shared the bed of kings; they were strong in New England and in the West, a decisive factor in the outcome. There were jackals, down-and-out ne'er-do-wells who always saw chaos as the best climate in which to better their personal fortunes; they were a factor excruciatingly familiar to loyalists, who paid dearly for what, had the war ended differently, were virtues.

There were the legalists, those self-governing and self-sufficient men who saw a wayward Parliament more than a king subverting a constitution and dictating to colonists as though they were children. They had read Montesquieu and Voltaire and, above all, England's own John Locke, who believed that liberty was a birthright and government a compact between the rulers and the ruled. They tended to be idolaters of Newton and science, deists in a religion of optimism. They were our Founding Fathers, the dominant factor in a revolution that was essentially conservative.

And there were a few from all rungs who sensed that they were on the brink of owning a continent and an exclusive destiny.

Chapter 17

The War and the West

THE DECISIVE AND REMEMBERED BATTLES of the Revolutionary War were fought on the Atlantic slope, precisely where England wanted her colonists and where, with French assistance, those colonists won their independence from an England less defeated than aware by the autumn of 1781 that victory was unattainable. But the war didn't stop there. It spread north to the uncertain ground between New York and Canada; it flowed over the mountains to the near West of the Carolina backcountry and the valleys of the upper Ohio. It even found its way farther west along the Mississippi River.

When men become sick of any war, they say it is a madness, that it makes no sense. The war in the West was that way early. While uniformed men were marching with precision and purpose in New Jersey and Pennsylvania, following prescribed maneuvers and listening for the command to fire the "perfect volley," the backwoods version raged on a smaller scale, a travesty of what was accepted in civilized climes, though such quaint chivalric survivals as "oaths of allegiance" and *parole* coexisted with guerilla tactics and the murder of innocents.

From the first, the western war lacked coherence. Colonials might be patriots, loyalists, or neutrals, or might shift position when their lives were at stake. British officers might be united in their loyalty to England, but of no one mind on how to prosecute the war. Indians of many tribes were forced to choose sides on the basis of short-range blandishments or long-run considerations of who would win and how tribal lands and survival would be affected.

333

Before war was formalized with a declaration, the Americans had hoped to keep the Indians across the mountains neutral, and they sent agents west to make agreements. Never was thinking more wishful. As always, the Amerind was an anvil to white men's hammers. But he had learned something in his long association with them. Englishmen were not all that likable as a rule, but they came to trade and with the best goods. The Americans — known to them variously as the Bostonians, the Long Knives, or the dirt-eaters — came after the earth, to clear it and plant wastefully on the domain of hunters. That the enmity was deep-seated and mutual is borne out by the words of Benjamin Franklin, a good and civilized man often called the most typical American of his time. After witnessing the tumult of a nocturnal mass Indian drunk, he cynically observed that "if it be the design of Providence to extirpate these savages in order to make room for the cultivators of the earth; it seems not improbable that rum may be the appointed means. It has already annihilated all the tribes who formerly inhabited all the seacoast."

It came as no surprise that most of the tribes in the near West went over to the side of Britain, some sooner, some later. In the South the Cherokees did so early and took a drubbing from the colonials in 1776. The Creeks and Choctaws were also enlisted but went into more effective action later. In the Old Northwest the Ottawas, the Wyandots, and the Miamis were ready allies of the English. In the middle, the formidable Shawnees and the indecisive Delawares kept out of the fray until senseless butcherings of innocent squaws and children by frontier yahoos pitted them, too, against settlers in western Pennsylvania and Kentucky. In this degenerate western war, stealth and savagery were the rule, and gains were measured not in territory seized and held, but in cabins and lodges burned, bushels of corn destroyed, livestock wantonly killed, prisoners and scalps taken. The beautiful Ohio River Valley was transformed into a scene of ugliness, the "Eden of Kentucky" into a purgatory where individual settlers fled their private gardens and were bottled up in fetid stations.

The British had been caught shorthanded in the Northwest when war erupted. Only five hundred regulars were garrisoned in the strongholds at Niagara, Detroit, and Michilimackinac.

"The Death of Jane McCrea" was based on an actual incident used as propaganda by the rebels. The innocent girl was scalped while going to join her soldier sweetheart.

*Rebel military hopes
in the West were
in the capable hands
of George Rogers
Clark, but shortages of
men and arms mostly
tied them.*

THE BETTMANN ARCHIVE

Nevertheless, they were well placed at the strategic Great Lakes, where they protected the fur trade and were provisioned with relative ease via the Saint Lawrence water system. Lacking her own men, Britain employed stand-ins, Indians for the most part, who required a liberal dole of presents and some education in how the red man's interest coincided with the king's across the ocean. Even hard-boiled career officers had difficulty adjusting to this bastardized style of war. Though a British officer or two might lead a party of Indians on their gory sorties, they had their hands full restraining the red men from taking scalps and torturing captives. A sickening business this bounty hunting—made more so when the random scalpings included as victims loyalist families trying to make their way to British territory.

The war was fated to spread to the farther West with the entrance of Spain into the contest in July 1779. A few rebels, however, gave fate a healthy shove by opening hostilities early, even prematurely. There was James Willing, the rascal commander of the *Rattlesnake,* who terrorized loyalists on the lower Mississippi in 1778 and established plunder as the first objective of battle. Head and shoulders above Willing was George Rogers Clark, America's "Hero of the West," who then as now had his detractors, but more than any other man on the scene furthered American claims to northwestern lands.

Clark was another expansion-minded Virginian, a redheaded major of the militia with a common weakness for tippling and an uncommon gift for command. Having gone to Kentucky in 1773 to found a settlement, he was back in Williamsburg late in 1777 to push a daring plan for taking the Illinois Country, where, his spies told him, the fertile plains had been virtually abandoned by British troops. Clark's motives and his achievements have been argued pro and con. What cannot be argued is that Governor Patrick Henry, Thomas Jefferson, and others with clout believed in him and approved his plan. He was promoted to lieutenant colonel in the Virginia militia and authorized to raise five hundred men for the avowed purpose of defending Kentucky; secretly his orders were to take the Illinois Country for Virginia.

But Clark never got his five hundred men. All he could muster was 178, mostly tried but poorly provisioned frontier fighters serving a three-month enlistment for a promise of three hundred western acres each if they were successful. The Virginia redhead was a man to make do, a believer in self, doubtlessly warmed, as were his backers, by the fresh flush of victory at Saratoga and optimistic about picking up good land for his own enrichment. His "dash" through the West began in May of 1778 when the little force rowed down the Ohio from Fort Pitt, getting word en route that France had declared war against England. The news was especially welcomed by Clark. Now he could hope for a kindly reception at his destination, which he had never seen.

Kaskaskia fell to Clark's buckskinned battalion on July 4, 1778, without a shot from a flintlock rifle. The town's five hundred Frenchmen were utterly surprised, none so completely as Philippe François de Rastel, Chevalier de Rocheblave, the unpopular British-appointed commander of the post, from which the English had withdrawn their regulars in 1776 to shave expenses. Rocheblave had been commandant of Sainte Geneviève after the Seven Years' War, but he had no stomach for Spaniards and later went over the river and to the English, who found him trustworthy and diligent in their interests. Clark packed him off to a Virginia prison.

With the remaining Frenchmen, who had sworn a pro forma oath of allegiance to Britain and were terrified of the ragged, unkempt American troops, Clark was magnanimous. Though a conqueror, he brought freedom, he assured them, and also the message that their France now sided with the rebels in a just cause. As for their religion, they were free to practice it as they wished. All they had to do was swear an oath of allegiance to his government. The charismatic Clark was delighted with the response: "In a few minutes the scene of mourning and distress was turned to an excess of joy, nothing else seen or heard — adorning the streets with flowers and pavilians of different colours, compleating their happiness by singing etc."

The nearby settlements of Prairie du Rocher and Saint Philippe and Cahokia meekly submitted to Clark's equable terms. The English Illinois Country with its nearly one thousand Frenchmen was now the American Illinois Country — at least temporarily. Clark did not have, and never would have, the men or the money to hold whatever land he had won with a show of force and meliorating speeches. What he did win that was lasting and more beneficial to his colony and the new Congress were the hearts of prominent men in the American Bottom. Father Pierre Gibault, the village priest at Kaskaskia, was one who took Clark at his word and Clark's cause as his own. Ten days after celebrating the American takeover, he journeyed to Vincennes, still nominally under British control, to pass the word quietly among Frenchmen that brighter days had come. When Clark dispatched a token force under Capt. Leonard Helm to Fort Sackville, they found an American flag flying over that strategic Wabash post.

A pair of well-off merchants also swung Clark's way: Gabriel Cerré of Kaskaskia liberally supplied his troops, while Francis Vigo, an Italian trader operating from Saint Louis with whom Clark struck a lifelong friendship, introduced the American colonel to Fernando de Leyba, the Spanish lieutenant governor at Saint Louis. Gracious notes were exchanged before Clark crossed the river to visit the Spaniard and his family at the official's residence. "Colonel Clark merits the best attentions of all the people in his jurisdiction, who are indebted to him for his affability, clemency, and upright administration of justice," de Leyba reported to Bernardo de Gálvez, his superior at New Orleans. Clark had an equally high opinion of de Leyba, writing that "he omitted nothing in his Power to prove his Attachment to the Americans with such openness as left no room for doubt; as I was never before in Compy. of any Spanish gent. I was much surprised in my expectations; for instead of finding that reserve thought peculiar to that Nation, I here saw not the least symptoms of it." De Leyba sealed the friendship with a commitment that later events would make slightly ridiculous. "He has offered me," Clark wrote to Governor Patrick Henry, "all the force he could raise, in case of an attack by Indians from Detroit, as there is now no danger from any other quarter."

Thus did the war gently crowd the river that drained half a continent. There was something absurd and ironic about how it began and how it would end and the nature of the parties to the shadowy conflict. Land that was Indian land by any but the imperial measure was being contended for by Englishmen and Americans and, in the summer of 1779, by Spaniards as well. But next to the atomized Amerind, the most plentiful folk sprinkled over the immense and indifferent valley were Frenchmen. For over a decade they had been orphaned by imperial France, which, even after declaring for the Americans, gave assurances it would not reclaim any former lands east of the Mississippi. So the strange surrogate war in the West assumed another paradoxical dimension. Frenchmen might hold the balance of power, but with no single flag to rally round, they took sides as circumstances decreed, and the battle rosters of rival forces were heavily weighted with French surnames.

Some fought for England; they were overwhelmingly Canadians and, as likely as not, had a stake in the fur trade. Some were firmly with the Americans because they hated England or had republican proclivities. Others, almost all of them west of the Mississippi, where they had been before the defeat of 1763 or where they had fled soon after, were loyal to Spain, in whose custody

THE MAKING
OF A STALEMATE
1778–1782

Sioux

◄∼∼∼∼∼∼∼	George Rogers Clark sweeps the Illinois Country for the Americans, French-occupied Kaskaskia surrendering to him, July 4, 1778.
◄ — — —	Henry Hamilton retakes Vincennes for Britain against token opposition in December, 1778.
◄ ▪ ▪ ▪ ▪ ▪ ▪ ▪ ▪	In a daring winter campaign, Clark takes Vincennes and Hamilton, February 25, 1779.
◄ · · · · · · · · · ·	British armed and led Indians from Ohio continually batter Americans on Upper Ohio (*indicates major American defeats.) Greatest Anglo/Indian victories came late in war, neutralizing Clark's successes farther west.
◄— ◄— ◄—	Massive British thrust (though largely composed of Indian mercenaries) led by Emmanuel Hesse descends the Mississippi River to take St. Louis but is repulsed, May 26, 1780.
◄∿∿∿∿∿∿	Meager Spanish force reinforces St. Louis from Ste. Geneviève.
◄■◄■◄■◄■	Joint Spanish-American force led by Col. John Montgomery vainly pursues Hesse's retreating army, burns Sauk villages on the Rock River.
◄— · · · ◄— · ·	Spanish force under Capt. Eugene Pourée captures British Fort St. Joseph and holds it a day (February 12, 1781).
◄◆◆◆◆◆◆	American army under Col. William Crawford is thrashed by combined Indian/English force in the valley of the upper Sandusky River in the spring of 1782.
◄— — — — —	George Rogers Clark (repeating a punitive campaign of 1780) assaults and burns the Shawnee strongholds of Chillicothe and Piqua in November, 1782, the last battle of the Revolutionary War.

British seize Spanish b◄
at mouth of Turkey Riv◄

British capture lead min◄
near modern Dubuque

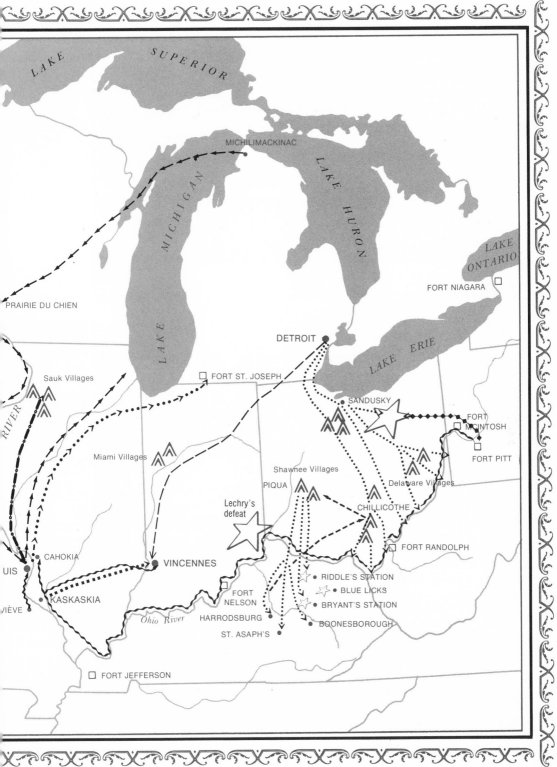

LAKE SUPERIOR

LAKE
MICHIGAN

LAKE HURON

LAKE ONTARIO

MICHILIMACKINAC

PRAIRIE DU CHIEN

FORT NIAGARA

DETROIT

FORT ST. JOSEPH

SANDUSKY

FORT McINTOSH

LAKE ERIE

FORT PITT

Sauk Villages

RIVER

Miami Villages

Shawnee Villages

PIQUA

Delaware Villages

CHILLICOTHE

Lechry's defeat

CAHOKIA

VINCENNES

FORT RANDOLPH

UIS

KASKASKIA

IÈVE

FORT NELSON

RIDDLE'S STATION

BLUE LICKS

BRYANT'S STATION

Ohio River

HARRODSBURG

BOONESBOROUGH

ST. ASAPH'S

FORT JEFFERSON

Henry Hamilton, the "Hair-Buyer General," led the counterattack against Clark, but he was too brash for his own good.

HARVARD UNIVERSITY PORTRAIT COLLECTION

they had been abruptly dumped. Still others, including many in the Illinois Country, tried to stay out of the way of the combatants, swearing oaths of allegiance to whatever dishevelled band came tromping into town, and with a Gallic shrug of the shoulders reversed themselves the next time it happened. All they really wanted was to be left in peace to do a little planting, a little hunting, a little trading—anything that didn't require too much hard work and allowed them a merry social life.

British officers who were responsible for prosecuting the war in the West were left smarting by Clark's clean sweep of the Illinois Country. It did little to unite them, though. Frictions between Canadian governor Guy Carleton and some of his subordinate officers commanding the western posts, and disagreement with Lord George Germain, secretary of state for the colonies, kept a forthright military policy from jelling. Even after Carleton was succeeded by Gen. Frederick Haldimand in 1778, that policy was unduly cautious, defensive even when bright offensive opportunities did come along.

One British officer stood apart from the rest. Henry Hamilton, lieutenant governor of Detroit, wasn't timid. He was impetuous. A year before Clark's strike, Hamilton had proposed a surprise attack on Spanish settlements that would not let up until New Orleans was taken, but Governor Carleton quashed it. Now, upon hearing of Clark's uncontested triumphs, Hamilton was spoiling for a fight. Retaking the Illinois Country posed no particular problem according to the intelligence he had gathered: "The Spaniards are feeble and hated by the French, the French are fickle and have no man of capacity to advise or lead them, the Rebels are enterprizing and brave, but want resources, and the Indians can have their resources but from the English if we act without loss [of] time." General Haldimand sent his vague blessing to the plan.

Known to the Americans as "the Hair-Buyer General" for his alleged payoffs for rebel scalps, Hamilton gathered a force of 160-odd whites (most of them French) and began collecting hundreds of Indians along the route of his difficult seventy-one-day march. Clark had meanwhile withdrawn his dwindling forces from the Wabash, leaving Captain Helm and three Virginians at Vincennes and a reminder to newly Americanized Frenchmen to be brave and true to their oath. Hamilton had amassed a force of five hundred by December 17, when he retook Vincennes with ease. The French inhabitants that had not fled quailed. They swore another oath to behave as loyal subjects of the king of England; Hamilton privately libeled them as a bunch of indolent drunks and took his pleasure from hauling down and stomping on the thirteen stars and red and white stripes of the rebel flag.

Hamilton had a sound strategy in mind. He intended to build a fort where the Ohio and the Mississippi joined to stop traffic between the Spaniards and their new friends, to clean out the Illinois of insurgents, and recoup the Mississippi trade, and then in the spring to drive south and link up with British forces from Pensacola and squeeze the life out of the rebel West. But the general's reach exceeded his grasp. The winter march had taxed his men, and the Indians had to be released to do their spring planting. So he curtailed operations for a time, contenting himself by sending messengers to John Stuart, the superintendent of Indian affairs for the Southern Department, to enlist the Creeks in the coming spring offensive, to rotate a party on the Ohio to interdict rebel communications, and to busy himself with refurbishing the defenses of Fort Sackville at Vincennes, which were in sad disrepair.

The diary of one of Hamilton's lieutenants, Jacob Schiefflin, contends that from the time his commander left Detroit, he fully intended to press on to New Orleans and run Bernardo de Gálvez and his minions off the continent. This seems too ambitious even for the headstrong Hamilton, though the idea did still tug at his mind, and on January 24, 1779, while still digging in at Vincennes, he put it in writing: "Though I have no doubt this minute of the existence of a Spanish as well as a French war, yet I have, as yet, no accounts by which I may venture to act on the offensive against the subjects of Spain, which I ardently desire, as there would be so little difficulty of pushing them entirely off the Mississippi."

Hamilton was in double error. War with Spain was not yet a reality, and when it became so six months later, the "Hair-Buyer" would be long gone, receiving rough handling in a Virginia prison. Hamilton also erred in releasing one of the captives taken at Vincennes, a trader from whom he had exacted a promise to say nothing to the rebels on his way home to Saint Louis. The man was Francis Vigo, Clark's friend. Vigo preserved his honor by going to Saint Louis first, but then he crossed the Mississippi and told Clark all. The American had all the instincts of an accomplished gambler. Though his men were few and poorly equipped, he sensed a tide at its flood, and fortune if he acted without delay.

No campaign of the Revolutionary War exceeded Clark's capture of Vincennes for pure heroics. He led his 172 men, nearly half of them French recruits, from Kaskaskia across 180 miles of prairie turned to quagmire by heavy winter rains. He had boats built to ferry his men across the swollen Wabash and exhorted his followers, who had gone days without food, with shouts and laughter. Greatly outnumbered if the French villagers stayed with Hamilton, Clark first sent a message to the town that appealed to "true citizens" who were "willing to enjoy the liberty I bring you" to keep to their houses. As for those who wanted to fight for the Hair-Buyer General, well, they would have to answer to his troops, of which, he left the clear and false impression, there were

The Americans' greatest victory in the West came when Hamilton gave over Fort Sackville to the daring Clark on February 25, 1779.

many. It worked. It worked so well that Hamilton was unaware of danger until balls began thudding into the walls of Fort Sackville. British cannon went silent as rebel sharpshooters fired from improvised breastworks. Hamilton held out one night and most of the following day, and then on February 25, 1779, he surrendered an amply stocked fort and seventy-nine officers and men — nearly half British regulars.

Such a splendid victory! As the news spread it became a shot in the raised arm for all Americans fighting for liberty and a cause of excessive gloom for British officers in the West. Of course, that raised arm harbored less than enough muscle to do what Clark knew had to be done: to take Detroit. That was the prop of all British strength in the West, and if it fell, so would all the Great Lakes dominoes. The prospect was one in which, Clark said, his "very soul was wrapt." He had the impertinence, and what turned out to be the subtle wisdom, of taunting the commandant at Detroit, Capt. Richard Lernoult, with a message carried by those at Vincennes he had freed. He was glad to hear that Detroit was

full of human beavers erecting ramparts against his coming offensive, "as it saves the Americans some expenses in building."
There was a side benefit to the Vincennes victory that Clark
could well savor: the Indians, who always respected force, now
had to have second thoughts about close dealings with the English. He had consistently been a hardliner toward the wavering
tribes. The giving of gifts was a waste of scarce goods. The display
of fear or indecision only invited assault. Now, with the upper
hand, he met with chiefs of the region and boasted of his power.
He proffered the carrot of peace but waved the stick of war. De-
jected officers at Detroit and Michilimackinac braced themselves
for attacks they felt could not be withstood. Their awe of Clark
would never again allow them to conduct the war with anything
resembling full confidence.

As bright as the western picture looked in the spring of 1779,
Clark would never taste the ultimate triumph of taking Detroit,
and American military fortunes in the West, which had peaked
at Vincennes, receded sharply through the duration of the war.
Illness plagued Clark's men, and the five hundred reinforcements
said to be on their way from Virginia never showed. He had no
choice but to hold on as best he could. His victory had only encouraged more settlers to stream into Kentucky, and they only
encouraged more devastation from Indian raiders out of the
British-controlled north. In September of 1779, Clark withdrew
from the conquered Illinois Country, recently made a county of
Virginia, and established his headquarters at the centrally situated Falls of the Ohio.

Behind him, Clark left John Todd, Jr., the civil magistrate appointed by Patrick Henry, and garrisons at Kaskaskia and
Cahokia with orders to accumulate stores for a campaign against
Detroit the following year. The smarmy brotherliness of May,
when the French were permitted to elect their own judges and
share with the citizens of Virginia "in the blessing of a free and
equal independence," was cold as a blue norther by December.
Yankee hucksters quickly showed up to do what they did best,
and the American troops (those who hadn't deserted) were not
too scrupulous about how they got their supplies. The dashing
and honorable figure struck by Clark had few imitators among

the Americans who stayed in the American Bottom as if it were their own — as indeed it was to remain.

Aside from the differences in language, religion, and mores, the hard matter of money, hard money, widened the breach between the two peoples. Oliver Pollock, the Irishman so devoted to the patriotic cause and who had financed Clark's operations from New Orleans, found his personal fortune and credit exhausted by July of 1779. That left Continental currency, which had been represented to the French inhabitants as redeemable at face value in silver. With the currency depreciated in the East to twelve cents on the dollar, a sudden deluge of paper inundated the Illinois Country. French merchants and traders wanted nothing to do with it, insisting that pelts be the medium of exchange, as had been earlier agreed. Magistrate Todd refused, and having no rare metals to back the worthless paper, he rattled the steel in his scabbard instead.

Clark's discontent could not match that of the French *habitants'*, but it, too, was growing. With his plans for Detroit shelved, he turned his attention in the spring of 1780 to an old project close to his heart — a fort at the mouth of the Ohio. There was a crying need for it. The British, he heard, were gathering strength and gearing up to retake the Illinois Country; a fort would also serve as a reminder to Spain of who owned that riverbank, lest she entertain any ideas about adding to her holdings. Thomas Jefferson, successor to Patrick Henry as governor of Virginia, directed his friend to build the post but appended a caution by now painfully familiar to Clark: "The less you depend for supplies from this quarter the less will you be disappointed by those impediments which distance and a precarious foreign Commerce throws in our way." In May of 1780, Clark located his Fort Jefferson five miles below the mouth of the Ohio, giving it a small garrison and introducing a few settlers. In the face of Indian attacks, hunger, and desertions, it would not be long for the western world.

Clark was right about the British. They were coming in the spring of 1780, fully recovered from the Vincennes setback and a brief seizure of the trembles. The scattered and poorly financed rebels had lost the initiative; those loyal to George III had for the moment a none-too-firm hold on it. With Spain now a declared adversary, it was time to dust off the grand old plan that would win both sides of the Mississippi—the contested east and the Spanish west—and open the way to Mexico itself.

There was only one large and nasty fly in the ointment: the plan had called for a far-reaching pincer movement, a force from Canada coming downriver to link up with Gen. John Campbell's seaborne force that was to enter the Mississippi and knock over New Orleans. That was no longer feasible. The lightning actions of Bernardo de Gálvez badly mauled the southern arm of the pincer soon after the state of war was formalized. Manchac and Baton Rouge on the lower Mississippi and Mobile on the Gulf Coast had fallen to the young Spaniard in quick succession, and General Campbell was penned up in Pensacola, suffering from an acute lack of ships and fortitude. The campaign nevertheless went forward on the northern front, where Spain was sickly thin and the Americans were in disarray.

The spring offensive of 1780 was three-pronged. A diversionary body of one hundred fifty whites and a thousand Indians under Col. Henry Bird left Detroit in early May for the Falls of the Ohio to "amuse Clark." Another group of Indians and Canadians rendezvoused at Chicago under Capt. Charles Langlade to work their way down the Illinois River toward the American Bottom. But the main force, estimated by the Spanish at 1,200 and officially put at 750 by the English, crossed the upper Mississippi in March and made the Far West for the first and only time during the Revolutionary War a full-fledged battleground.

The end-around was the brainchild of Patrick Sinclair, the lieutenant governor of Michilimackinac, who believed he was taking dead aim on an easy victory. The actual leader of the expedition was Emmanuel Hesse, a former military officer turned trader. Somewhere around three-fourths of the polyglot motley was composed of Menominees, Winnebagoes, Sauks, Foxes, Ottawas, and—the rubicund hard core perennially friendly to the British—the Sioux, led by the great chief Wabasha. For the occasion the British dressed him in scarlet military raiment and elevated him to the rank of captain. The composition of the army was an example writ large of the essential nature of war in the

West and the methods the English strategists used in waging it.

The Hesse contingent got off to a productive start. A detachment under Lt. Alexander Kay captured an armed Spanish boat and its crew of twelve at the mouth of Iowa's Turkey River. Then Kay turned some twenty miles to the southeast and surprised a group of lead miners near present-day Dubuque. "Seventeen Spanish & Rebel Prisoners" were taken, along with fifty tons of lead ore, stores of furs, tobacco, and rum. Sinclair was elated by the results, but apparently one or more of the miners escaped and paddled down the Mississippi to spread the alarm, though fear had already surfaced in Saint Louis and Sainte Geneviève in anticipation of an attack.

Lieutenant Governor de Leyba, mortally ill and pessimistic about defending Saint Louis, had nevertheless begun fortifying the town months before. Five cannon from abandoned Fort Carlos III at the mouth of the Missouri were removed to Saint Louis. His appeal to the eight hundred poor and mostly French inhabitants for donations netted him six hundred piasters, with which he hoped to build four defensive towers. As the British force drew closer, de Leyba summoned Lt. Don Francisco Cartabona and his small force from Sainte Geneviève to join him. Cartabona arrived on May 13, and when the *chasseurs* came in from the fields, the defenders numbered 29 regulars and 281 volunteer militia, including a couple with Anglo-Saxon names. Only one defensive tower was built, on the west side of town, where the five cannon were installed. Trenches were dug on the north and south perimeters and manned. The terrified women and children were herded into the governor's house and put under the protection of Lieutenant Cartabona and twenty men.

At 1:00 P.M. on the twenty-sixth of May, 1780, Hesse's mongrel army darkened the northern horizon, firing their pieces and filling the air with bloodcurdling cries. For the next two hours, Saint Louis took the full fury of a frontier assault, and held. The attackers had not expected to find a tower, atop which the ailing de Leyba stood, nor fire from cannon which he directed. The valor of those in the trenches also came as a surprise. These were not the easy pickings advertised.

Hesse's force broke off the engagement to wander and savage

HAROLD OWENS AND MISSOURI STATE CAPITOL, JEFFERSON CITY

The war crossed the Mississippi in force on May 26, 1780, when a British-led army of Indians was repulsed at Spanish St. Louis.

the countryside, dismembering and disemboweling farmers and farm animals where they found them. Spanish officials in later declarations would bitterly denounce the atrocities, which, when widely known, would earn Britain the contempt of the *mundo filosófico.* As for casualties suffered, Spain's tally of 21 dead, 7 wounded, and 25 made prisoners actually ran less than a British report that listed 70 killed, 34 taken prisoner, and 43 scalped. Against this, Hesse lost only three men with two wounded, which raised an embarrassing question: Why did he retreat? Sinclair was beside himself, but he did not lack for alibis. The perfidious Sauks had deserted at a critical time, and many of the erstwhile French-Canadian traders had been guilty of treachery, sowing disunity and condoning cowardice among the Indians they led. Wait till next year, Sinclair warned. It would be done come April, but only with the dependable Sioux under arms this time.

There was probably another reason for Hesse's inglorious retreat. Immediately after withdrawing from Saint Louis, he had marched to the Mississippi where the Illinois emptied its waters, expecting to join the supportive column of Captain Langlade for another go at de Leyba's makeshift citadel. Langlade had been there and had prepared to reduce Cahokia just hours before Saint Louis took its battering. But to his dismay, he found himself confronting none other than George Rogers Clark! The tiger was not at the Falls of the Ohio where he was supposed to be. He was loose in the West! After a brief skirmish, Langlade made a hasty departure for home. Hesse's Indians doubtlessly learned that Clark was in the vicinity; that was cue enough to clear out of the territory — fast. Indeed, Clark immediately organized an army of pursuit, numbering more than three hundred Americans, Illinois Frenchmen, and Spaniards from Saint Louis, and named Col. John Montgomery to head it. Montgomery set off up the Mississippi and marched overland to Sauk and Fox villages on the Rock River, failing to overtake any of the raiders. So, following the standard frontier operating procedure, he put the torch to the deserted Sauk and Fox villages instead.

By the summer of 1780 the war in the West was marked by exhaustion, attrition, and indecision, and seemed incapable of being won by anyone. Governor de Leyba died of his illness on June 28. That left the inhabitants of Spain's West temporarily leaderless while still nursing the wounds wrought by the British offensive. Rumors that the English would soon be back circulated daily. Fifteen hundred British and Indians were on their way from Detroit. Two thousand Frenchmen and Indians were coming to annihilate them all. Eight hundred Sioux had gone west to enlist the Missouri River tribes to wreak their fiendish vengeance on Saint Louis. The savages had even told the English how to reach Santa Fe easily by way of the Platte; not even Mexico was secure anymore. Terrified by such talk, the mostly French inhabitants of Spanish Upper Louisiana pleaded with Governor Gálvez for protection. Barring that, they warned, they would have to evacuate the town.

Across the river Clark began his slow and piecemeal withdrawal from the West he had won. While he was gone, his Fort Jefferson had known six days and six nights of demonstrative displeasure from Chickasaw and Choctaw warriors of the south, who had not been advised of this encroachment on their hunting grounds. By the following June it would be given up, some of its hungry settlers drifting into the Illinois Country to the less demonstrative displeasure of Frenchmen. The abandonment of Fort Jefferson would rank down the list of personal worries for Clark when it happened. More Americans had crossed the mountains into the Ohio Valley by the fateful summer of 1780 than ever before. But that only meant more trouble in Kentucky and its environs, because the tribes north of the Ohio, manipulated expertly by the British, were more united and hostile than ever, having it pretty much their own way during 1781. Clark again settled himself at the Falls of the Ohio, closer to where he was needed, and ordered most of his men out of the Illinois posts.

In many ways the Americans were their own worst enemies. Officers and merchants conspired in sticking moneyless Virginia with bills to be paid in silver she did not have. Land sharks, grafters, and currency speculators practiced their self-serving arts while the new West seemed to crumble around their heads. Disgruntled and unpaid soldiers deserted. Widows and orphans were made daily in Kentucky and western Pennsylvania as Indian attacks increased in frequency and ferocity. Although Governor Jefferson and, after 1779, even General Washington took an active interest in extending the war in the West, there were never enough troops and guns to go around. Field-grade officers vied with each other for the glory of crushing the savages or — that deed of deeds — capturing Detroit. Some came out of the East, unused to war as it was waged in the West, and walked into ambuscades, had their forces cut to pieces, and if they were unlucky enough to be taken prisoner, learned in one ghastly lesson how the red men dealt with the enemy.

Clark was a lesser factor than he had hoped to be. He was made a general by Virginia, but the troops and equipment he was promised never seemed to arrive at the same time, were sidetracked elsewhere, or were nonexistent. He persevered as the western anchor of Kentucky, of greatest use to the infant nation as a paper tiger always on the verge of bearding the weakened lion away from his den. That radiant vision of Detroit prostrate never left Clark, but the best he would do was to invade, in November of 1782, the Scioto River villages of the redoubtable Shawnees — "the first in at a battle, the last at a treaty" — which netted him few killed and few prisoners among the fleeing inhabitants. Nevertheless, Chillicothe and five other towns were burned to the ground in the last battle of the Revolutionary War.

The years 1780 to 1782 had seemingly every reason to be sterling years for the British in the Northwest. The rebels were in general retreat along the front before Indians almost solidly with the British. Yet the same Indians who could terrorize the enemy from Fort Pitt to Saint Louis had to be kept in presents, and General Haldimand had difficulty balancing, or at least justifying, the books. After the luckless Hamilton, no British officer approached Clark in imagination and the willingness to risk defeat for victory. As a consequence, Clark was endowed by them and their hired guns with a reputation beyond what he had earned — a man to avoid and, because constant rumor had him coming their way, to over-defend against.

The truly deflating news reached Haldimand's subordinates in the West in April of 1782: Cornwallis had surrendered his army at Yorktown. As jarring as that was in itself, it meant help that might have come from Montreal would be diverted to weakened British forces in New York. Since peace talks were said to be under way, the best thing to do was shore up and stave off, and make the Great Lakes forts of Detroit and Michilimackinac double-safe. General Haldimand did not intend to give the rebels any claims by conquest to the prime fur country.

In the final years of the bloody stalemate, only one man in the West improved his country's status. Francisco Cruzat inherited panic and despair when he took over for the deceased de Leyba in September of 1780. He had served a term as lieutenant governor of upper Louisiana before de Leyba and had been beloved by its people. Now he was back in Saint Louis to bring sanity and some new thinking. Unlike de Leyba, he did not care for Clark or the Americans. Though he put on a pleasant face in dealings with them, he did not trust them. All he had to do was look across the river at the Illinois French — Clark's cat's-paws — who had been leached from and left to fend for themselves if and when the British came again. Their treatment had been contemptible and would not be repeated west of the river — not if he had anything to do with it. And he made it his business to do all he could about it. Under his direction Saint Louis sprouted an eighteen-foot-high stockade with six-inch walls to greet those British who had promised to return in 1781. Spies were sent deep into enemy territory to keep Cruzat posted. He distributed gifts to the Indians as freely as his limited resources would allow, and while he was never able to match the "enemy [who] scatters presents by handfuls among these barbarous tribes," yet by the spring of 1782 he had more than a hundred tribes coming to Saint Louis for handouts and Spanish protection.

The British return remained a rumor. Cruzat insured against its becoming a reality in February of 1781, when he borrowed a page from George Rogers Clark's book. Fivescore men, evenly divided between red and white, were dispatched under the leadership of Capt. Eugène Pourée eastward into the winter heart of disputed territory that even Clark had never seen. On February 12, 1781, Cruzat's men disarmed the small British garrison at Fort Saint Joseph east of Lake Michigan and held it for twenty-four hours, taking nine prisoners, burning stores, and raising the Spanish ensign over what was formally proclaimed Spanish territory. Spain in Michigan? Cruzat's purpose behind the wildcat raid was to destroy provisions slated for use in the anticipated attack on his Saint Louis and to cow Indians leaning toward the British. The quixotic hoisting of the Spanish flag also gave his nation an extra throwaway card at the peace table. The war in the West answered to no logic. Why should the peace?

A FLEETING TWENTY YEARS after the glorious year of 1763, England was back in Paris, looking across the diplomatic table at the familiar faces with their fixed grins and flexible insincerity. How much had changed! Some of those familiar faces had been kin, country cousins. Yes, much had changed.

Of whatever stature were those patriots who fought the day-by-day natal war, they were dwarfed by a trio of men who won the first peace in dazzling fashion and would cast long shadows across the continent. There was the beaming, benevolent Benjamin Franklin—the Platonic American with the international reputation as scientist and sage, whose agile intelligence guided

"Franklin Urging the Claims of the American Colonies Before Louis XVI," by George Peter Alexander Healy, circa 1847.

the negotiations. There was John Adams, as sound of mind as New England's rocky mantle, testy and abrasive, who had the effrontery to plainly state to the Comte de Vergennes that France needed America as much *au contraire*. Finally, young John Jay of New York, a legal beagle, his suspicious nose detecting every foul scent emanating from Europe's rotten diplomatic chambers.

None was what you would call an innocent abroad in 1783. Each had crossed the Atlantic years before even the preliminary settlements were signed. Franklin had spent years in London as a colonial lobbyist before being sent to France in 1776 to represent the breakaway colonies. Adams arrived in 1778, first upsetting the French with his obstinacy, then wangling loans from the Netherlands, one of the five commissioners appointed by the Continental Congress in 1781 to conclude the peace. Jay alighted in Spain in January of 1780, hat in hand, pleading for money and help from the Count Floridablanca, the archconservative principal minister who was in his soul more staunch an enemy of the young republic than any Briton.

There are always two concurrent wars: the one fought on the land and on the sea, and the one fought by diplomats far from the scene of strife. Thus it had been necessary to send envoys to Europe as soon as hostilities seemed certain. How else could the Americans protect their interest? How else be a party to those preliminary sparrings, the feeling-out phase when ambassadors kept abreast of what their opposite numbers would settle for at a given time? In 1779, Floridablanca had tried to blackmail England into handing over Gibraltar by promising to stay out of the war that family-member France was desperately trying to get her into. When England balked, she entered the war, not as a friend of those rabble who threatened her western colonies in North America, not willingly at the bidding of the Bourbon relative, who also showed latent republican tendencies, but for herself. She wanted total possession of the Gulf Coast and—in war if not in peace—Gibraltar. In formal exchanges with Britain, Spain persistently referred to the thirteen as "colonies," not as the independent states they insisted they were.

What is often forgotten is that the United States did not spring full grown from the ear of ancient Athens as a champion of democracy and justice. The representatives of the Continental Congress in Europe through the war years learned all about the cold shoulder, Old World *hauteur,* the interminable wait in the bureaucratic anteroom. Enemies of England did not embrace rebellious sons of England, save for a small scattering of bookworm liberals outside diplomatic circles who saw something messianic in men who pledged their lives, property, and sacred honor in resisting the oppression of kings.

Catherine II of Russia, packager of the 1780 Pact of Armed Neutrality that placed England in unspecified peril if she did not respect the free transport of non-contraband in neutral bottoms, had no interest in Americans or their cause. The kingdoms of Denmark, Sweden, and Portugal, and the German states decidedly disapproved of those who would tamper with the divine right of kings. Frederick of Prussia, shabbily treated by England in the Seven Years' War, was amused to see his faithless ally on

*Charles Gravier,
Comte de Vergennes,
did not play fair
with his American
"friends," nor did
they with him.*

CULVER PICTURES

the rack, but that did not keep him from refusing to receive the American Arthur Lee. When British agents stole Lee's official papers, Frederick did nothing. Lee fared no better in that lair of the spider of Europe—Austria. Not only would the Court refuse to recognize the independence of the colonies, it would not even let the friendly French ambassador introduce Lee.

Only in France did Americans have many true friends. From there, at least, the intelligentsia and the ordinary man on the Paris street looked west, not east, and saw a new dawn breaking, feeling for the first time bonds of the heart that the leaders of the respective nations, then and ever after, would be reluctant to admit.

Vergennes was not one of those admiring Frenchmen, however. He belonged to the *ancien régime*, no promoter of *liberté*, let alone *égalité* and *fraternité*. Crippling Britain was his overriding aim, and to do that he had to draw heavily on his considerable skills in bottom-drawer diplomacy. He had engineered the Treaty

*A New Yorker
of Huguenot stock,
young John Jay
was rebuffed in
Spain and smelled
betrayal in France.*

of Alliance with the Americans, which mutually pledged that neither nation would cease hostilities and conclude a separate peace without the partner's consent, and that the independence of the American colonies was absolute — a point upon which both were agreed for completely different reasons. For Vergennes that was not enough. He wanted Spain in the fray, too, needing her navy to reach parity with English sea strength. That was not easy, not with the tough Floridablanca managing Carlos's affairs of state. The secret Convention of Aránjuez, signed by the two members of the Family Compact on April 12, 1779, reflected more the stubborn Spanish count's will than the facile French count's wishes. Yes, Spain would go to war, but on the side of France, not the rebellious provincials — or whatever they were now calling themselves. Under no circumstance would their independence be recognized. The price for this? Gibraltar, of course, and no peace was possible until delivered. France's good offices also were wanted in safeguarding Spain's interests in the

Mississippi Valley, the American West, where rebel activity was as worrisome as their damnable insistence on using the river. Vergennes must have blanched, maybe swallowed once. The West — yes, well, he would see what could be done to lend a hand out there.

When Jay arrived in inhospitable Spain, his antenna picked up bad vibrations. Something was up between the Bourbon pair, something that Vergennes had not divulged to the Continental Congress. A tumor of distrust took hold on the Franco-American alliance, and in the year 1780, when the war news was not pleasant, it grew. Headline-hunting Catherine of Russia and the Machiavellian Kaunitz of Austria found their offer of mediation, of applying sweet reason to this European unpleasantness, not unpalatable to France. Great Britain would settle with her colonies separately, of course, and follow the formula of *uti possidetis* ("keep what you have"). What Britain had was New York City and Long Island, parts of New England, big pieces of interior North and South Carolina, almost all of Georgia, and the Great Lakes country. Those belonging to the European family would convene in Vienna and resolve there the larger differences.

Vergennes was set to go, with assurances to the Americans that he would look to their interests for them; but Adams, the accredited American plenipotentiary, saw a sellout. Nothing doing. Britain would have to withdraw all her troops from the colonies before there could be any truce. Adams and Jay were separately coming to the same conclusion: Europe was corrupt and France not to be trusted.

In fact, England was in no mood to go to Vienna or withdraw anything in 1780 or deep into 1781, until October and Yorktown, after which Lord North's ministry collapsed and Englishmen were generally in the market for peace at the best price. Franklin received overtures in the spring of 1782 from the phoenix Lord Shelburne, risen again to power from the ashes. Would the Americans entertain a private settlement? One kept in the family, so to speak? Yes, they would. Nothing seemed more proper to Shelburne at the moment than to drive a wedge between England's errant sons and perfidious Gaul.

The earnest meetings begun in Paris in September of 1782

between the Americans and Shelburne's delegate Richard Oswald have been called unethical and worse by some. The French Alliance forbade any separate peace with Britain. Yet it would be no act of mercy to absolve Jay, Adams, and Franklin from seeking their own accords. Vergennes's two ministers living in America during the war, Alexandre Gérard and his successor, the Chevalier de la Luzerne, had with bribery and sweet talk subverted the gullible Continental Congress into weakening the hands of its all-too-capable commissioners abroad; France could be trusted to manage American affairs was the unheeded wisdom sent to Franklin, Adams, and Jay. Those same French ministers advised Americans to curb their territorial appetites, preparing them in a general way to do without those western lands to which Spain had preferential rights, by conquest if nothing else. As peace drew near, the collusion of Spain and France became ominously clear. In the summer of 1782, Jay had informal meetings in Paris with the Spanish ambassador, the Count Aranda, and Vergennes's secretary, Joseph Matthias Gérard de Rayneval. The map was spread out. The lines were drawn. All Spain wanted was West Florida, the east side of the Mississippi all the way to the Ohio, land northwest of Lake Erie — just about everything that would "coop us up within the Allegheny Mountains," as Benjamin Franklin put it. Jay broke off discussions.

Vergennes had his hands full trying to placate his two polar allies, but in favoring Spain in the American West, he was following the pragmatic wisdom of prior French diplomacy. He wanted America independent of Britain all right, but he also wanted it kept small, feeble, dependent on France. As deft a juggler as Vergennes was, he simply had too many balls in the air. Early in September he sent Rayneval on a secret mission to London, where the British were informed that France felt American demands for a settlement were excessive, opening the door to private arrangements that the United States need never be told about. Jay got wind of it. He smelled another rat. With Adams resolutely behind him and Franklin following after his zealous juniors, the trio extricated themselves from the tangled skein of deception and double cross. With few qualms, they entered into direct negotiations with the English in Vergennes's capital.

Like the Spaniards' terms, what the Americans either asked for or demanded robbed the word *modesty* of meaning. They wanted Canada, indemnification for Americans who had lost property in the war, favorable trade considerations from wealthy mother, and some form of official apology for "distressing" the colonies that would help heal the late wounds. What the quondam colonies insisted upon was only slightly less a dream: first, of course, the granting of unqualified independence; then the withdrawal of British troops from the lands of the thirteen colonies, the right to fish the cod lode off Newfoundland, a guarantee of free navigation of the Mississippi, and the cis-Mississippi West all the way to the crumbling banks of that river and south along it to thirty-one degrees, the boundary of West Florida, which Britain might keep if Spain did not demand it by right of conquest. One suspects they would have asked for the moon itself if they thought it was drained by the Father of Waters.

In the preliminaries of peace signed on November 30, 1782, the republican pup got less than it barked for, but much more than it had reason to expect. Independence was granted. Blurred fishing "liberties" were extended. The promise of a total military withdrawal was made, if not immediately implemented. The boundary on the north was roughly the lake-and-river border of today that stretched all the way to the Lake of the Woods. Above all the new nation got its West—the West partly won by Spain in battle, the West partly won and then abandoned by George Rogers Clark, the West partly in the secure hold of General Haldimand and his frontier fort commanders.

Vergennes chided Franklin for this breach of faith. The old fox from Philadelphia admitted guilt to a minor indiscretion but pointed out that this separate peace was in the preliminary stage — contingent upon a general agreement among all the belligerents. He regretted any slight harm that might have been done. With a coyness that the French cynic had to relish, he added: "The English, I just now learn, flatter themselves they have already divided us. I hope this little misunderstanding will therefore be kept a secret and that they will find themselves totally mistaken."

Vergennes took it all in stride. He was aware of what was transpiring under his nose. He had one good reason to encourage

The winners, from left: Jay, Adams, Franklin, Henry Laurens, Franklin's grandson. The English signers would not sit for Benjamin West.

it by ignoring it after the news came that the long-awaited Franco-Hispanic assault on Gibraltar had failed. The British rock had held. Wasn't then the private American settlement a prod to Spain to accept less than Floridablanca wanted? To forego dragging out this war, which like most wars had emptied the Bourbon treasuries?

Europe resolved its quarrel on September 3, 1783, and the Anglo-American preliminary treaty became a part of the general settlement. The imperial Old World went through its hackneyed ritual of petty redistribution. Spain got East and West Florida, the island of Minorca, and the restriction of British hardwood harvests to the coast of Honduras. France got Tobago, a restoration of the minute Saint Lawrence Gulf islands of Saint Pierre and Miquelon, slave-running control in Senegal, and damned little in India.

England held on to Gibraltar and Canada. Et cetera, et cetera.

Under this multi-continental tent of colony-swapping and ac-commodation, a new nation had been delivered on the fertile earth of North America. Conceived in Europe, it fairly squawled its independence, portending a break with a past that dated to the Renaissance. Things would never be the same, as was prophesied by London's *Morning Post* in December of 1782, just after the preliminary articles of peace were signed:

> As soon as the Thirteen Colonies are established in the form of a separate state, tens of thousands will emigrate from all parts of Europe and repair the losses of the war with a rapid increase of population. The pride of empire will awaken, and conquests will be multiplied. . . . Florida and all the Spanish possessions on the banks of the Mississippi will fall before them; and as they increase in power, that power will reach the limits of the South-ern Oceans, and dispossess the Europeans of every hold upon the great continent of America.

La Luzerne observed more succinctly to Vergennes that "the Americans in pushing their possessions as far as the Lake of the Woods, are preparing for their remote posterity a communication with the Pacific."

Yes, and the posterity was not so very remote. Momentarily weak, poor, disunited, the imperial infant still had life and room to grow and a direction to go—which was west. For what was in the run of time no more than a protracted moment, the child paused to gulp one deep breath before plunging into the shadow of its continent.

Epilogue

THE MEXICAN POET OCTAVIO PAZ describes history as having all the reality of a nightmare and credits the romantic side of man with trying to make sense of what makes no sense. The idea is disturbing. Man must believe in a past that has at least some semblance of order and meaning, if for no other reason than to imagine he knows himself and where he has been.

The tangled story of the American West during the twenty years following the close of the Revolutionary War tempts one to agree with Paz. There is a nightmare quality to the events of those two decades. The war had settled nothing about the eventual ownership of the trans-Mississippi lands; it had only complicated things by creating a new nation to challenge the three Old World contenders for the prize. Once more, the Mississippi Valley became the stage for the sound and the fury, the setting for a muddle of transient schemes and dreams, conspiracies and betrayals, plots and counterplots with bewildering subplots.

Yet through it all, the shadow was slowly lifting from the dark three-fifths of the continent as white men of various nations and motives began to close in on the mystery. Spaniards on the Pacific coast explored the inland valleys of California. New Mexico at long last was enjoying a marginal peace and prosperity. The trails blazed by the French into the depths of the southern plains were being reopened under Spanish auspices, and Pedro Vial in 1792 and 1793 traversed what, two generations later, would roughly conform to the Americans' Santa Fe Trail. To the north, where the Missouri River comes down from the Yellowstone, Spain sent traders to compete with British interests in the harvest of furs.

December 20, 1803: New flag over New Orleans; the way west is opened.

Britain had been humbled by the war that divested her of thirteen North American colonies, but to nowhere near the extent that her multitudinous enemies might have wished. A late-comer to the notion of westward expansion, England now pursued it across Canada with a celerity reminiscent of the early French explorers, the economic edge in peltry as well as curiosity her constant goads. Alexander Mackenzie made a centuries-old dream come true in the summer of 1793 when he traveled the Peace, Fraser, and Bella Coola rivers and tasted the salt of Pacific tides. The full breadth of the continent had at last been crossed; the western sea had been reached.

Americans, united by the term but divided by much else, also pushed westward, chiefly into the cis-Mississippi lands they owned, or thought they owned, by the treaty of peace signed in Paris in 1783; the resistance of Indians, Spaniards, and English-men merely slowed their progress. As auguries for the future, there were those few who crossed the dividing river and became horse traders in Texas, fur traders along the Missouri, sanitized settlers (or so Spain hoped when she reluctantly invited them) in such places as New Madrid, just below the Ohio, and just west of the Mississippi. To find that the pull of the West went deep, to the very bowels of the new nation's new men, one need look no far-ther than Daniel Boone. The apotheosis of the frontiersman, the man who had hacked out the Wilderness Road, the coonskin-capped prototypical American with the compulsive need for few neighbors and ample elbowroom, resettled in Spanish Missouri and would travel as far as the Rockies before he died. Of course, what Boone and many a Spanish and English Johnny-come-lately saw of the West had already been seen, known, and ap-preciated by Frenchmen before them.

The surnames of white men in the West after 1776 were more than ever a printout of the larger international struggle for its ownership. As before, the fate of the American West was being determined elsewhere, by well-dressed men in civilization's well-appointed conference rooms far from migrating bison herds, subhumid skies that seemed to shrink horizons, Indians who were getting their first look at pale-skinned explorers, and the parallel ranges of the Rocky Mountain massif and the vast desert beyond, which seemed to a man on foot or horseback to go on forever.

On paper it all belonged to Spain until 1801. But that was on paper, and Spain was generally known by those who periodically revised deeds of imperial ownership to be on the run. As long as Carlos III was on the throne, Spain did not lack able ministers, but circumstance assigned them impossible tasks, a series of holding actions against prime foes who from year to year were never the same. Immediately after the Revolutionary War the enemy was identified as American. So Spain decided in 1784 to economically strangle the half-million Americans then living west of the Appalachians by closing the Mississippi to their shipping. The tribes of the lower Mississippi were armed and encouraged to war on the approaching tide of American settlers. Spies were paid well to wean frustrated westerners away from their eastern countrymen.

But the time came when Spain's fears were transferred from Americans to Englishmen. After Cook's crew delivered that first haul of sea-otter pelts to China, the northwest coast of America became a popular spot for profit-seeking merchantmen. English, Portuguese, Russian, and American ships began putting into a coast that was rightly, if vaguely, Spain's, by virtue of her explorations of it in 1774 and 1775. In 1789 a Spanish officer at Nootka Sound seized two British ships and sent them and their crews to detainment in Mexico. Spanish treatment of the English intruders was actually scrupulous if not kid-gloved, but England went into a jingoistic frenzy over the "brutalities" conjured up by pamphleteers. In fact, first minister Pitt and his loyal opposition were in a pugnacious mood and prepared to browbeat Spain out of everything they could. The ultimatum was sent that Spain courted war if she did other than grovel at London's boots by admitting that the northwest coast was open to anyone with the ships to get there, and that she further concede the preposterous notion that occupation, not discovery, was the basis of territorial claims.

The astute Count Floridablanca pointed out that under such a principle England's own discoveries in the South Pacific were vulnerable and that any nation's unoccupied coast was fair game for another. But he dealt from a position of weakness. Carlos III had died in 1788, succeeded by a retiring and timid Carlos IV, whose meddlesome queen attracted a host of inept courtiers. The world was changing too fast for weary Spain. When she turned to France for help against England, in keeping with the Family Compact, it was not forthcoming. The Bastille had been stormed in 1789. Louis XVI was himself retrenching; he sent his regrets. Spain, as Floridablanca realized before he was sacked by his inferiors, was on her own and badly in need of a transfusion. John Bull bullied Spain into signing the Nootka Convention of October 1790, in which Spain yielded almost everything England wanted and almost nothing she deserved. Spain, England, and the world had gone to the brink of war; Spain had blinked and taken a giant step backward into the twilight of her long imperial day.

Britain had settled a score with Spain at Nootka for siding against her in the late war. From her stronghold in fur-rich Canada, English traders continued to roam Spanish territory west of the Mississippi and north of the Missouri. In the East she kept a cold, uncompromising eye on her erstwhile colonists. All had not been forgiven. The prodigal sons would be made to crawl back home, and English policy was calculated to make life miserable for them if they did not. American shipping was harassed on the high seas. In the Old Northwest, British agents set the Indians against American settlers, and Britain held fast to the Great Lakes forts of Niagara, Detroit, and Michilimackinac in contravention of the Paris accords.

Frail and friendless, an infant America bided its time in a perilous world, slowly gathering strength. The original colonies with claims to land over the mountains began surrendering them in 1780, and with the passage of the Northwest Ordinance of 1787, a formula was found that would admit new states to the sickly confederacy, which in 1789, with the ratification of the Constitution, became one nation with one military force and a chance to survive the cradle.

The new nation's West remained an open wound. Indian wars raged with an intensity greater than before, and Spanish and English agents circulated among the restless settlers, fanning separatist sentiment among the short-tempered long-rifle-toters, who demanded the right to use the Mississippi to sell their whiskey, wheat, and salt pork, and believed easterners generally out of sympathy with their wants. It was a time to be thankful for small favors, chief of which was that Spain owned the West. Yet even here there was worry. "My fear," wrote Jefferson to a friend in 1786, "is that they are too feeble to hold it til our population can be sufficiently advanced to gain it from them piece by piece."

The Nootka confrontation between Spain and England had presented the Americans with both an opportunity and a cause for further concern. Various options were discussed. President Washington favored neutrality at all costs. Secretary of State Jefferson viewed neutrality as a club with which to wring concessions in the West—the opening of the Mississippi by Spain or the evacuation of the Great Lakes forts by England. Alexander Hamilton, secretary of the treasury and the foremost of American anglophiles, counseled against an alliance with Spain—a certain loser—and advised instead joining with Britain in chasing Spain all the way to Mexico. He had it on good authority that England was preparing to launch an attack from Canada down the Mississippi Valley; since the United States was powerless to stop this violation of its western territory, it might as well align itself with a winner and save face if nothing else. There was much logic to Hamilton's plan. But it would also leave a powerful Britain in the West, a revolting prospect to the republican-minded Jefferson.

The war scare evaporated with the Nootka Convention, and the Americans gained little from the crisis, thanks in part to the indiscreet Hamilton, who informed his British contacts that American neutrality was assured and thereby dashed what bargaining power the young republic had. Yet, an important lesson had been learned: Europe's troubles were America's blessings. When events on the Continent distracted the Great Powers, it was time for a studiously neutral United States to grab what little it could. It might be humiliating to play the jackal at the quarrels of lions, but survival meant doing just that, and those who presided over the destinies of the new nation—Washington, John Adams, Jefferson—played it well.

The supreme event, the distraction of distractions, had begun in Paris in 1789 and thereafter slowly gained its awesome momentum. As the Nootka crisis was cooling, the ongoing French Revolution entered a white-hot phase. In Paris the tumbrils were rolling, along with aristocratic heads, and in 1793 an unstable but truculent France declared war on England and Spain, as well as Holland. Though the revolutionaries had drawn from the experience of English-speaking North Americans, their break from the past was far more drastic. The Girondists spoke for all mankind and made it clear that the toppling of kings was an item of export. It was a nervous time for Europe's monarchies, a time to fear France and to pare enemies to a minimum.

The United States could be counted as the only possible friend of France. Indeed, the Jeffersonian faction had loudly cheered the bloodstained freedom fighters who were purifying their land and advancing the rights of man. But the opposition Federalists were at the helm. Washington and Adams were horrified at the excesses of the revolution and steered a course of careful neutrality, while American diplomats made the rounds.

In the autumn of 1794, John Jay secured a treaty with England that was as damned at home as the 1783 treaty had been praised. He failed to get Britain to quit seizing American shipping, but he did keep the peace, obtaining some trading concessions and the promise that Britain would vacate the Great Lakes forts she had promised to leave in 1783. Had not France been on a tear, he would probably never have got that much.

More favorable diplomatic fallout came the American way the following year when Spain pulled out of the war against France and prepared to rejoin her no longer recognizable bedmate. Since such a move was sure to incur the wrath of Britain, Spain was obliged to mend other fences. So in October of 1795 the hapless Spaniards concluded a treaty with Thomas Pinckney that gave the Americans free run of the Mississippi, renewable privileges of deposit for their wares in New Orleans, a hold put on Indian war parties, and a southern readjustment of the West Florida boundary to the thirty-first parallel — everything, in short, that the Americans could have asked for.

Improved relations with England and Spain were offset by a deterioration of those with France. Citizen Edmond Genêt had come to America in 1793 as minister plenipotentiary of the French republic. The hotheaded young man had barely touched land when he took to the streets and incited radical republicans to action. He was prepared to finance with French funds an American attack on Spanish Florida and Louisiana, and sundry other mischiefs against the vile monarchies. But Genêt was astonishingly lacking in tact. When President Washington informed him he meant the United States to remain neutral, the fiery Frenchman threatened to go over his head to the people with his case. That was more than Americans were willing to tolerate. The pendulum of opinion was already swinging away from France. The Reign of Terror was too red for most American tastes, and Genêt's unspeakable conduct resulted in American protests to France and the dismissal of Genêt from his post.

There was another ominous turn to the French Revolution that disturbed Americans looking westward. Parisian patriots might loudly cry their devotion to *liberté, égalité,* and *fraternité,* but the abstractions were not to interfere with the holding of overseas colonies. Whereas the corrupt *ancien régime* of the kings Louis had dealt itself out of imperial struggle for the American West, the republicans of France dealt themselves right back in again after 1793. They wanted western Louisiana back, and after Spain rejoined the unhappy family in 1796, she started feeling the heat. French motives became clearer with the arrival in America of French agents, most notably Gen. Victor Collot, who floated the Mississippi River in 1796, taking extensive notes and making elaborate maps with an eye to future ownership. Collot did not go undetected in that confusing place at that confusing time; the French spy was watched closely by Spanish spies, English spies, and American spies. Even Thomas Jefferson, the long-time admirer of France, turned away from his old friend now that his other love, the West, had come between them.

By 1798 relations with France were scraping bottom. Jay's treaty with England was rightly construed by the French as a slap in the face. After July of that year more than three hundred American ships had been taken by the French fleet, and an American mission to Paris had been humiliated in the notorious XYZ Affair. The popular clamor for revenge on France was courageously ignored by President John Adams, who, like Washington before him and Jefferson after him, saw wisdom in swallowing hard and waiting for a brighter day.

That day was not far off. Napoleon Bonaparte had come to

power in France. The first consul brought order to the chaotic republic, renewed prowess to the French army, and headaches to France's many enemies. Her friends did not fare much better with the forceful Corsican. In October of 1800, France called in its marker from fading Spain. At San Ildefonso a secret treaty returned western Louisiana to its previous owners, with Bonaparte's assurances that only France could put muscle in that buffer protecting the Spanish farther west and Mexico to the south, and that France would never give it away to another. In exchange, Carlos IV was to get the throne of Tuscany for his needy son-in-law.

Napoleon wanted Louisiana the way he wanted anything that belonged to someone else, but he also had plans for it. It was to be the provider, the granary, for the profitable French islands of the Caribbean, particularly Santo Domingo, just as soon as order was restored there and the rebellious slaves led by the self-styled black Bonaparte, Toussaint L'Ouverture, were brought into line.

But even as Bonaparte was finalizing the secret treaty that would put France back in the American West, American politics took an abrupt change in direction. Adams and the Federalists were voted out of power, and by the barest of margins Thomas Jefferson became the third president of the United States. Rumors of Louisiana's change of hands were circulating freely and posed for Jefferson his first crisis. A weakened Spain on the western flank was bad enough. A puissant France with empire in mind was incalculably worse and, as such, unacceptable. Indirect evidence that France was, indeed, the closet owner of Louisiana fell swiftly into pattern. In October 1801, Napoleon concluded a temporary peace of convenience with Britain after seven years of war to free the seas for an expedition to quash the black uprising in Santo Domingo. The upstart ex-slave Toussaint was taken soon enough, but his militant followers put on a show of resistance that astounded the French expeditionary force, and before victory was within reach, the dread yellow fever made its grim appearance and more than thirty-five thousand Frenchmen, including their commander, General Leclerc, had succumbed. Meanwhile, three thousand French troops and civil administrators began assembling in Holland with orders to proceed to Louisiana as soon as the winter ice melted and permitted a transatlantic sailing. The international boil was coming rapidly to a head.

Jefferson fretted and entered the bluffers' game. When Spanish officials still stationed in Louisiana revoked American privileges of deposit in New Orleans in the autumn of 1782 (some have maintained it was purely a local decision, others that Madrid ordered it, still others that it was at French instigation), trans-Appalachian westerners were ready to shoot their way to that port or secede, whichever would relax the stranglehold on their river and their livelihoods. Jefferson gingerly walked the middle, urging patience to his western wards while letting Napoleon know that his trigger-happy westerners were on a frayed leash and about to take New Orleans from whomever had title to it. In March of 1803 he sent special envoy James Monroe to join Robert Livingstone in Paris to buy the port that would preserve the union. The pair had money in their pockets and they were ready to spend it: ten million dollars for New Orleans and however much of West Florida they could wangle.

The year 1803 was the best of times to be an American in Paris, where the destiny of the West again rendezvoused precisely on a twenty-year schedule, as it had in 1763 and 1783. Napoleon was momentarily desperate. The fiasco in Santo Domingo had rendered Louisiana superfluous for the time being. Many more thousand flowers of the French army would have to wilt in a tropic hell to put the power of France back in the New World. With another war against England inevitable and a matter of months away, the first consul decided to cut his losses. He suddenly directed Barbé-Marbois, minister of the treasury, and the masterful Talleyrand to see what the Americans might pay for *all* of Louisiana. Talleyrand's offhand inquiry astonished the hard-of-hearing Livingstone, but he avidly discussed it with Monroe when the latter arrived in Paris two days later. Could this be true? All of Louisiana! The Americans rushed to payment— fifteen million dollars for all of Louisiana (two-and-a-half million more than France was prepared to settle for)—and the bargain was sealed.

Foreign minister Talleyrand was a reluctant party to the sale. He saw wisdom in avoiding war with England and holding onto

Louisiana. But Napoleon played a rash game, a card at a time. England would force war whether France wanted it or not, he argued. Louisiana would be indefensible when Britain cut the sea-lanes. Moreover, the fifteen million dollars would come in handy to finance a planned cross-channel invasion of the ancient enemy's homeland in the imminent war. If that should fail, well, at least the United States, a fellow republic, would be loosed on lands that England wanted. England perforce would have to commit armies to protect her holdings in North America, armies that could not be deployed in Europe. Beyond that, there was the cynical implication that, should France prevail, the world would be hers, including the American West. Treaties, after all, were only tide-me-overs until armies determined who got what.

Britain's spies made her privy to the negotiations in Paris, and she was not averse to living with France out of North America again. As for Spain, the treachery was beyond her rage, and the loss of the rest of her West less than twenty years away.

Only after the signatures were dry did Livingstone ask Talleyrand what the boundaries of Louisiana were. "You must take it as we received it," was the foreign minister's enigmatic response. The subtle implications were not lost on the wise: the extent of the American West was for the Americans to decide, at the expense of England and Spain one could be sure. "You have made a noble bargain for yourselves," said Talleyrand, "and I suppose you will make the most of it."

Though there were still dark days ahead, and trials that would try their souls, the Americans were legally across the Father of Waters. And make the most of it they most emphatically would.

Bibliography

In researching the early history of the American West, the writer is faced with a few problems by no means unique but nevertheless troublesome. Those who went west of the Mississippi before the nineteenth century were not Anglo-Americans who left records in English that have since been gathered in museums and libraries. They were "foreigners," and that is perhaps why general histories of the pre-American West are so few. *We* weren't there yet, and *they* didn't go out of their way to supply us with records.

This is especially true of the Amerind, by far the most numerous of eighteenth-century westerners, who left no written records at all. Consequently, I have relied heavily on the splendid work of anthropologists and ethnologists with an interest in reconstructing the Indian past and on the relatively few firsthand contemporary accounts of contacts between white man and red.

Anthropologists using new scientific measuring tools have steadily pushed backward in time man's presence on earth and in the New World. The application of those techniques coupled with some rather basic deductions, has pointed to early man knowing more, doing more, and being more than has heretofore been thought possible. It is tempting (and not so very much out of line) to believe that the same holds for more recent men — particularly Frenchmen — when they penetrated the trans-Mississippi lands in the seventeenth and early eighteenth centuries. The scarcity of French material on the West is due to a number of factors. The first who came were mostly illiterate. Even when not, they were usually there illegally, and it was in their self-interest to cover their tracks. Beyond that, it is likely that valuable documents (in French and Spanish) are still gathering dust in Old World collections, museums, and archives, untranslated and, for all purposes, lost.

Of the contemporary French literature available, I found the books of Jean-Bernard Bossu and Le Page du Pratz especially revealing of what life was like in eighteenth-century Louisiana. *The French in the Mississippi Valley* and *Frenchmen and French Ways*, both edited by John Francis McDermott, are invaluable to understanding the problems, failures, and achievements of France in the American heartland. Henri Folmer's works are most helpful in tracing some of the early penetrations into the western plains, while William J. Eccles' *France in America* is the best recent overview of the French New World experience.

The early Spaniards (bless their compulsive, meticulous record-keeping ways) have been far more generous with us. I have relied very heavily on the voluminous works and translations of Herbert E. Bolton, which remain indispensable. His renowned student, John Walton Caughey, fills in the void of Lower Louisiana during the Revolutionary War, while Abraham P. Nasatir has been my primary authority on events in the Upper Mississippi Valley in the late eighteenth century. The translations of documents by A. B. Thomas have been favored in treating eighteenth-century New Mexico; Warren L. Cook's recent *Flood Tide of Empire* is both a readable and comprehensive treatment of Spanish activity in the north Pacific.

There is understandably a much larger literature on the English and Americans in the Colonial and Revolutionary periods, yet here, too, that dealing with the West few had reached is skimpy. Generally, works listed here are limited to those that treat western lands and events just prior to, during, and after the Revolutionary War.

The bibliography is broken down to correspond with the major parts of the book. This is for the convenience of the general reader and the scholar, and is admittedly somewhat arbitrary, for many books and articles span two or more sections of the whole. Of the total entries, a sizeable number are journal articles. This seemed obligatory because so much good material of narrow focus reposes in the scholarly quarterlies, seldom referred to in popular histories.

Where there is a difference of opinion among historians (e.g., the route of the explorer Claude du Tisné, the same for the brothers Vérendrye, whether La Salle on his ill-fated last voyage missed the Mississippi delta or fully intended a landfall in modern Texas), I have taken sides not on the basis of hard evidence, which is lacking, but on what simply seems to me to have been more likely.

Finally, many more sources were consulted than there was space to list here. I have included only those that seemed most basic, engaging, and relevant to the scope of the book. Selectivity, of course, justly invites protest over omissions. I can only hope that those omissions were all by choice, not neglect.

GENERAL AND BACKGROUND
Brebner, John B. *Explorers of North America, 1492–1806*. New York: Macmillan, 1933.

Cheyney, E. P. *The European Background of American History, 1300–1600*. New York: Harper & Bros., 1904.

Dorn, Walter L. *Competition for Empire, 1740–1763*. New York: Harper & Bros., 1940.

Gorshoy, Leo. *From Despotism to Revolution*. New York: Harper & Bros., 1944.

PART I: FANTASYLAND
Carver, Jonathan. *Travels through the Interior Parts of North America in the Years 1766, 1767 and 1768*. 3d ed. London: C. Dilly, 1781.

Cline, Gloria G. *Exploring the Great Basin*. Norman: Univ. of Oklahoma Press, 1963.

Coxe, Daniel, Esq. *A Description of the English Province of Carolana*. Reprinted by the Sutro Branch of the California State Library. Occasional Papers Report Series no. 11, San Francisco, February 1940.

Crouse, Nellis M. *In Quest of the Western Ocean*. New York: Wm. Morrow & Co., 1928.

Deacon, Richard. *Madoc and the Discovery of America: Some New Light on an Old Controversy*. London: Muller, 1967.

Espinosa, José Manuel. "The Legend of Sierra Azul." *New Mexico Historical Review*, IX, 113–158.

Gilbert, Sir Humphrey. *A Discourse of a Discoverie for a New Passage to Cataia*. London: Henry Middleton, 1576.

Hale, Edward Everett. *The Queen of California . . . from the Sergas of Esplandian*. San Francisco: Colt Press, 1945.

Hammond, George P., and Rey, Agapito, trans. *Expedition into New Mexico Made by Antonio de Espejo, 1582–1583 . . . .* Los Angeles: Quivira Society, 1929.

Hammond, George P. "The Search for the Fabulous in the Settlement of the Southwest." *Utah Historical Quarterly*, XXIV, 1–19.

Hennepin, Louis, *A New Discovery of a Vast Country in America*. Ed. by Reuben G. Thwaites, 2 vols. Chicago: McClurg, 1903.

Lahontan, Louis Armand de Lom d'Arce, Baron de. *New Voyages to North-America*. Ed. by Reuben G. Thwaites. 2 vols. Chicago: McClurg, 1905.

Nunn, George E. *Origin of the Strait of Anian Concept*. Philadelphia: privately printed, 1929.

Pratz, Le Page du. *The History of Louisiana*. London: T. Becket, 1774.

Purchas, Samuel. *Purchas His Pilgrimes*. 4 vols. London: W. Stansby, 1625.

Turner, Robert K. "Coxe's A Description of Carolana." Virginia Univ. Bibliographical Society's *Studies in Bibliography*, 1956–1957, pp. 252–255.

Tyler, S. Lyman. "The Myth of the Lake of Copala and Land of Teguayo." *Utah Historical Quarterly*, XX, 313–329.

Wagner, Henry R. "Apocryphal Voyages to the Northwest Coast of America." *Proceedings of the American Antiquarian Society*, 41, pt. 1, 179–234.

Wagner, Henry R. "Some Imaginary California Geography." *Proceedings of the American Antiquarian Society*, XXXVI, pt. 1, 83–129.

Wheat, Carl I. *Mapping the Trans-Mississippi West, 1540–1861*. 6 vols. San Francisco: Institute of Historical Cartography, 1957–1963.

PART II: AN INDIAN SUMMER
Brandon, William. *The American Heritage Book of Indians*. New York: American Heritage, 1961.

Catlin, George. *Letters and Notes on the Manners, Customs, and Condition of the North American Indians*. 2 vols. New York: Tosswill & Meyers, 1841.

Ewers, John C. *The Blackfeet: Raiders on the Northwestern Plains*. Norman: Univ. of Oklahoma Press, 1958.

Ewers, John C. *Indian Life on the Upper Missouri*. Norman: Univ. of Oklahoma Press, 1968.

Forbes, Jack D. *Apache, Navaho and Spaniard*. Norman: Univ. of Oklahoma Press, 1960.

Forbes, Jack D. *Native Americans of California and Nevada*. Heraldsburg, Calif.: Naturegraph Publishers, 1969.

Forbes, Jack D. *Warriors of the Colorado: The Yumas of the Quechan Nation and their Neighbors*. Norman: Univ. of Oklahoma Press, 1965.

Gunther, Erna. *Indian Life on the Northwest Coast of North America . . . .* Chicago: Univ. of Chicago Press, 1972.

Hagan, William T. *American Indians*. Chicago: Univ. of Chicago Press, 1961.

Haines, Francis. *The Nez Percés: Tribesmen of the Columbia Plateau*. Norman: Univ. of Oklahoma Press, 1955.

Heizer, Robert F., and Mills, John E. *The Four Ages of Tsurai. A Documentary History of the Indian Village on Trinidad Bay*. Berkeley: Univ. of California Press, 1952.

Heizer, Robert F., and Whipple, M. A., eds. *The California Indians, A Source Book*. 2d rev. ed. Berkeley: Univ. of California Press, 1971.

Hodge, Frederick W., ed. *Handbook of American Indians North of Mexico*. 2 vols. Washington: Govt. Printing Office, 1912.

Hoebel, Edward A. *The Cheyennes: Indians of the Great Plains*. New York: Holt, Rinehart, 1960.

Hyde, George E. *Pawnee Indians*. Denver: Univ. of Denver Press, 1951.

Kroeber, Alfred L. *Handbook of the Indians of California*. Washington: Govt. Printing Office, 1925.

Leacock, Eleanor B., and Lurie, Nancy O., eds. *North American Indians in Historical Perspective*. New York: Random House, 1971.

Lowie, Robert H. *The Crow Indians*. New York: Farrar Rinehart, 1935.

Mathews, John Joseph. *The Osages: Children of the Middle Waters*. Norman: Univ. of Oklahoma Press, 1961.

Newcomb, William Wilmon, Jr. *The Indians of Texas: From Prehistoric to Modern Times*. Austin: Univ. of Texas Press, 1961.

Roe, Frank Gilbert. *The Indian and the Horse*. Norman: Univ. of Oklahoma Press, 1965.

Spicer, Edward H. *Cycles of Conquest: The Impact of Spain, Mexico, and the United States on the Indians of the Southwest*. Tucson: Univ. of Arizona Press, 1962.

Steward, Julian Haynes. *Aboriginal and Historical Groups of the Ute Indians of Utah*. New York: Garland, 1974.

Steward, Julian Haynes. *Basin-Plateau Aboriginal Sociopolitical Groups*. Washington: Govt. Printing Office, 1938.

Teit, James A. *The Salishan Tribes of the Western Plateaus*. Ed. by Franz Boas. Washington: Govt. Printing Office, 1930.

Underhill, Ruth M. *The Navajos*. 4th rev. ed. Norman: Univ. of Oklahoma Press, 1967.

Underhill, Ruth M. *Red Man's America: A History of Indians in the United States*. Chicago: Univ. of Chicago Press, 1953.

Unrau, William E. *The Kansa Indians. A History of the Wind People, 1673–1873*. Norman: Univ. of Oklahoma Press, 1971.

Wallace, Ernest, and Hoebel, E. Adamson. *The Comanches: Lords of the Southern Plains*. Norman: Univ. of Oklahoma Press, 1952.

Wissler, Clark. *Indians of the United States*. Rev. ed. by Lucy Wales Kluckhohn. Garden City: Doubleday, 1966.

PART III: THE FAILURE OF FRANCE

Belting, Natalie Maree. *Kaskaskia Under the French Regime*. Urbana: Univ. of Illinois Press, 1948.

Bossu, Jean-Bernard. *Travels in the Interior of North America 1751–62*. Trans. and ed. by Seymour Feiler. Norman: Univ. of Oklahoma Press, 1962.

Caldwell, Norman Ward. *The French in the Mississippi Valley, 1740–1750*. Urbana: Univ. of Illinois Press, 1941.

Charlevoix, Pierre François-Xavier de. *History and General Description of New France*. Trans. with notes by John G. Shea. 6 vols. New York: 1900.

Charlevoix, Pierre François-Xavier de. *Letters to the Duchess of Lesdiguieres . . . .* London: R. Goadby, 1763.

Crouse, Nellis M. *La Vérendrye: Fur Trader and Explorer*. Ithaca, N.Y.: Cornell Univ. Press, 1956.

Delanglez, Jean. *The French Jesuits in Lower Louisiana (1700–1763)*. Washington: Catholic Univ. of America, 1935.

Eccles, William J. *France in America*. New York: Harper & Row, 1972.

Folmer, Henri. "Contraband Trade Between Louisiana and New Mexico in the Eighteenth Century." *New Mexico Historical Review*, XVI, 249–274.

Folmer, Henri, trans. and ed. "De Bourgmont's Expedition to the Padoucas in 1724." *Colorado Magazine*, XIV, 121–128.

Folmer, Henri. "Etienne Véniard de Bourgmont in the Missouri Country." *Missouri Historical Review*, XXXVI, 279–298.

Folmer, Henri. *Franco-Spanish Rivalry in North America, 1564–1763*. Glendale, Calif.: Arthur H. Clark, 1953.

Folmer, Henri, trans. and ed. "The Mallet Expedition of 1739 through Nebraska, Kansas and Colorado to Santa Fe." *Colorado Magazine*, XVI, 161–172.

Lemaître, Georges E. *Beaumarchais*. New York: Knopf, 1949.

Lewis, Anna. "Du Tisné's Expedition into Oklahoma, 1719." *Chronicles of Oklahoma*, III, no. 4.

Lewis, Anna. "La Harpe's First Expedition in Oklahoma, 1718–1719." *Chronicles of Oklahoma*, II, no. 4.

Lyon, E. Wilson. *Louisiana in French Diplomacy, 1759–1804*. Norman: Univ. of Oklahoma Press, 1934.

McDermott, John Francis, ed. *The French in the Mississippi Valley*. Urbana: Univ. of Illinois Press, 1965.

McDermott, John Francis, ed. *Frenchmen and French Ways in the Mississippi Valley*. Urbana: Univ. of Illinois Press, 1969.

McDermott, John Francis, ed. *Old Cahokia*. St. Louis: St. Louis Historical Documents Foundation, 1949.

Morton, Arthur S. *A History of the Canadian*

West to 1870-71. Toronto: T. Nelson & Sons, 1939.

Pénicaut, Andre. *Fleur de Lys and Calumet*. Ed. by Richebourg G. McWilliams. Baton Rouge: Louisiana State Univ. Press, 1953.

Phares, Ross. *Cavalier in the Wilderness: The Story of the Explorer and Trader, Louis Juchereau de St. Denis*. Baton Rouge: Louisiana State Univ. Press, 1952.

Priestley, Herbert I. *France Overseas Through the Old Regime; A Study of European Expansion*. New York: D. Appleton-Century, 1939.

Vérendrye, Pierre Gaultier de Varennes de la. *Letters . . . .* Trans. and ed. by Lawrence J. Burpee. Toronto: Champlain Society, 1927.

PART IV: RESURGENT SPAIN

Bancroft, Hubert Howe. *Works*. 39 vols. San Francisco: A. L. Bancroft, 1882-1890.

Bannon, John Francis, ed. *Bolton and the Spanish Borderlands*. Norman: Univ. of Oklahoma Press, 1964.

Bobb, Bernard E. *The Viceregency of Antonio María Bucareli in New Spain, 1771-1779*. Austin: Univ. of Texas Press, 1962.

Bolton, Herbert E., ed. *Anza's California Expeditions*. 5 vols. Berkeley: Univ. of California Press, 1930.

Bolton, Herbert E., trans. and ed. *Athanase de Mézières and the Louisiana-Texas Frontier, 1768-1780*. 2 vols. Cleveland: Arthur H. Clark, 1914.

Bolton, Herbert E. *The Mission as a Frontier Institution in the Spanish-American Colonies*. El Paso: Texas Western College Press for Academic Reprints, 1960.

Bolton, Herbert E., and Stephens, H. Morse, eds. *The Pacific Ocean in History*. New York: Macmillan, 1917.

Bolton, Herbert E. *The Spanish Borderlands: A Chronicle of Old Florida and the Southwest*. New Haven: Yale Univ. Press, 1921.

Bolton, Herbert E., ed. *Spanish Exploration in the Southwest, 1542-1706*. New York: Scribner's Sons, 1930.

Bolton, Herbert E. *Texas in the Middle Eighteenth Century: Studies in Spanish Colonial History and Administration*. Berkeley: Univ. of California Press, 1915.

Caughey, John Walton. *Bernardo de Gálvez in Louisiana, 1776-1783*. Berkeley: Univ. of California Press, 1934.

Caughey, John Walton. *History of the Pacific Coast*. Los Angeles: privately printed, 1933.

Chapman, Charles E. *The Founding of Spanish California: The Northwestward Expansion of New Spain, 1687-1783*. New York: Macmillan, 1916.

Chapman, Charles E. *A History of California: The Spanish Period*. New York: Macmillan, 1921.

Cook, Warren L. *Flood Tide of Empire: Spain and the Pacific Northwest, 1543-1819*. New Haven: Yale Univ. Press, 1973.

Concha, Fernando de la. "Advice on Governing New Mexico, 1794." *New Mexico Historical Review*, XXIV, 236-254.

Cutter, Donald C., ed. *The California Coast: A Bilingual Edition of Documents from the Sutro Collection*. Norman: Univ. of Oklahoma Press, 1969.

Dominguez, Fr. Francisco Atanasio. *The Missions of New Mexico . . . .* Trans. and ann. by Eleanor B. Adams and Fr. Angelico Chavez. Albuquerque: Univ. of New Mexico Press, 1956.

Dunn, William E. "The Apache Mission on the San Saba River." *Southwestern Historical Quarterly*, XVII, 379-414.

Dunn, William E. "Spanish Reaction Against the French Advance Toward New Mexico, 1717-1727." *Mississippi Valley Historical Review*, II, 348-362.

Garcés, Francisco. *On the Trail of a Spanish Pioneer: Diary and Itinerary of Francisco Garcés . . . .* Trans. by Elliott Coues. 2 vols. New York: F.P. Harper, 1900.

Hammond, George P., and Rey, Agapito, ed. and trans. *Don Juan de Oñate, Colonizer of New Mexico, 1595-1628*. Albuquerque: Univ. of New Mexico Press, 1953.

Houck, Louis. *A History of Missouri from the Earliest Exploration and Settlement Until the Admission of the State into the Union*. 3 vols. Chicago: R. R. Donnelley & Sons, 1908.

Houck, Louis, ed. *The Spanish Régime in Missouri: A Collection of Papers and Documents . . . .* 2 vols. Chicago: R. R. Donnelley & Sons, 1909.

James, James Alton. "Spanish Influence in the West during the American Revolution." *Mississippi Valley Historical Review*, IV, 193-208.

Jones, Oakah L., Jr. *Pueblo Warriors and Spanish Conquest*. Norman: Univ. of Oklahoma, 1966.

Kinnaird, Lawrence, ed. *The Frontiers of New Spain: Nicolás de Lafora's Description, 1766-1768*. Berkeley: Quivira Society, 1958.

Kinnaird, Lawrence, ed. *Spain in the Mississippi Valley, 1765-1794: Translations of Materials in the Spanish Archives in the Bancroft Library*. Washington: Govt. Printing Office, 1946.

Palóu, Fr. Francisco, O.F.M. *Historical Memoirs of New California*. Ed. by Herbert E. Bolton. 4 vols. Berkeley: Univ. of California Press, 1926.

Priestley, Herbert I. *José de Gálvez: Visitor-General of New Spain (1765-1771)*. Berkeley: Univ. of California Press, 1916.

Simmons, Marc, *Spanish Government in New Mexico*. Albuquerque: Univ. of New Mexico Press, 1968.

Tamarón y Romeral, Pedro. *Bishop Tamarón's Visitation of New Mexico, 1760*. Ed. by Eleanor B. Adams. Albuquerque: Historical Society of New Mexico, 1954.

Thomas, Alfred B., trans. and ed. *After Coronado: Spanish Exploration Northeast of*

New Mexico, 1696–1727 . . . . Norman: Univ. of Oklahoma Press, 1935.

Thomas, Alfred B., trans. and ed. *Forgotten Frontiers: A Study of the Spanish Indian Policy of Don Juan Bautista de Anza* . . . . Norman: Univ. of Oklahoma Press, 1932.

Thomas, Alfred B. "Massacre of the Villasur Expedition at the Forks of the Platte Rivers, August 12, 1720." *Nebraska History*, VII, 68–81.

Thomas, Alfred B., ed. *The Plains Indians and New Mexico, 1751–1778: A Collection of Documents* . . . . Albuquerque: Univ. of New Mexico Press, 1940.

Thomas, Alfred B., trans. and ed. *Teodoro de Croix and the Northern Frontier of New Spain* . . . . Norman: Univ. of Oklahoma Press, 1941.

PART V: THE DIVISIBLE EMPIRE

Abernethy, Thomas P. *Western Lands and the American Revolution*. New York: D. Appleton-Century Co., 1937.

Adams, John. *The Works of John Adams*. Ed. by Charles Francis Adams, 10 vols. Boston: Little, Brown, 1850–1865.

Alden, John R. *A History of the American Revolution*. New York: Knopf, 1969.

Alvord, Clarence W. *The Mississippi Valley in British Politics*. 2 vols. New York: Russell & Russell, 1959.

Alvord, Clarence W. *The Illinois Country, 1673–1818*. Chicago: McClurg, 1922.

Barnhart, John D. *Henry Hamilton and George Rogers Clark in the American Revolution*. Crawfordsville, Ind.: R. E. Banta, 1951.

Bemis, Samuel Flagg. *The Diplomacy of the American Revolution*. New York: D. Appleton-Century, 1935.

Billington, Ray Allen. *Westward Expansion: A History of the American Frontier*. 3d ed. New York: Macmillan, 1967.

Burpee, Lawrence J., ed. "The Journal of Antony Hendry (Henday), 1754–1755." *Proceedings and Transactions of the Royal Society of Canada*. 3d ser., 1907, Sec. II.

Caughey, John Walton "Willing's Expedition Down the Mississippi, 1778." *Louisiana Historical Quarterly*, XV, 5–36.

Cook, Captain James, and King, Captain James. *A Voyage to the Pacific in 1776, 1777, 1778, 1779, and 1780*. 4 vols. London: J. Stockdale, 1784.

Degler, Carl Neuman. *Out of Our Past: The Forces That Shaped Modern America*. New York: Harper & Row, 1959.

Franklin, Benjamin. *The Writings of Benjamin Franklin*. Collected and ed. with a life and intro. by Albert H. Smyth. 10 vols. New York: Macmillan, 1907.

Gates, Charles M., ed. *Five Fur Traders of the Northwest* . . . . St. Paul: Minnesota Historical Society, 1963.

Hammond, George P., Hackett, Charles W., and Mecham, J. Lloyd, eds. *New Spain and the Anglo-American West*. 2 vols. Los Angeles: Lancaster Press, 1932.

Harlow, Vincent T. *The Founding of the Second British Empire, 1763–1793*, 2 vols. New York: Longmans, Green, 1952–1964.

Hemphill, W. Edwin. "The Jeffersonian Background of the Louisiana Purchase." *Mississippi Valley Historical Review*, XXII, 177–190.

Hinkhouse, Fred J. *The Preliminaries of the American Revolution as Seen in the English Press, 1763–1775*. New York: Columbia Univ. Press, 1926.

Hutchins, Thomas. *An Historical Narrative and Topographical Description of Louisiana and West-Florida*. Gainesville: Univ. of Florida Press, 1968.

James, James Alton, ed. *George Rogers Clark Papers, 1771–1781*. Springfield: Trustees of the Illinois State Historical Library, 1912.

James, James Alton. *The Life of George Rogers Clark*. Chicago: Univ. of Chicago Press, 1928.

James, James Alton. "Louisiana as a Factor in American Diplomacy, 1795–1800." *Mississippi Valley Historical Review*, I, 44–56.

James, James Alton. *Oliver Pollock: The Life and Times of an Unknown Patriot*. New York: D. Appleton-Century, 1937.

James, James Alton. "The Significance of the Attack on St. Louis, 1780." *Proceedings of the Mississippi Valley Historical Society Association*, II, 208–217.

Jefferson, Thomas. *Notes on the State of Virginia*. Ed. with intro. and notes by William Peden. Chapel Hill: Univ. of North Carolina Press, 1955.

Jefferson, Thomas. *The Writings of Thomas Jefferson*. Ed. by Andrew A. Lipscomb. 20 vols. Washington, 1905.

Johansen, Dorothy O., and Gates, Charles M. *Empire of the Columbia: A History of the Pacific Northwest*. 2d ed. New York: Harper & Row, 1967.

LaFargue, André. "The Louisiana Purchase: The French Viewpoint." *Louisiana Historical Quarterly*, XXIII, 107–117.

Morgan, Edmund S., ed. *The American Revolution: Two Centuries of Interpretation*. Englewood Cliffs, N.J.: Prentice-Hall, 1965.

Nasatir, Abraham P. "The Anglo-Spanish Frontier in the Illinois Country During the American Revolution, 1779–1783." *Journal of the Illinois State Historical Society*, XXI, 291–358.

Nasatir, Abraham P. "The Anglo-Spanish Frontier on the Upper Mississippi, 1786–1796." *Iowa Journal of History and Politics*, XXIX, 155–232.

Nasatir, Abraham P. "Anglo-Spanish Rivalry on the Upper Missouri, 1790–1804." *Mississippi Valley Historical Review*, XVI, nos. 3 and 4.

Nasatir, Abraham P., ed. *Before Lewis and Clark: Documents Illustrating the History of the Missouri, 1785–1804.* 2 vols. St. Louis: St. Louis Historical Documents Foundation, 1952.

Nasatir, Abraham P. "Ducharme's Invasion of Missouri: An Incident in the Anglo-American Rivalry for the Indian Trade of Upper Louisiana." *Missouri Historical Review,* XXIV, nos. 1, 2, and 3.

Parish, John Carl. *The Persistence of the Western Movement, and Other Essays.* Berkeley: Univ. of California Press, 1943.

Parker, John. *The Great Lakes and the Great Rivers: Jonathan Carver's Dream of Empire.* Lansing: Historical Society of Michigan, 1965.

Peckham, Howard H. *Pontiac and the Indian Uprising.* Princeton Univ. Press, 1947.

Price, A. Grenville, ed. *The Explorations of*

Captain James Cook in the Pacific . . . . New York: American Heritage, 1958.

Rogers, Robert. *A Concise Account of North America.* London: Private printing, 1765; New York: Johnson Reprint, 1966.

Rossiter, Clinton. *The First American Revolution: The American Colonies on the Eve of Independence.* New York: Harcourt, Brace & World, 1956.

Smith, Henry Nash. *Virgin Land: The American West as Symbol and Myth.* Cambridge: Harvard Univ. Press, 1950.

Sosin, Jack M. *The Revolutionary Frontier, 1763–1783.* New York: Holt, Rinehart and Winston, 1967.

Sosin, Jack M. *Whitehall and the Wilderness.* Lincoln: Univ. of Nebraska Press, 1961.

Index

383

Body type: Melior and Bookman by Applied Typographic Systems, Mountain View, California.
Display faces: Tiffany Demi Bold and Melior Open by Applied Typographic Systems; Tiffany
Heavy and American Extra Bold by Atherton's Advertising Typography, Inc., Palo Alto, California. Printing and binding by Kingsport Press, Kingsport, Tennessee.